MW00331425

GROWING UP
in the
CITY OF THE SAINTS

Glimpses of America in Salt Lake City During the 1950s and 60s

Gordon Shepherd & Gary Shepherd

Endorsement Reviews

Growing up in places very different from Salt Lake City, these vignettes of boyhood nevertheless had me recognizing and recalling moments long forgotten. The adventures and misadventures narrated and reflected upon by the Shepherd brothers are unique but hauntingly universal.

Charles Harvey, Professor Emeritus,
University of Central Arkansas

I met Gary and Gordon at Lincoln Jr High, and we are still friends. The sensitive way their experiences with old companions are presented in the stories of this book will evoke nods of appreciation, with both smiles and tears.

Kathy Carling Wilson, Utah landscape artist and owner,
Trolley Art & Antique

The Shepherds write wonderful essays about growing up, including humorous antics with friends, family tensions, schools and teachers, playing sports, etc. Their well told memories are almost guaranteed to resonate and stir personal recollections in all readers.

Bruce Haggard, Distinguished Professor Emeritus,
Hendrix College

The Shepherds provide us with stories of identical twin brothers growing up in Salt Lake City in the '50's and '60's and also stories from their adult lives reflecting those youthful foundations. This is a book that will put a smile on your face and, at times, a lump in your throat.

Chris Spatz, author of
Exploring Statistics: Tales of Distributions

The intertwined lives of Gordon and Gary Shepherd provide beguiling glimpses of growing up in Salt Lake City. The Shepherds draw the reader into times and places that no longer exist but which sparkle back into life with their captivating writing.

Lavina Fielding Anderson, author of
Mercy Without End: Toward a More Inclusive Church
and former editor of the *Journal of Mormon History*

One cannot read the Shepherd's anecdotes and reminiscences without reflecting upon one's own childhood, including both fond memories and regrets. Their stories bristle with universal themes that will appeal to all readers. Be prepared to feel a range of emotions.

Ted Boyer, former chair of the Utah State Utilities Commission

Putting their two nearly-identical heads together, Gary and Gordon Shepherd have recalled details, personalities, and subtle relationships that create depth and empathy in their vignettes. Their willingness to share the joys and disappointments in their common experiences has resulted in a memoire rich in detail and humanity.

Kay Helstrom Gaisford, former adjunct teacher in Business and
Computers at Mesa Community College

For Our Children

Lynne, Pamela, Natalie, Robert, Bethany, and Snow

Growing Up in the City of the Saints
Glimpses of America in Salt Lake City During the 1950s and 60s

©2021 Gordon Shepherd

All rights reserved. This book or any portion thereof may not be reproduced or used in any manner whatsoever without the express written permission of the publisher except for the use of brief quotations in a book review.

print ISBN: 978-1-09838-892-8
ebook ISBN: 978-1-09838-893-5

Contents

PREFACE   1

I. Memoir Vignettes of Growing Up in Salt Lake City   7

1. BLIGHTED AREA
   This Was America   9

2. REQUIEM FOR A BOYHOOD FRIEND   15

3. DISQUISITION ON PLAYING MARBLES
   FOR KEEPS AT LIBERTY ELEMENTARY   27

4. THE POLIO PLUNGE AND OTHER WATERY MISADVENTURES   41

5. JOUSTING WITH THE PHANTOM   51

6. GETTING ACQUAINTED WITH
   THE STOKERMATIC SALESMAN   67

7. THE AVON LADY   75

8. LEARNING COMMUNITY AND DEMOCRACY
   FROM FREDDY THE PIG   81

9. REGRETFUL REMINISCENCE OF A DOOMED KID   89

10. JUST THROW TO MY MITT!
    When Baseball Was Our Passion, Season I   99

11. WILLFUL DISOBEDIENCE AND THE LAST FOXTROT   107

12. FREE RANGE KIDS AND BOYHOOD BRUSHES
   WITH THE GRIM REAPER   115

13. WHAT ABOUT GIRLS?   131

14. SHOWDOWN AT HIGH NOON
   The Last Fist Fight   143

15. THROWING PAPERS FOR *THE SALT LAKE TRIBUNE*
   AND OTHER BOYHOOD JOBS   149

16. ARE YOU IN OUR DREAMS?
   Role Model Apparitions From our Youth   163

17. MORE THAN A GAME
   When Baseball Was Our Passion, Season II   173

18. NATIONALITY AMERICAN   183

19. COPS AND EGGS   193

20. ALL THE SMART GIRLS BECOMING WOMEN   201

21. WE THOUGHT THE WORLD WOULD BE BETTER   207

22. TEEN SPIRIT
   Youthful Idealism and The Spirit of Democracy   221

23. SMALL MOMENTS OF GLORY
   When Baseball Was Our passion, Season III   231

II. Moving On and Coming Back Home   241

24. FATEFUL DECISION   243

25. WELCOME Y'ALL TO BRAVO COMPANY!
   Boys In Training for Uncle Sam   249

26. FAREWELL Salt Lake City, May 17, 1964   259

27. MEXICO   273

28. HELLO SOCIOLOGY   287

29. MORMON PASSAGE   297

30. OF WIGS AND ROLLER COASTERS:
   Wherein the Phantom Demonstrates his gentle side   313

31. THE CAPTAIN GOES DOWN WITH THE SHIP   317

32. HERE COMES THE SUN
   Talking with Student Survivors at Kent State   323

33. VIETNAM FROM A SOLDIER'S POINT OF VIEW   335

34. STILL TWINS AFTER ALL THESE YEARS   351

35. SOMEONE LIKE OUR SISTER SUE   357

36. ON THE ROAD AGAIN   365

36. FROM DUST TO DUST   373

38. MUSICAL ILLITERATES
   Getting By with a Little Help from Our Friends   381

39. FATHER AND SON REUNION   387

40. SHEIK CAPUTO AND THE BIG DUGOUT IN THE SKY   391

41. AUTHORS MEET CRITICS IN THE CITY OF OUR BIRTH   403

42. THE LITTLE GIRL WHO LOVED THE LIBRARY   411

EPILOGUE   419

CHAPTER IMAGES AND ILLUSTRATIONS

Chapter 1 *Blighted Area*

1. Salt Lake City central city area.

Chapter 2 *Requiem for a Boyhood Friend*

1. Salt Lake childhood home on Herbert Avenue. 2. Sondra and Roberta Swenson. 3. Ron Swenson.

Chapter 3 *Disquisition on Playing for Keeps at Liberty Elementary*

1. Liberty Elementary School. 2. Different types of marbles. 3. Proper marble shooting technique.

Chapter 4 *The Polio Plunge and Other Watery Misadventures*

1. Wasatch Warm Springs. 2. Liberty Park swimming pool. 3. Gary and Gordon at Bear Lake. 4. The Boise River.

Chapter 5 *Jousting with the Phantom*

1. Marjorie Shepherd with sons Don, Gary, and Gordon. 2. Alvin Shepherd with sons Don, Gary, and Gordon. 3. LDS Los Angeles Temple mural paintings by Robert L. Shepherd. 4. Robert L. Shepherd home on Highland Drive. 5. Highland Drive swimming pool. 6. Early Don Shepherd pen and ink

drawing. 7. Don Shepherd high school painting. 7. Don Shepherd University of Utah illustration class projects. 8. Oil painting portrait of Don Shepherd.

Chapter 6 *Getting Acquainted with the Stokermatic Salesman*

1. 1933 Utah State freshman football team. 2. Red Cross Feld Director Alvin B. Shepherd. 3. Water color painting of Shepherd family homestead near Parley's Canyon.

Chapter 7 *The Avon Lady*

1. Marjorie Coombs's missionary farewell portrait.

Chapter 8 *Learning Community and Democracy from Freddy the Pig*

1. Old Salt Lake City Public library.

Chapter 9 *Regretful Reminiscence of a Doomed Kid*

1. Morris Hulse. 2. Steve Kemp and Guy Snarr. 3. Liberty Elementary traffic patrol.

Chapter 10 *Just Throw to My Mitt!*

1. Gordon and Gary with Lorin Larsen. 2. Gordon showing off his bicep.

Chapter 11 *Willful Disobedience and the Last Foxtrot*

1. Gary's sixth grade Christmas drawing. 2. Owen Wood. 3. Kathryn Keat. 4. Gordon in his Sunday clothes.

Chapter 12 *Free Range Kids and Brushes with the Grim Reaper*

1. Gary and Gordon in Provo backyard. 2. Kingdom Hall Church. 3. Cathedral of the Madeline. 4. Buckingham Apartments.

Chapter 13 *What About Girls?*

1. Carol Jean Christensen. 2. Fifth grade Valentine card. 4. Gold and Green Ball crown bearers. 5. Lynell Ipsen. 6. Kim Novac and William Holden in the movie Picnic.

Chapter 14 *Showdown at High Noon*

1. Fourth East apartment houses. 2. Background scene of the last fistfight.

Chapter 15 *Throwing Papers for the Salt Lake Tribune and Other Boyhood Jobs*

1. Melvin and Margaret Coombs' wedding portrait. 2. Salt Lake Tribune route area. 3. 1956 Mercury Monterey.

Chapter 16 *Are You in Our Dreams?*

1. Lincoln Junior High. 2. David Triptow and Dailey Oliver in1957 junior high track meet. 3. Coach Hal Harcastle and 1959 Lincoln Junior High Green Team. 4. Coach Dean Papadakis and 1959 Lincoln Junior High White Team.

Chapter 17 *More than a Game*

1. Gordon and Leo Sotiriou getting ready for a game of over-the-line. 2. Fred Richeda. 3. 1958 Cops League team. 4. Kenny Caputo hitting at Municipal Ball Park.

Chapter 18 *Nationality American*

1. Gary and Gordon with Janis Yano at 55th high school reunion. 2. 1960 South High production of the Mikado. 3. Janice Yano as a sophomore student. 4. Gary campaign poster by Bob Aoki. Jancie Yano Aoki as an adult woman. 6. Irene and Lillian Yano. 7. Aoki brothers. 8. Dave Shiba and Matzi and Terry Mayeda. 9. Eddie Aoyogi, Katheleen Sako, Sue Tohinaka, and Bruce Tokeno.

Chapter 19 *Cops and Eggs*

1. Ari Ferro, Donna Schippaanboord, and Kathleen McLean. 2. 1940 De Soto. 3. Old Salt Lake City Police Department.

Chapter 20 *All the Smart Girls Becoming Women*

1. 1962 South High Honors at Entrance students. 2. 1961 South High Scribe election issue.

Chapter 21 *We Thought the World Would Be Better*

1. Mike Ellis and his "Big Daddy" football helmet. 2. Football coach, Dale Simons. 3. Mike Ellis all-state football. 4. Mike Mitchell 1961 football co-captain. 5. Wayne Miller scoring against Granite High. 6. Wayne Miller South High outstanding athlete.

Chapter 22 *Teen Spirit*

1. Holy bedlam in South High auditorium. 2. South High front steps and interior foyer. 3. Election posters. 4. Gary campaign speech.

Chapter 23 *Small Moments of Glory*

1. Baseball coach, Dale Simons. 2. Gordon and Gary cartoons for South High Scribe. 3. Dennis Steiner. 4. Derks Field.

Chapter 24 *Fateful Decision*

1. Gary and Gordon in army dress greens.

Chapter 25 *Welcome Y'all to Bravo Company!*

1. Seargent Owens. 2. Gary and Gordon in army basic training drills. 3. Gordon and Gary in army field fatigues with M-14 rifles.

Chapter 26 *Farewell*

1. Liberty/Liberty Park Ward Chapel. 2. Alvin and Marjorie Shepherd. 3. Gary and Gordon missionary farewell portrait.

Chapter 27 *Mexico*

1. Gordon and Gary in Mexico. 2. Map of Mexico. 3. Gordon and Gary with missionary companions in Mexico.

Chapter 28 *Hello Sociology*

1. Lauren Shepherd after graduation from the University of Utah. 2. Lauren and Gary leaving for Michigan.

Chapter 29 *Mormon Passage*

1. Front cover of Mormon Passage.

Chapter 30 *Of Wigs and Roller Coasters*

1. Lagoon roller coaster. 2. Don Shepherd as an art instructor at the University of Utah.

Chapter 31 *The Captain Goes Down with the Ship*

1. South High School in 1931. 2. Mr. Backman, 1931. Dr. Backman, 1961.

Chapter 32 *Here Comes the Sun*

1. Ohio National Guard firing on Kent State University students. 2. Kent State student survivor, Tom Grace. 3. Gail Roberts at the Kent State Victory Bell. 4. Daffodils growing near Kent State Victory Bell.

Chapter 33 *Vietnam from a Soldier's Point of View*

1. Vietnam Veterans Memorial Wall. 2. RMO token gift.

Chapter 34 *Still Twins After All These Years*

1. Page from Rodney Stark's Sociology text discussing identical twins.

Chapter 35 *Someone Like Our Sister Sue*

1. Alvin Shepherd holding Susan as a baby. 2. 1958 Shepherd family portrait. 3. Sue, Gordon and Gary. 4. Gary and Sue with Golden Retrievers.

Chapter 36 *On the Road Again*

1. Howard Ashby and Sally Post in South High production of Calamity Jane. 2. Paul Eddington. 3. Bill and Jack Gehrke. 4. Salt Lake City at night.

Chapter 37 *From Dust to Dust*

1. Vince Khapoya. 2. Izzy and Vince Khapoya at Bryce Canyon. 3. Bryce Canyon.

Chapter 38 *Musical Illiterates*

1. Phillip Starr. 2. David Lingwall.

Chapter 39 *Father and Son Reunion*

1. Tim Christensen.

Chapter 40 *Sheik Caputo and the Big Dougout in the Sky*

1. Ken Caputo. 2. John Caputo. 3. Frank "Sheik" Caputo.

Chapter 41 *Authors Meet Critics in the City of their Birth*

1. Front and back covers of book on Jan Shipps. 2. Jan and Tony Shipps.

Chapter 42 *The Little Girl Who Loved the Library*

1. Lavina and Paul Anderson's Roberta Street home. 2. Lavina Fielding Anderson. 3. Lavina inside her home.

Epilogue

1. Hope for the Future.

PREFACE

If people are famous, having made significant contributions to important fields of human endeavor, or if they have led unusual or adventurous lives, especially in connection with important historical events, there is a likely audience not only for biographies about them but also for their own memoirs or autobiographies. Otherwise, why should anybody outside of a person's family or close friends be interested in reading histories or stories about somebody not known to them?

The two of us can scarcely claim to be famous and, by and large, we have lived fairly conventional lives without direct or substantial connections to important historical events. Why should anybody beyond a few close friends or family members give a hoot about what we offer in the way of reminiscence stories in this volume? Fair question. Perhaps, we tell ourselves, our writing is intrinsically compelling and, in reflecting on our own experiences, we succeed in addressing some universal human concerns that resonate with the experiences of a wide range of other people—especially those who grew up in our era of American history in the 1950s and 60s. We, of course, would like to think that these "perhaps" propositions are more or less true as justifications for the writings we offer in this book. But that is for others to decide.

We don't pretend in this little volume to have written treatises on religion, history, or politics. Nor have we attempted to compose a full-blooded autobiography. But our writing does contain parts of all these genres, especially some fundamental elements of autobiography and memoir. However, in contrast to the detailed chronology of a conventional autobiography of a single person, this book consists of a set of memoiristic vignettes that capture shaping moments and events in our lives as twin brothers growing up in a particular time and place. Rather than a sustained narrative, we offer a series of moments and glimpses in the unfolding of our interwoven experiences over time. Though oddly unorthodox, perhaps the term "*we*moiristic" would be more accurate for describing the pieces in this volume. This is because the content of every story in the collection references both of us acting together—from our earliest childhood years growing up in Salt Lake City through adulthood in which our occupational careers as academic sociologists were conjointly formed by extensive collaboration in both teaching and other scholarly ventures. True to our shared experience, we narrate our reminiscences by employing plural pronouns (we, us, our), while occasionally shifting to "Gary" or "Gordon" when appropriate.

We intend for each vignette to stand coherently on its own merits while also being organically related to the others in the collection as a whole. There's a rough chronological order in the sequencing of our stories, though many of them employ flashbacks or fast-forwarding techniques that produce a certain amount of chronological overlap. This results in minor redundancies, but the principal effect is to reinforce the thematic connection between different formative episodes in our lives that we have selectively written about. We have included in our reminiscences occasional dialogue between us and various other people. We, of course, did not sound-record these exchanges and keep a record of them. In some instances, we have fairly clear or even vivid recollections of exactly what was said. In others, we recall the essence of what was said—even if not the exact words—and have exercised a modest amount of literary license in order to humanize our remembrances and convey to readers key elements of the events that most decisively informed our experiences.

Even though there is considerable diversity of specific content across these writings, we believe they are undergirded by a broad thematic consistency revolving around a subset of America's promissory ideals—often unrealized in practice—which challenge our civic conscience today more than ever: community, democracy, diversity, tolerance, and racial, ethnic, and gender equality. If one is looking for an underlying thesis in our personal vignettes, it would be that, however vital our DNA as biological beings might be in predicating our personal development and life course, as socialized human beings, there are always crucial environmental factors that add their essential weight to the outcomes of our lives and social identities. The fact that we were born identical twins did not provide anyone with a crystal ball for forecasting our futures or anticipating how and in what ways our lives would remain so intertwined over the course of time. In retrospect it's easy for people to say, "Of course, you're identical twins. *That* explains it." In reality, though, our shared DNA does not at all explain the particulars of who we are and why and how we have conducted our lives.

Crucial environmental factors that emerge in our stories include our conflicted relationship with an older brother close to us in age, our inherited Latter-day Saint faith strongly supported by significant kinship attachments, our proclivity for cultivating closely shared friendship networks, and especially the shaping influence of the public schools we attended on our core values growing up. These influences were, of course, framed by a particular time and place, which jointly contributed their own fundamental imprint on our lives. The time was the post-World War II era of the 1950s and early 1960s. And the place was Mormon-dominated Salt Lake City, Utah ("Mormon" being the nickname by which members of the Church of Jesus Christ of Latter-day Saints are popularly known). Needless to say, time imposed other impactful influences on our lives, shaping us in different ways as we moved away from Salt Lake—graduate studies, marriage, children, job opportunities, etc. In this book, however, it is the experiential factors that selectively pertain to earlier stages of our lives that we emphasize most.

The 1950s were a time of resurgent national confidence, optimism about the future, and strengthening of the belief in American exceptionalism and our country's benevolent goodness. These proudly ethnocentric attitudes covered over the growing frustration and resentment of Americans of color who were still denied equal civil rights, increasingly antiquated Victorian ideas about women's roles in society, and the restless rebelliousness of a booming youth culture no longer attached to patriotic sacrifice in a war economy. These subterranean strains eventually erupted in the divisive protests and conflicts of the 1960s. All of this, of course, was an important part of our own experience growing up in Salt Lake City, and these contradictions of American history are both alluded to and directly depicted in our various essay accounts.

Salt Lake City, like other American metropolitan areas of the postwar era, looked to the future with optimistic confidence concerning the prospects of progressive growth and material prosperity for all Americans. Unlike any other capitol city in the United States, however, Salt Lake City was fundamentally the center of a Mormon community, with a unique history in relationship to negotiating the boundaries between church and state. Headquartered in Salt Lake City, the Church of Jesus Christ of Latter-day Saints (or LDS Church) was, in the 1950s, vigorously implementing steps to dramatically increase its postwar membership worldwide by pumping member resources into the expansion of its lay missionary program—which more and more depended on the voluntary services of post-high school youth. Needless to say, our family history and deep ties to the LDS faith tradition through active involvement in local Mormon congregations in Salt Lake, had a decisive impact on our religious socialization and subsequent decisions to serve LDS missions to Mexico for two years in the early 1960s. When we returned from Mexico, the world of our boyhoods and youth had been upended. How we experienced the social upheavals of the 1960s is subsequently reflected in several of our collaborative vignettes in the second part of the book.

Corresponding to the rough chronology of our vignettes, we have divided the book into two parts. Part I is entitled *Memoir Vignettes of Growing Up in Salt Lake City*. The backdrop for many of the stories we tell in this section of the book portrays us as Mormon boys absorbing lessons shaped by the historical context and subculture of the time and place in which we grew up as twin brothers. The two of us were virtually inseparable, cultivating and sharing the same friends, the same interests and adventures, and the same life-lessons. Readily acknowledging our youthful self-righteousness and ethnocentrism, common themes that emerge from our writings about shared experiences growing up include early understandings of cooperation, friendship, community, democracy, inclusiveness, and equality—fundamental values that we continue to embrace as adults.

Part II is entitled *Moving On and Coming Back Home*. This section provides further autobiographical glimpses as our lives continued to unfold in parallel fashion. Our accounts spotlight the two of us moving beyond childhood and adolescence through fulfillment of U.S. military obligations in the Utah National Guard, acceptance of missionary assignments for the LDS Church in Mexico, and our subsequent pursuit of graduate training and occupational careers outside of Utah as academic sociologists. As academics, we both formed habits of critical thinking that soon led us to abandon our inculcated Mormon faith commitments. At the same time, we developed shared teaching and research interests in the sociology of religion (including the sociology of Mormonism) and movements for social change. Like most people, our lives as adults continued to be shaped by the cultivation of new friends and colleagues over time, some of whose stories we include in this volume. But we also have persisted in valuing and sustaining contacts with our past and, as indicated in our last several stories, are drawn back to the city of our youth in the current century to reconnect with family and old friends.

While this collection of writings is far from being exclusively devoted to Mormon or LDS Church topics, it certainly is marinated in the values and experiences we grew up with as Mormon kids in Salt Lake City in the 1950s and 1960s. That said, we hope that a broad audience of readers—both

Mormon and non-Mormon—will find value and some pleasure in our memoiristic accounts. In addition to readers who grew up when and where we did, we optimistically trust that others, who grew up elsewhere and in different eras than ours, will encounter some universal, coming of age experiences that resonate with their own. Even though our personal narratives are highly selective, if we have written them with sufficient clarity and skill they should also reveal a diverse mixture of different kinds of people and personalities over time whose lives have impinged in meaningful ways on our own. And, if authentically composed, our accounts of those who enter our narratives should faithfully reflect alternating moments of human nostalgia, good will, regret, humor, indignation, sadness, and even tragedy, but also, we trust, some rays of hope.

Last but not least, we offer appreciative thanks to our tolerant wives, Faye and Lauren Shepherd, both of whom have endured listening to or reading many rough drafts of our writing, while also making helpful suggestions and correcting some of our careless errors along the way. With much appreciation we also thank a number of other readers of our manuscript drafts for their feedback and helpful suggestions, including: Lavina Fielding Anderson, Jana Riess, Carol Jean Christensen Cordy, Kay Helstrom Gaisford, Janet Burton Seegmiller, Marian Peck Rees, Linda Baily Ogden, Bruce Haggard, Chris Spatz, Charles Harvey, Ted Boyer, and especially Pamela Shepherd. As for any remaining inaccuracies in our recollection of individuals and events, we alone are responsible.

I.

Memoir Vignettes of Growing Up in Salt Lake City

I.

BLIGHTED AREA
This Was America

In 1997, the two of us attended a conference session of the Society for the Scientific Study of Religion in Montreal, Canada. One of the session presenters was employed by the Church of Jesus Christ of Latter-day Saints Research Division. His talk focused on the changing demographics of the urban neighborhoods in and around Salt Lake City, the capital of Mormon Utah. The church researcher projected a PowerPoint slide on the screen which labeled and color-coded a Salt Lake City map in terms of different socio-economic sections of the city. Both of us looked closely at the projected map. Salt Lake City was our place of birth, the place where we had spent our childhood and youth before leaving Utah to pursue graduate training and academic careers out of state. We peered at the slide and then did a double-take. There in the middle of the map, highlighted in ghastly gray, were the neighborhoods of our youth. The gray section of the map was labeled "Blighted Area."

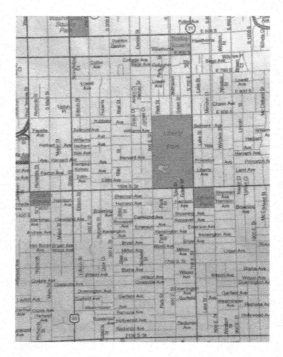

Salt Lake central city area around Liberty Park.

Say what? *Blighted Area?* Por favor. For us, growing up in the central city neighborhoods of downtown Salt Lake during the 1950s had been the Garden of Eden on Earth. Sure, there were problems and occasional ugliness there. As we got older, we realized we lived in the central city environs of an expanding metropolitan area. We knew that times had changed, that inner-city populations were declining, that homes and property values in the Liberty Park area had also declined while crime rates had gone up. Even as younger kids we knew there were much wealthier areas of town on the East Bench and in the rapidly growing suburbs south of Salt Lake City proper.

But *Blighted* area? That blunt designation hurt. As kids we took pride in the modest, well-cared for homes and flower bestrewn working class neighborhoods where we lived; in the older, distinctively styled LDS chapels with their elaborate stained glass windows that anchored designated ward neighborhoods every few blocks; and especially in the public schools we attended—Liberty Elementary (on Third East between Ninth and 1300 South), Lincoln Junior High (on the corner of 1300 South and State Street), and a half a mile further down the road (at 1575 South State), South High School—where we expanded understanding of our ABCs, the birds and the bees, and valued civic lessons from growing up with ethnically diverse friends.

The schools we attended and the LDS Liberty/Liberty Park Ward where we went to church with our parents were housed in buildings that were aging, even then. Liberty Ward opened its chapel doors in 1909; Liberty Elementary was built in 1917; the construction of Lincoln Junior High was completed in 1921; and Depression-era South High, lovingly crafted by Works Progress Administration workers for central city kids the age of our parents, opened its doors in 1931. During the mythical age of our youth in the 1950s and early 60s, all of these structures underwent significant remodeling in naïve anticipation of sustained, if not increased local growth. The Liberty Ward chapel's sanctuary was virtually gutted, remodeled, and refurbished with tastefully modern interior furnishings; Liberty Elementary acquired a brand-new auditorium/gym; ditto Lincoln Junior with the installation of a big, new gym and refurbished library; and South High was enlarged substantially with a new library, a new gym, competition-sized natatorium, and a fifty-yard expansion of new classrooms to extend the school's already lengthy brick profile on South State Street.

The urban demographics of rapidly evolving American cities being what they are, however, a scant few decades later, the old Liberty Elementary was demolished (but replaced with a new school building for Title I families in the 21st century); Lincoln was likewise demolished and its former footprint overlaid with a strip-mall of random business enterprises and their corollary parking lots; and South High, where we learned our most lasting lessons of democracy, was shuttered in 1988. For four years the old campus was a virtual ghost town complex on State Street until it was converted into Salt Lake City Community College's South City campus in 1992.

When we were growing up, our central city schools were attended by Greek, Italian, Mexican, Japanese, Lebanese, and African American kids with surnames like Bizakis, Kyriopoulos, Ligeros, Pappas, and Sotiriou; Caputo, Ferro, Pignataro, Richeda, and Sartori; Archuleta, Balderas, DeVargas, Grego, Martinez, and Sisneros; Aoki, Aoyagi, Mayeda, Shiba, and Yano; Kaleel and Malouf; and yes, with solidly American "slave names" like Crawford, Davis, Ellis, and Miller that had been imposed on the kidnapped ancestors of our African American friends. And, of course, we had plenty of Northern European classmates as well—some of whose parents' native language wasn't English and who spoke with foreign accents. Among our friends, these included kids with names like Ekberg and Swenson (Swedish), Brandl, Dahl, Ebert, and Ruth (German), Johannessen and Loyberg (Norwegian), Schipaanboord, Van de Sluis, Van Der Wouden, and Vander Veur (Dutch).

For us, even in Mormon Salt Lake City, this was America. Sure, most of our classmates like us grew up in Mormon households and on Sundays bowed their heads with their families in neighborhood Mormon chapels. But not the Greek Orthodox or Italian Catholic kids we knew and not many of the Mexican, Japanese, or Lebanese kids either; and certainly not our black friends, whose religious roots were mostly Southern and Baptist and whose fathers would have been denied ordination to the LDS lay priesthood because of their race.

But to us—at our public schools and playgrounds—these ethnic and religious distinctions didn't seem to make a whit of difference. When we say *us*, we specifically mean Mormon white kids who were admonished by responsible adults at church and school to be fair and just to all and, in a taken-for-granted manner, we thought we were. Majority populations usually do. People typically prefer nostalgia to history and re-remember themselves and their past in a rosier light than the facts warrant. We certainly don't exclude our accounts of the good old days from that caveat.

But the facts are, we *were* exposed to democratic principles of justice and equality, and these values *were* strongly emphasized, especially in the public schools we attended. Mere exposure to community values does not, of course, mean that everyone embraces them with equal fervor and sincerity. But we're not speaking for everyone. We're speaking for us and how we believe our experiences growing up in central Salt Lake City affected our thinking and fundamental attitudes later in life. We don't think our retrospective musings in this regard are sheer confabulations.

We weren't paragons as individuals. We were as selfishly immature as other kids our age, had our fair share of family troubles, and were saturated with the same provincialism, unthinking prejudices, and discriminatory practices of the times as everyone else. In the abstract language of social theory that we both learned later as adults, we were deeply ethnocentric in our convictions of the inherent superiority of our local churches, schools, community institutions, and middle/working class way of life. Our ethnocentrism was the product of growing up in a miniature "gemeinschaft" world in which community bonds were based on primary relationships of personal loyalty, trust, and reciprocity. What's wrong with that? Well, the ethnocentrism part, of course, is a universal human problem that arguably has justified, if not generated, virtually every ethnic, religious, and cultural conflict in history. So that needs to be considerably allayed. But the loyalty, trust, and reciprocity parts are what make life sweet and worth living.

Despite our youthful ethnocentrism, what we gained by growing up in the "blighted area" of Salt Lake City in the 1950s and early 1960s was making friends with a diverse set of kids of differing ethnic, racial, and religious backgrounds. We were fortunate in our friends. If we learned nothing else from our diversified, gemeinschaft associations at Liberty, Lincoln, and South, it was that cultivating personal loyalty, trust, and reciprocity transcended race and religion; that the children's children of slaves and immigrants from the different corners of the world could find common cause as fellow citizens and human beings in our country and in our communities.

For us growing up as kids, even in Mormon Salt Lake City, *this was America*. Is it so today in the City of the Saints? Is it so in our country, the

United States of America? Is it what the friends and young people of our generation learned and continue to prize? We fervently hope so, but you'd have to ask them. Sadly, we have our doubts.

2.

REQUIEM FOR A BOYHOOD FRIEND

Gary quickly scanned the brief obituary notice our sister Susan had clipped for him. He and his wife Lauren were home for a summer visit to see family and old friends in Salt Lake City. Sue lived on H Street, high enough in the Avenues neighborhood so that one can view the wide expanse of the Valley of the Great Salt Lake from east to west and north to south, which Brigham Young had claimed for the Mormons (never mind the resident Indians) in 1847. The obituary was for Ronald Victor Swenson—our oldest boyhood friend. It said there would be a gravesite service at 11:00 a.m. in Wasatch Lawn Memorial Park at 3300 South and Highland Drive—about an eight-mile trip from Sue's house. Wasatch Memorial Park is a sixty-five-acre cemetery grounds, just west of Parley's Canyon (named for one of Brigham's fellow apostles, who explored the possibilities of constructing a road—now Interstate 80—down the canyon in 1848). Rearing up like sharks' teeth on adjacent sides of Parley's Canyon are the fortress-like Wasatch Mountains that had initially given the Mormon pioneers a false sense of protection from Babylon America in the middle of the 19th century.

It was just a little past 10:30 a.m., so there might still be enough time for them to make it if they hurried. They had no map of Wasatch Lawn's complicated burial quadrants, nor had there been any directions specified in the obituary. On this sunshine drenched day, however, there seemed to be only one active burial service underway—in a far-flung corner of the cemetery— and Gary, Lauren, and Sue drove toward it. They parked off the side of a curving road on a slight hill right above the burial service site and began trudging down the grassy slope toward a small knot of mourners clustered around the casket and freshly dug grave. They had arrived late and stood quietly unnoticed on the outskirts of the small gathering. A woman was speaking a few modest words in memory of the deceased, and her voice sounded familiar: it was Sondra Swenson, Ron Swenson's oldest sister.

Ron Swenson became our first boyhood friend when our parents moved back to Salt Lake City from God-forgotten Cowley, Wyoming, following several of our dad's unsuccessful business ventures in sales. It was the summer of 1949. We were five-year-old twin brothers and on the verge of starting kindergarten that fall at Liberty Elementary School on Third East, right around the corner from our humble, bungalow home at 312 Herbert Avenue. That summer was when we met Ron, who was a year older. Ron lived a half a block north of Liberty School on Third East, but we first met him in "the field," a big, vacant lot between Herbert and Williams Avenues that abutted Ron's backyard fence. In later years some apartments were erected in this lot. But when we were growing up "the field" is where we habitually joined with Ron and other neighborhood pals to play army or cowboys and Indians or even Robin Hood or Knights of the Round Table, depending on what movie we had seen most recently.

Left, our father, Alvin Shepherd (Shep), shoveling snow off the walk-in front of 312 Herbert Avenue circa, 1955. Right, a contemporary image of 312 with foliage and garden plots now sprouting in place of grass.

We remember, after we first met Ron in the field, going to his home and calling loudly for him on the back steps of his house in the prescribed manner of the times: "Rhaa-ahnnnn! Can you come play?!" Ron's mother opened the screen door, and she was exasperated: "That little bugger!" she heatedly exclaimed. Apparently, Ron had made some kind of mess in the bathroom, locked the door against his mother, jumped out the bathroom window, and had headed for the field. Ron's mother actually became one of our favorites among our friends' mothers. She seemed a little younger and more candid than most moms, smiled easily, semi-cussed a little, and sometimes chatted good-naturedly with us while she drank her morning coffee. Most of the moms we knew would have looked askance at drinking a cup of Postum, let alone coffee.

Ron's father was a WWII vet who worked on the west side of the city for the Rio Grande Railroad. Of Swedish ancestry, Mr. Swenson was darkly handsome instead of blonde, quietly observant, and, unlike our father and the fathers of our other Mormon friends in the neighborhood, smoked Camel cigarettes. He had mechanical skills, tinkered with car engines, and built elaborate model train sets as a hobby. Barely noticeable, unless you looked for it, his right thumb was scarred and deformed from a battle wound received in the war. He let Ron's mother take charge of the house and kids but reprimanded with quiet authority when he deemed it necessary. We liked him, too.

A year ahead of us in school, Ron was stricken with Rheumatic Fever when we were in first grade, and he ended up being "held back" a year. For us, however, that misfortune had its positive side: we were best friends, and it meant that Ron would now be a member of our grade cohort at Liberty for the duration of our elementary education. That Halloween, with Ron restricted to bed rest at home, we trick-or-treated for him and brought him back a big bag of candy, which Mrs. Swenson eyed warily before telling us it was okay for him to keep. Later, when we were nine, Ron suffered a relapse. This time his parents obtained a tutor for him to keep him abreast of his studies at home, where he was confined strictly to his bed. We remember the big black and green "horse pills" (as he called them) that he struggled to choke down every day.

For six months we made almost daily, afterschool visits to see Ron. He had Lincoln logs and a metal erector-set to play with, and he began, painstakingly, putting together plastic WWII model planes. From our visits with Ron, we learned all about British Spitfires, Japanese Zeroes, and American Mustangs as he carefully glued the parts, positioned the decals, and painted the fine details. When we talked about what we were going to be in life, Ron said he was going to be an engineer.

Ron was well enough to return to school in the fourth grade around Thanksgiving time, 1953. Mrs. Lawrence had given the class a poetry assignment to write about what Thanksgiving Day meant to each of us. We were anxious for Ron to do well, and he did, sort of. That is, he had rehearsed the lines he composed and recited them to the class in a resolute voice when it was his turn: "On Thanksgiving Day we work and work, and we never shirk, on Thanksgiving Day." We all applauded.

A few years later, both of us became obsessed with sports, especially baseball. We spent hours poring over Hall of Fame batting and pitching statistics and could quote verbatim the names and lifetime records of baseball's immortals. We got a baseball bat and mitts for our birthday in the fifth grade, and, when spring arrived, we learned how to both pitch and be a catcher, taking turns to catch the other's fastballs with an opposing team's batter swinging away six inches in front of our young, scrunched-up faces.

A year older, a little taller, and a little bigger, Ron had decent shoulders and what we enviously thought was a good build. We thought he looked a little like the Yankee's famous Iron Horse, Lou Gehrig—like a first baseman—so Ron got a mitt for his birthday too, a first baseman's glove. We spent time showing Ron how we thought he should field his position at first base, how to switch his feet to cover the bag and maximize his stretch when a baserunner came charging down the line. He in fact began playing first base on our little league team while the two of us were "batterymates," switching every other game as pitcher and catcher.

In the summers we played baseball, drank Dr Pepper at Ron's house (forbidden at home by our parents because of its caffeinated contents), and slept out most nights in sleeping bags with Ron and some of our other neighborhood friends: sometimes in Ron's back yard, sometimes in ours, and sometimes on Liberty School's old playing field. Lying on our sleeping bags at night we vividly remember gazing at the cloudless, black diamond Salt Lake City sky and gratefully thinking that we were the luckiest kids on the planet.

One Friday summer night, we, Ron, and two other school buddies—Udell Stones and Alvin Ebert—were walking home from watching a WWII war movie that had been shown in the amusement hall of the old Liberty Ward chapel, a half block west of Liberty Park. At the corner of Herbert Avenue and Third East there was another vacant field-lot, within equidistant shouting range of both Ron's house and ours. The lot was filled with large, tall clumps of grass which, when grasped firmly and yanked stoutly up by the roots—with a heavy, clinging clod at the end—could then be hurled at an adversary, exploding in a satisfying burst of dirt and grass when it hit its mark.

Sweaty and satiated with our WWII combat games of throwing grass-clods at each other, Swenson (we had commenced calling one another by our last names), Ebert, and Gordon left the field and began strolling north on Third East. In the meantime, Gordon had yanked up the biggest grass-clod yet and was dangling it by his side as they walked. "Hey, Shepherd," Ebert called out, "see if you can hit this car." Two hundred feet in front of us shined the headlights of an approaching vehicle. "Sure," Gordon said, and anticipating the exact moment of intersection, launched his weighty grass-clod missile on an arc toward the street . . . BLAM! Right in the middle of the car's windshield! And, almost instantaneous with the explosion of dirt that showered them, they heard SCREEEECH! as the car's driver slammed on the brakes.

We all took off running. (That is, Swenson, Ebert and Gordon did; Gary and Udell Stones were still dueling each other in the field.) Both Ebert and Swenson were faster runners than Gordon, who momentarily slipped as they were about to round the corner on Williams Avenue. "I'm doomed!" Gordon thought, as Swenson and Ebert sped ahead. He could hear the heavy footsteps and adult swearing of an angry man breathing down their necks. So, instead of following Swenson and Ebert, who, under the glare of streetlights, were now pounding neck and neck down the middle of Williams Avenue, Gordon cut through some bushes of the house on the corner and ducked around to the backyard of the house next door. He stood there breathlessly waiting to see which way his pursuer would come, so he could scat in the opposite direction. But instead, he heard more shouting from the street; it was Swenson and Ebert who were being chased, not him anymore. "*Stop! It's the police!*" he heard, as the staccato sound of footsteps in flight continued down the street. "The Police?! Holy shit! Who did I hit?!" Gordon wondered out loud.

It turned out that the approaching headlights Gordon had impulsively tossed his dirt-clod missile at belonged to a Salt Lake City Police car. Swenson and Ebert stopped running and meekly surrendered to the irate cop who had chased them down.

Back at the scene of the crime, the cop's partner had jumped out of the driver's side of the car and grabbed both Gary and Udell by the scruffs of their necks while they stood stunned and dumbfounded, entirely baffled by what had just happened, close to the side of Third East where the squad car had screeched to a halt. The second cop, spewing curses, tossed them unceremoniously into the back seat of his car. When the first cop returned with Ron and Al Ebert in tow, they were all deposited with great trepidation to join Gary and Udell in the back seat. The two cops then wheeled their dirt plastered vehicle around and headed for downtown Salt Lake City—with all the delinquents in custody but one: Gordon.

Gordon stood paralyzed in the backyard on Williams Avenue until it was plain that, in the dark and confusion, *nobody had even seen him.* He was home free! He hopped the backyard fence, found himself back in the vacant lot, cut through the weeds, and made a beeline for 312 Herbert Avenue, which was on a diagonal across the street. Our parents called out from the living room where they were absorbed in watching General Electric Theater on television: "How was the show?"

"Great!" Gordon answered and went straight to bed.

An hour or so later, Gary slipped into our small bedroom. "Where the heck were you?!?" he hissed, as he crawled under the covers of the rickety bed we shared. Gordon didn't have a good answer for him, but Gary was actually more interested in narrating what had happened after Gordon fled the scene than venting recriminations against him. He said the cops drove straight to downtown police headquarters on State Street and First South, parked in front of the old red brick Victorian-looking structure, and herded everyone up the steps and through the imposing entrance while bystanders gawked on the sidewalk. Inside, they were ushered into a small interrogation room.

Initially, Ron, Al, and Udell all thought Gary was Gordon and were waiting loyally for him to confess. Instead, Gary shook his head and said he had no idea what had happened. The cops suddenly turned-on Ron Swenson: "You're the biggest, you were running the fastest! You have the dirtiest hands! You're the *leader*, aren't you?! Admit it!" Ron, of course, his rheumatic heart quaking with fear, denied he was the leader of anything. In their turns, Al and Udell also disclaimed guilt while furtively casting anxious glances at Gary. But they all resisted the pressure to rat him out. We weren't a gang; it was just a little war-play in the field, and a stray dirt clod went further than intended, Officer Krumpke.

Well, it didn't take too long for the two arresting officers to discern that what they had in hand were some pre-adolescent boys who were guilty of a little mischief, but who didn't seem to represent a dire threat to community safety. Their decision? Not to book us *or* call anybody's parents; they had scared us enough to learn a lesson, they said. "And this guy"—exclaimed the bigger of the two cops, effortlessly hoisting Udell off the floor and holding him aloft with one beefy arm —"is too little to belong to a gang anyway!" Maybe, just maybe, they recalled themselves at our age when they too were rambunctious, impulsive boys and decided to cut us a break. But, had our skins been black or brown, would we have been treated in such a surprisingly forbearing way? We surmise not.

But not even call our parents? That *was* surprising to us, even back then in 1950s Salt Lake City, for which we were eternally grateful. What they did do was drive Gary, Ron, Al, and Udell back to the corner lot on Herbert Avenue and Third East, drop them off with a warning to keep their noses clean and not to throw things at cop cars again. That was it. Our parents never did find out about what happened that night.

When we hit adolescence, things began to change. Now there were girls, of course, and parties and dances. We were all a little bashful, but Ron was more than reticent or shy around girls; he couldn't seem, even with timid diffidence, to talk to them or flirt with them. Not that Ron was entirely ignorant about girls; his two sisters, Sondra and Roberta, grew into beautiful young women. Both of them—Sondra, willowy and blonde, and Roberta, dark like her father with luscious brown eyes and eyelashes—had plenty of male suitors asking for dates. Ron was as horny as the rest of us, but as a teenager he never had a single date that we know of, not one. Maybe spending eighteen months of your life in bed as a child affects your self-esteem in ways we don't fully understand or appreciate.

Sondra and Roberta Swenson, early 1960s.

Whatever the case, Ron did become clothes conscious. His father got him part-time jobs at the railroad, and, instead of frequenting the department store bargain basements where we had all shopped previously with our parents, he began spending his earnings on fashionable items (like soft-spun jersey wool pullover shirts at Hibbs menswear store and Florsheim loafers at Al Homan's Shoe Shop). He cultivated his taste in music and began listening to cool jazz records instead of pop tunes and rock 'n' roll on the radio. He also learned auto-mechanics from his father but disparaged American jalopies to work on and favored European sports cars instead. His first car was a vintage, 1946 MG, whose entire engine he removed and reassembled. He then traded up for a 1958, Austin-Healey Sprite.

By the time we got to high school in 1959, the two of us were hanging out with the jocks and the kinds of earnestly civic-minded students who joined clubs, staffed the school newspaper, poetry magazine, and student yearbook; participated in school plays and debates; sang in the A'Cappella choir; played in the orchestra and band; and engaged in numerous other extra-curricular activities for which South High was famous. In our 1961-62 senior year, Gary was elected student body president, and Gordon became the sports editor of the *South High Scribe*.

Ron, on the other hand, gravitated to other friendship networks, toward kids who were more cynical and less actively involved in student activities. He didn't attend sporting events, and he never joined a student organization. A mystery to this day is the fact that Ron's photo-portrait never appeared alongside those of his cohort classmates in any of our high school yearbooks, including our senior year. In the official annals of our high school history, Ron Swenson was a complete cipher.

But we were still friends and kept in contact outside of school, especially in the summer when Ron and Gordon would play tennis regularly on the public courts at Liberty Park. Every summer Saturday—when Ron wasn't working—they would motor twenty miles north of Salt Lake in his Sprite on Highway 89 to go swimming at Lagoon and look at the girls. But Ron hung back and would never introduce himself or talk to any of them, even when we knew them from school. He would always pump Gordon for information afterwards, however, asking him how they looked closeup in swimming suits and what they had said.

When, at the age of 20, we both accepted LDS mission calls to serve for two years in Mexico, Ron dutifully attended our missionary farewell from the Liberty Park Ward. When writing to us while we were in Mexico, he would say things like, "Hallelujah, Brother Shepherd! and, "I've been trying hard, but I still haven't gone to Hell!" which delighted us. Ron's irreverent sense of humor was one of the things we prized most in our friendship.

After two years of Spartan abstinence from worldly pursuits south of the border, we returned home to a very different world. Young people our age were radically redefining the salient issues of the 1960s. The counterculture was thriving on the west coast and elsewhere; "psychedelic" drug experimentation was becoming widespread among middle class white kids—not to mention recreational marijuana; the civil rights movement was engulfed in violence and becoming increasingly militant; and student protest against the Vietnam War was already separating children from their parents and deeply dividing the country. A bit taken aback by the abrupt transformation of the 1950s America of our youth, but irresistibly drawn by the tides of change, the two of us continued our educations at the University of Utah, got married, and pursued out-of-state graduate studies in sociology. We stayed in touch with some of our childhood friends but not with Ron. He seemed to disappear from our cognitive maps.

At the lonely Wasatch Lawn burial site for Ron Swenson, Sondra continued her modest eulogy: "But let's not dwell on the unhappy times," she said. "Let's remember the good days for Ron when Gary and Gordon Shepherd used to come to our house as Ron's best friends during his school years. Those were the best years of his life, the only years when he was really happy." Gary sank his chin into his chest.

After the informal service concluded, Gary stepped forward and made himself and Lauren and Sue known to the Swensons standing around the grave. From them Gary learned that, after high school, Ron went to work for the railroad. Over time he became increasingly lonely and alienated. For several years he rented an apartment and lived by himself. Finally, he moved back home to live in his parents' basement. It also became increasingly apparent that he had other problems. He spent a lot of time in bars by himself. Eventually he was diagnosed as being schizophrenic. After that, he never left his parents' basement on Third East until his untimely death on August 5, 1994, at the age of 51.

Dear Ron, we want to thank you for your friendship. You were our first and most loyal friend in boyhood. Those were important times for us. We regret we didn't do more to stay in touch as we got older. We could have, but we didn't. Forgive us. Perhaps you already have. We still dream about you sometimes at night, as though you were still with us. We consider that to be a kind of blessing, and perhaps a sign of your forgiveness too. Thanks.

Ron Swenson, in happier days on the Liberty School playing field, where we would sleep out on summer nights and practice baseball during the day.

3.

DISQUISITION ON PLAYING MARBLES FOR KEEPS AT LIBERTY ELEMENTARY

Arguably, archeological excavations of the playgrounds of our ancient forebears and the games they played, which are no longer understood or appreciated, have value for curious students in contemporary times. Perhaps in decades to come an ambitious archeology student will attempt to write her thesis or Ph.D. dissertation on the antiquated American sport of playing marbles for keeps. Until then, here is our childhood remembrance.

A year or two after we moved on from Salt Lake City's Liberty Elementary to Junior High at Lincoln, the old dirt section of the Liberty playground was blacktopped. That spelled final doom for the marble-playing culture that had prospered at Liberty for decades. But we always believed that the *real* end to our beloved tradition was caused by sadly misinformed and grinchy schoolboard officials who decreed that we couldn't play marbles for keeps on school property anymore. Let us explain.

In the spring of every year—before school, after school, and at recess— the old dirt section of Liberty's playground was dominated by boys, of every grade-level, playing marbles. Girls were concentrated on the sidewalks play- ing hopscotch, jacks, jump rope, or swinging on the tricky bars. Focused on their own interests and criteria for assessing peer standing, girls seldom, if ever, were tuned in to the esoteric rules and standards for playing marbles that engrossed their male counterparts (and vice versa for boys regarding girls' games). What follows will highlight what we learned as boys at Liberty Elementary about playing marbles. What we knew or appreciated about contemporaneous girls' games on the playground is, admittedly, very little.

**Liberty Elementary at 1085 South, Third East in Salt Lake City
in the early 1950s.**

The importance of there being *dirt* on the playground for boys, of course, was so they could draw circle-rings for their marbles with a handy stick or broken pencil stub. The size of the ring depended on the skills and number of players involved. Let us emphasize skills and players. As we passionately understood our boyhood marble games, they were competitive games of skill, and the players who played them knew what they were doing. They were *not* games of chance, we insisted, and did not involve contestants who won the jackpot by getting "lucky" or employing devious chicanery. Sure, on some rare occasion, a novice player might luck-out and somehow win a single game from an experienced player. But, over the long run of many games, true talent would always tell.

Playing for keeps, instead of "funsies," meant to us that you were willing to risk your prized marbles in a challenge to your skill and mastery of the game. And when you won, you could take genuine pride in your hard-earned winnings, i.e., other kids' marbles. That, of course, is what eventually got us into trouble and led to the ban on playing for keeps. But more on that later.

As in other competitive sports, local reputations for shooting marbles were built, challenged, and therefore in need of being regularly defended, confirmed, or overturned. If there was a big game, involving some of the school's best marble players, word would quickly circulate, and a crowd would form around the ring to watch the unfolding drama of triumph and loss. Big marble matches were an alternative form of excitement to school-yard fights and were much less likely to get anybody in trouble or sent home with a bloody nose.

Even though these were competitive contests there was seldom any trouble from sore losers at marbles, because there were *rules*. If you were going to become a reputable marble player, stick your own marbles in the ring, and test your skills in competitions for keeps, you were expected to know and play by the rules. But the rules were not written down; they were unwritten directions and specifications that were an essential part of our oral tradition, and they had to be learned if you were going to play marbles at Liberty Elementary. This does not mean, however, that every game was played in conformity to a standard set of unspoken rules. Not at all. Negotiating and determining *which* rules would apply to a particular game was part of the deal.

An exposition of the possible rules which boys negotiated and under which they competed for one another's marbles is in order, but first let's talk more about the marbles themselves and the accoutrements that went with them. For simplicity's sake, let us say there were three main types of marbles: stickups, taws, and inappropriate marbles.

Stick-ups were the marbles one put into the ring, and, once they were in the ring, they were called "dates." Dates referred to the *number of stickups* one would "ante up" in the ring. If you knocked out the number of marbles you put in the ring (regardless of whether they were your marbles or the other kids'), it was said that you had won "your dates." Dates were the minimum you played for. Any marbles you knocked out of the ring after dates were your winnings to keep (and the other kids' losses). Stickups, by the way, were cheap marbles made from inexpensive glass, that could be easily nicked and chipped, and which could be purchased at the local five and dime in small plastic bags for less than a quarter.

Taws were the shooter marbles that one fired, betwixt thumb and forefinger, into the ring to knock out stickup marbles. Generally speaking, most serious players had numerous stickups in their possession or stockpiled at home but possessed relatively few taws. Taws didn't look like stickups. They usually were a little bigger, a little heavier, not made of cheap glass, and featured unusual colorings. Some taws were made of glass but of a different style, texture, and quality than stickups. Stickups looked virtually all the same and were literally a dime a dozen. Taws stood out, each one having distinctive qualities and characteristics. The best (and most expensive) taws, in fact, weren't made of glass at all; they were marbles made from *flint*. Polished and gleaming like gemstones, they were showcased in little, cotton lined boxes behind glass countertops at higher end drugstores and could be purchased for a buck or two apiece (small fortunes for us at the time). Unless you were an idiot, you never used a flint as a stick up for dates in a game of keeps.

Parenthetically we should mention that Gordon's favorite taw was a "cherry flint," so called for its ruddy coloring; Gary's was a grey and red "bullseye" flint. But we didn't buy them from a store. Gordon traded 300 of his hard-earned stickups for his—carefully counted out of a big Folger's coffee can—from an older kid who possessed other flints and who wasn't that interested in actually playing for marbles anyway. Gary won his in an unusual game of "knockout-kills-takes-dates + taw" (to be explained later).

Inappropriate marbles were marbles that, in respectable games, were disallowed as either taws or stickups. These included boulders pee-wees, aggies, and steelies. Boulders were oversized marbles that were too big to shoot as a taw and too big as a stickup to knock out of a ring. If hit dead center, pee-wees could be knocked *out* of a ring, but as marbles they were worthless and certainly could not be shot as taws to knock anything else out of the ring. Aggies were made of baked clay, tended to be a bit misshapen, and probably were relics from fathers' and grandfathers' marble playing days. And steelies? Steelies were marbles (or ball-bearings) that were made of steel: too dense, too heavy, and no good for either taws or stickups.

Bullseye flint, glass taw, and stickup marble.

The standard accoutrements were also pretty basic, consisting of marble bags and knuckle pads. Marble bags were relatively small pouches with draw strings. Some kids (like us) simply put the marbles they planned to use for the day in an old sock with a knot tied at the end. The thing was, you wanted to take enough stickups with you to cover your dates in projected matches when you got to school, but not so many as to weigh your jeans down or spill out of your pockets. You would also take several of your favorite taws on the theory that you might shoot hotter with one rather than another on any given day. And of course, you counted your marbles carefully before leaving home in the morning and then again upon returning in the late afternoon, so that you could accurately determine your winnings (or losses). Winnings were always marbles in excess of your dates, which would be stored in the aforementioned coffee can or some other suitable container.

Knuckle pads ranged from store-bought (e. g., a tiny rabbit pelt) to homemade (e.g., a woman's used powder puff applicator or a flat piece of sponge swiped and cut-out from your mom's cleaning supplies). The purpose of knuckle pads is virtually self-explanatory. Most marble shooting required you to lay your knuckles on the ground. Without a protective pad to lay them on, they would be cracked and bleeding in no time. A few kids might even deploy something akin to kneepads to keep their knees from getting skinned up or their jeans from getting worn and shredded at the knees. But most of us just wore old jeans that were frequently patched by our moms.

In addition to the types of marbles and accoutrements acquired and displayed as recognized markers of a player, there were also important shooting techniques and skills that had to be perfected in order to compete at the higher levels of the game. First and foremost, you had to learn how to shoot a marble off your knuckle. Novice players and (we presumed) "girls" shot off their fingernail instead of their knuckle. This was called "fudge-knuckle." Shooting fudge-knuckle was a dead giveaway that you were not a serious player. (Heaven knows what faux pas boys committed when they tried playing hopscotch, jacks, or jump rope.) Shooting from your knuckle required learning how to stuff your shooting thumb into a tight grip applied by your middle, ring, and pinky fingers. Your taw could then be balanced on the exposed knuckle of your thumb and held in place by your index finger. "Knuckle power" was a function of how hard you squeezed your gripping fingers and the subsequent velocity with which you fired your taw by springing your thumb from its grip. Knuckle power was essential. It determined whether or not you could shoot through big rings with the best players. If you had good knuckle power you could hit a stickup at a distance of five feet or more and send it flying out of the ring.

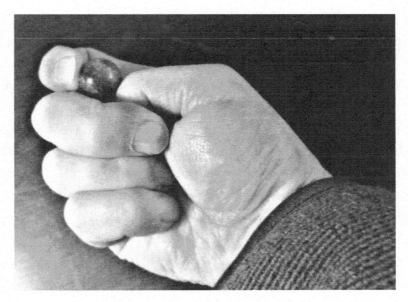

Shooting from knuckle.

It was really quite remarkable with what force good players could shoot their taws. Among boy marble players, knuckle power was the sports equivalent of having a live fastball in baseball. But, of course, just as in baseball, a lively fastball isn't the same thing as pitching strikes, neither did knuckle power necessarily coincide with shooting accuracy in a game of marbles. The best players could not only shoot their taws with power but also with accuracy. Accuracy was the result of constant practice, regular play, and, one supposes, a certain amount of genetically inherited eye-hand coordination. In our experience, the most accurate shooters were probably kids who later in life went on to become artists, surgeons, tennis players, or pool sharks.

Case in point: The best player at our ethnically diverse little school was a Mexican American kid by the name of Mike Martinez. Stocky and short in stature, Mike turned out to be an outstanding athlete. As we got older, he quarterbacked our little league football team, transferred to East High as a teen where he played linebacker and kicked winning field goals, and, sure enough, excelled at tennis, winning the state high school tennis championship in 1962-63. As a younger marble player at Liberty elementary,

Mike was without peer; hardly anybody dared risk their marbles playing for keeps against him. Like a marksman at a rifle range, Mike sighted his taw by resting his chin on his shoulder, squinting his left eye shut, and then, with his right eye focused and steady, he gazed down the length of his arm to the top of his knuckle as though affixing the crosshairs of a scope squarely in the middle of a target: SMACK. A stickup would fly out of the ring at high velocity while Mike's taw spun dead in the center of the ring. Highly consistent in his aim and knuckle power, Mike Martinez was the undisputed playground champ whose American *bona fides* we never thought to question.

That said, we can now summarize some of the basic *rules* for regulating the placement of stickup dates in the center of a ring and for knocking them out by shooting your taw in a game of keeps. First things first. How did games commence? They commenced by one kid approaching another kid on the playground and asking, "Wanna play a game of marbles?" If the kid knew you and your reputed skill level—usually the case—he might say, "Naa, I don't think so," or, "Sure, let's lag." (If for some reason he didn't know you or vice versa, but he had a marble bag on him and you could infer he was a player, the negotiations were up for grabs).

"Let's lag" meant, "let's decide who gets to shoot first," which—as in pool games—bestows an advantage. The procedures for lagging required that a straight line first be drawn in the dirt. Crouching five or six feet back of the line, players would take turns shooting their taw at the line; the taw closest to the line determined who shot first. (Note: one could also lag by standing up and gently casting, underhand, one's taw toward the line, but this was considered gauche form and less likely to be accurate, to boot). The advantage for the lag-loser, however, was that he got to say what the rules were, selectively choosing from the cultural repertoire of common rules, both prescriptive and proscriptive. If the kid who won the lag didn't like the proposed set of rules, he could always quibble or change his mind about wanting to play, but that also would be considered gauche, and he would be viewed as a boo-baby.

Before starting the game, three other things had to be settled: Were you going to play for keeps (almost always) or funsies? What were the dates going to be? And how big was the ring going to be? In pre-game negotiations, dates usually varied between three to five stickups. There were no hard and fast rules about the size of the ring. If kids were younger, however, and/or novice players, the ring would be smaller, with a diameter of three to four feet. If just two kids were playing who were older and more experienced, the ring would be larger but a kind of "medium larger," with a dimeter of five to six feet. If it was a big game with multiple, skilled players, the ring would be significantly larger, with a diameter of between eight and ten feet.

To play in these latter games meant, as already stated, that you had to have enough knuckle power to shoot your taw four or five feet to the center of the ring and hit a stickup with sufficient force to knock it at least another four or five feet out of the ring in order to claim it as your own. If you hit a stickup, but it didn't go out of the ring, it was still in play and could be shot at by the next shooter at what usually would be a shorter distance. But if your taw knocked a stickup *out* of the ring, not only did it belong to you, but you also got to keep shooting until you missed (just like shooting pool). Now, there was one very important potential condition to what we just said, so let's return to the rules.

Rules need names and, in the oral tradition of our playground culture, some of the rules for marbles had odd names—names like: ups, spins, tony-in, and knock-out-kills. There were many other potential rules, but those were the main ones.

"Ups" allowed you to shoot your taw standing up or, as was usually the case, by steadying your shooting wrist on your knee, rather than crouching on the ground with your knuckles in the dirt. The point about claiming "ups" was that shooting position would give your taw more velocity (playing marbles is essentially about physics, after all). This rule allowance was predictably favored by players with weaker knuckle power to compensate for their disadvantage when playing stronger players. Of course, shooting from an up position was markedly less accurate and virtually never resorted to by good players. And it goes without saying that all shots from outside the ring, whether from ups or with knuckles on the ground, had to be taken without the player's shooting hand going over the ring line. To do so was a transgression called "snudging" and, in the event that a snudged shot resulted in striking one of the marbles placed as dates in the center of the ring, it resulted in disqualification of the shot—assuming, of course, that the players all agreed that snudging had occurred. And if players didn't agree that snudging had occurred? Well, theoretically, that's the same problem for schoolyard basketball games where kids must call their own fouls, traveling, or out-of-bounds violations. Theoretically, somebody could take their ball and go home if they insisted that only they were ever right, but that rarely happens. There may be a certain amount of arguing, cussing, and even yelling but usually cooler heads prevail, an agreement is reached, and the game continues. The same was true in marbles.

Another way for weaker players to even the odds was the tony-in rule. If the kid calling rules said "tony-in," it meant that when it was his, or any other player's turn, he could shoot his taw softly for the center of the ring, without necessarily hitting anything, and be allowed to keep it in place where it had stopped rolling until it was his turn to shoot again. This meant, of course, that he would be much *closer* to the stickups on his next turn and consequently more likely to hit one of them out of the ring.

That particular advantage could be countered, however, by the "knock-out-kills" rule. If knock-out-kills was in force, another player could shoot your *taw* out of the ring after you had tonyed-in. If this happened, the game was over, and you lost all your dates. As previously alluded to, a more severe variation of this rule was knock-out-kills-takes-dates + taw, meaning that you could not only lose all your stickup dates on one shot to an opponent, but your *taw* as well (God forbid if it was a *flint* taw), and very few players would agree to play to that rule.

But prior to concluding, let us consider the single most demanding marbles game rule which, in marblesese, separated the sheep from the goats: the "spins" rule. If you played spins, your taw not only had to knock a stickup out of the ring for you to keep it, but your taw also had to remain *inside* the ring. If it didn't, you had to place the stickup back in the center of the ring, and it was the next player's shot. Deflected marbles that glanced or ricocheted off your taw and went out of the ring along with your taw didn't count.

The sweetest shot in marbles happened when your taw *spun dead* after connecting with a stickup in the center of the ring. To spin dead meant your taw hit a target marble square in the middle, not a glancing blow on its side or top. This is the equivalent of hitting a pitched baseball flush in the center of the barrel of the bat, or, in a game of pool, the cue ball splattering the triangularly racked object balls in all directions by hitting the lead ball dead center. When a taw spins dead, it literally spins on the exact spot occupied by the target marble a split second previously. In turn, this means that the shooter can continue shooting his taw, but now his taw is in the *center of the ring*. It's quite possible at that point for an expert shooter to "clean the ring" by systematically knocking out all the remaining stickups with short range, dead-on, spin shots. That was the gold standard of marble playing culture. When it happened, it was something to behold. This, as we already recounted, was the kind of shooting that made Mike Martinez such a formidable opponent among his playground peers.

In the big games with the best players, the spins-rule was always in effect; and in covariation, so too were these basic proscriptions: *No* ups, *no* tony-in, and consequently *no* knock-out-kills. Maybe a few kids lost all their marbles and their taws as well because of poor skills and bad rule-making decisions. And maybe they were the same kids who complained to their mothers, who complained to the teachers, who passed on their complaints to anxious schoolboard officials, who decided they had to outlaw playing marbles for keeps on school property. But we must reiterate: The best players in the best games knew what they were doing and learned to accept defeat as well as victory. What was the point of playing for funsies?

It certainly may be argued that the latent function of boys learning to play marbles for keeps was to introduce them at an early age to the business realities of the world they were destined to inherit—to the material world of commerce and trade, of savings and investment, profit and loss, of entrepreneurship and shrewd calculating, of sizing up your competitors in the market and learning how to make the rules work to your own advantage. In a word, learning to play marbles for keeps induced boys to imbibe deeply of the *spirit of capitalism*, so that America could depend on its next generation of Republican businessmen leaders to run its banks, factories, real estate markets and investment houses, not to mention its local grocery stores, insurance companies, and country clubs throughout the land.

Yeah, okay, maybe so.

But we think there were more important latent lessons and consequences. Conflict, it may be argued, is what happens in human interaction when there are no rules or, if there are rules, what happens when they are systematically disregarded and unenforced. In contrast, competition occurs when people with conflicting interests are effectively regulated in their conduct by acceptance of shared rules that limit what they can and cannot do in pursuit of their own interests. When rules break down, competition becomes conflict. *Cooperation* occurs when people make alliances with others in order to improve their shared benefits in either competition or conflict with others.

Speaking of cooperation, did we mention that another aspect of marble playing culture was playing with a *partner*? Partner or team games, of course, increased the number of potential players and consequently the number of marbles at stake in the center of the ring. If you had a good partner, and he or you spun dead in the center of the ring with your taw, you could really clean house together, because you would share equally your winnings, regardless of who knocked the marbles out. At the same time, as in most forms of cooperation, *individuals,* who could otherwise do better for themselves in personal competition (or conflict), must be willing to sacrifice some of their own potential gains for the good of the team. Apropos to marbles, Gordon had a great partner, Lorin Larsen, whose skills were arguably even better than his. Gary's partner, Dave Lingwall, was less skilled but a good friend. Predictably, Lorin and Gordon won more marbles on average than Gary and Dave, whereas Gary's partner, Dave, ended up with more marbles than he would otherwise have won on his own. So, both Gary and Dave profited and, in the end, strengthened a friendship. That's how cooperation works.

And also, by the way, we held kids in distain who only cared about increasing their marble supply and not about the sport itself and what was required to play it well. These tended to be kids who preferred to play "pots," for instance. Pots was a pseudo marbles enterprise that required very little skill and was predicated largely on the hope of simply acquiring marbles per se, somewhat akin to the wishful expectation of vacation gamblers feeding coins into slot machines and hoping to win a jackpot by sheer luck. We will not even bother to elaborate the rules of this game, such as they were.

The thing about our marble rules for skilled players is that they taught us respect for rules—respect, that is, for the kind of *rules that we ourselves could choose and take ownership of*— rules that served to define a status meritocracy among peers based on both competition and cooperation, talent and integrity. Had they understood this, perhaps our anxious schoolboard officials would have allowed us to continue playing for keeps. In any case, hustler kids who didn't respect the rules, who tried to cheat or didn't play by the rules or complained and made excuses for themselves when they lost, were held in contempt, no matter if they (or their parents) could afford rabbit pelt knuckle pads or a dozen flints or hundreds of store-bought marbles.

Actually, there were few if any kids of that description at Salt Lake City's Liberty Elementary School when we attended there. Indulge us a small thought experiment on this final point: Imagine that Fred C. Trump of Queens, New York lived in Salt Lake City in those days, and for some unfathomable reason he permitted his churlish son, Donald J., to attend Liberty Elementary. We wonder how well Donald J. would have made out in the marble-mania culture of our youth? As a kid, would the future, self-appointed lord of the Mexican border have dared to match his skills for keeps against Mike Martinez? Would he patiently have invested the time and effort to develop the necessary skills in the first place? And if he had, would he have proved himself to his peers by adhering to the proud playground rules of marble culture? Would any of the boys at Liberty Elementary have trusted Donald J. sufficiently to share their dates and partner with him to divide their potential winnings equally? Or would he have connived to be a "winner" by other, less righteous means?

Just ask'n. Who knows? After all, in our most cherished fantasies we are permitted to imagine how, at critical turning points, individuals and their world might have been changed for the better. Realistically, though, we'd wager every marble we ever won that Donald J. would never have made the grade among our peers at Liberty Elementary—or at any of the other school playgrounds of Salt Lake City's public schools in 1950s America—let alone successfully challenge Mike Martinez to a game of keeps. Wanna bet your marbles against us on that?

4.

THE POLIO PLUNGE AND OTHER
WATERY MISADVENTURES

Our family moved to Salt Lake City from Cowley, Wyoming in the spring of 1949. We were five years-old and slated to begin kindergarten at Liberty Elementary in the fall. One of our earliest memories after arriving in Salt Lake is a family outing to the old Wasatch Warm Springs Plunge on 800 North Beck Street—a cavernous and decaying structure that was intensely humid, reeked of chlorine, and housed a large indoor swimming pool that drew its waters from an adjacent hot spring that burbled up to ground surface in the adjacent foothills of the Wasatch Mountains.

Wasatch Warm Springs at 840 North Beck Street and Main pool, circa 1950.

It was the first time in our young lives that we had been in a real swimming pool with deep water, and we loved it. Spaced several yards apart from each other in the shallow end of the pool, Mom and Dad would push our little bodies between them, and we would splash happily forward into waiting arms. Before long, we were able to propel ourselves a shortish distance from a standing start in the shallow end to the guttered and tiled bank a few yards away.

We perfected our beginning swimming skills on our own later that summer at the Liberty Park public swimming pool. The first time or two, we splashed around in a small wading pool off to the side of the main, big pool. After watching older kids in the big pool, we migrated there and, starting in the shallow end, quickly discovered that we could stay afloat in the water and swim forward by imitating the movements of the older kids. From then on, swimming at Liberty Park became a regular summer activity.

The wading pool at Liberty Park and jumping off the diving board, circa mid-1950s.

To illustrate, let's take a typical hot day in Salt Lake City that could have been one of any hundreds of similar summer days from 1950 through 1954. On this typical day we had just gone to collect Ron Swenson from his house on Third East and approximately Tenth South. Then the three of us headed for our almost daily swim. Oooh, oooh, ow! All three of us sang out these little yelps in unison as we took quick, high arched steps in our bare feet across the hot, pebbly asphalt surface of the street. Once on the other side, we briefly soothed the burned pads and toes of our feet on the small strip of soft grass that lined the sidewalk in front of our 312 Herbert Avenue home. Herbert Avenue extended another two city blocks east until its interruption at Liberty

Park on Fifth East. The park and its outdoors public swimming pool were our destination, and we continued our eastward trek on the hot sidewalk, hopping onto grass patches along the way whenever these were available. We wore only swimsuits and a small towel tied around our waists. At Fifth East, we waited for a break in car traffic, then made another hot-footed dash over street asphalt to the wide, welcoming swaths of green grass at Liberty Park.

We squinted and scanned ahead to see how many other kids might already be lined up outside the entrance of the public swimming pool that was stationed at an angle another 200 yards ahead, just south of the park's public tennis courts. It was important to be among the first 50 boys in our line: What was called a "plunge," or scheduled swimming period, was set for every hour, and only a fixed number of kids—about 100—were allowed in the pool during each plunge. (One line was for boys, and a second, parallel line was for girls.) We jokingly called swimming at Liberty Park the "Polio Plunge." It was the 1950s and, until the Salk vaccine became widely available in the summer and fall of 1955, upward of 50,000 mostly youthful victims of polio in the United States alone were falling prey to the devastating virus each year. The exact cause of the virus was not widely known at the time, but some local rumors suggested that swimming in a crowded public pool with a bunch of scruffy kids from God knows where could be a contributing factor. Nevertheless, we figured that if our parents didn't forbid us, it must be OK. Those were the days when kids pretty much ran free during the summer months. We spent a lot of our time roaming around Liberty Park—an eighty-acre oasis in the old residential center of Salt Lake City that featured ancient trees, expansive lawns, tailored gardens, children's playgrounds, ball fields, picnic grounds, tennis courts, an amusement park, a boating lake, and the Tracy Aviary. And of course, the swimming pool.

We arrived at the pool around 12:40 p.m. to await entrance to the next plunge at 1:00 p.m. We shifted our bare feet back and forth waiting on a graded, hot concrete strip leading up to the doors while the two lines grew behind us, curving at the end of the concrete onto a worn patch of lawn and dirt. We could hear sharp retorts of a whistle at 12:55 p.m. and loud yells, "Everybody out!" After swimmers from the previous plunge had all straggled out through the entrance, two young adult lifeguards, who to us appeared to be like bronzed Greek gods, signaled the lines to move forward while calling out the numbers of entrants, "one, two . . ." until reaching the designated cut-off point of fifty for each line. Boys turned to locker rooms on the left and girls went to a separated room on the right. On the boys' side, some of the kids were dressed in street clothes and had to take time to put their things in lockers. But we who arrived already stripped down, with no hindering baggage, headed directly into the required shower area. We rushed through the jets of water spewing from shower heads positioned prior to the dressing room exit, just enough to show that our suits were wet, and our legs and feet were dripping, and emerged out onto the pool deck.

Ron had not learned to swim previous to our first taking him with us to the park. But we taught him what we had already learned: All he had to do was relax, hold his breath, move his arms and kick his legs, and he could even open his eyes under water if he wanted. We stayed with him in the shallow end of the pool and kept encouraging his efforts. Ron was bigger and stronger than we were and doggedly determined. Before long, he was able to swim on his own, and swimming became one of the pleasures of his life.

When we were a little older, we headed straight for the low diving board, taking three steps forward on the board, the last one a bounce at the board's end, and launched up and forward, self-consciously trying to keep our legs together, our back arched, and our toes pointed in the proper form that we had learned from reading and observation. The water was shockingly cold after roasting in the sun, but we kept our downward dive momentum under the water and skimmed the ten-foot-deep bottom before angling up to the surface. We had learned how to cut our arms and cupped hands through the water, while paddling with our legs and feet from behind, and swam back to the pool's edge. After the first few years of summer swimming, we had screwed up our courage and confidence enough to edge out onto the end of the high diving board, about 10 feet above the water. We would then attempt to perform jack-knives or swan dives and ask breathlessly of each other after a finished dive, "Was that a good one? Did I do it right?

"The two of us were pretty scrawny . . ." Gordon (left), and Gary (right), swimming at Bear Lake, Utah at about age seven.

Ron was sturdily built as a kid, but the two of us were pretty scrawny. After repeated dives and fast swims back to shore, we would be a bit shaky, our lips would turn purple, and we would seek rest on the hot surface of the pool deck, stretching out fully on our stomachs, arms close to our sides, drying off and baking in the sun, eyes closed, smelling the faint odors of cement and chlorine mixed together, and vaguely hearing the shouts and splashes from the pool as we dozed off for a few minutes—tactile, sensory memories that remain potent after all these years. By summer's end, our hair would be bleached blonde, and our normally fair-skinned bodies transformed into a dark tan. Our grandmother Shepherd would exasperatedly admonish us that we had "turned brown as berries," a color which she apparently disapproved of.

Two things interrupted our days of summer swimming at Liberty Park. First, halfway through the fourth grade, our family moved from our central city Salt Lake home to spend a year living in and taking care of the home of our Uncle Bob and Aunt Olive on Highland Drive in the suburb of Holladay. So, in the summer between fourth and fifth grade, we were cut off from our regular Liberty Park swimming routine. Second, during our one-year absence from Salt Lake, we started acquiring other interests that would soon turn our time and pre-occupation away from being summer park rats toward overdosing on library books and playing little league baseball (but more on these emerging interests elsewhere in this volume).

Our Uncle Bob's property included a beautifully terraced swimming pool and lounging deck overlooking a wooded area below. But filling the pool with water and maintaining it properly for the one summer we lived on Highland Drive was a financial step removed from our family's ability to manage. Money was tight, and, at the time, our dad had a sales job that took him to Idaho every week. While he was gone, we three young boys were not seen as reliable caretakers of a complex pool and water system, even if the chemicals and higher water bills had been affordable. The pool stayed empty, serving only as a repository for leaves and other yard debris we raked into it.

Though we no longer had daily summer access to swimming at Liberty Park, we enthusiastically embraced any irregular opportunities to go swimming that arose. The Winder Ward, where we now attended church meetings, afforded such an opportunity that summer through its younger LDS youth group (The Primary Children's Association): a group outing to Saratoga Springs—an amusement park with a large outdoor swimming pool that was located on the northwestern shores of Utah Lake.

We regret to say that our move to Holladay activated a latent tendency to be wiseacres and to embellish our recitations of alleged accomplishments back in central Salt Lake to our new friends in the Winder Ward (and at the William Penn Elementary School). En route to Saratoga Springs in the backseat of our primary class instructor's car, we bragged of our swimming and diving prowess and especially aimed these boasts at Craig Lawson, a boy we perceived to be unwelcoming to us as the new kids on the block. Once in the pool at Saratoga, we began teasing Craig to go up on the high dive with us. Craig was short and a bit chubby and, as it turned out, didn't even know how to swim. But, we said, no problem. We would go first, then wait for him in the water below the diving board. He could just jump—wouldn't even have to try diving—and we would be right there to help him make it back to shore. So Craig climbed up the rungs to the top of the high dive with us. We dived off, then waited in the water, paddling in place, looking expectantly upwards. Craig hesitantly crouched forward into view, then, as we waved and encouraged him on, he grimaced, closed his eyes, clutched one arm across his chest, held his nose with the hand of his other arm, and jumped.

Gary was closest to Craig when he hit the water and then popped up like a cork, with a wide-open mouth, a gasp, and bugging eyes. He instantly launched himself towards Gary, embracing him with a neck-strangle-hold and began trying to climb Gary's upper body as they both sank below the pool surface. Gary was struggling and taking-in water through both his mouth and nose. But as soon as they went under the surface, Gary instinctively raised his arms straight up, and Craig's slippery flesh was magically untethered from around Gary's neck. Up Gary popped behind Craig, who, he could see, was now being grappled by Gordon. In a flailing, splashing ball of arms and hands, we managed to steer Craig back to edge of the pool and helped push him from the water up onto the deck, where he laid breathing hard for what seemed a long time.

Did we learn anything from this little debacle, in which we had endangered and, at a minimum, publicly embarrassed a classmate? Maybe, hopefully. Vivid recollections of what happened and why, 65 years later, suggest that it made an impact. Nevertheless, it apparently was not enough of a lesson at the time to forestall another dangerous watery episode involving Gary that occurred not long after the Saratoga incident. It happened this way.

Gary accompanied Dad on a sales trip to Boise, Idaho, where they stayed overnight at a friend's home on the outskirts of town. The friend had sons of his own, one of whom was just a year younger than Gary. The next morning, while Dad visited with his friend and friend's wife, the younger son was more or less assigned to befriend Gary and show him a good time. They were both initially awkward but before long discovered they shared certain sporting interests, including swimming. As it happened, the family home was situated on a bluff overhanging the Boise River—a one-hundred-mile-long tributary of the Snake River, famous for its salmon fishing. Gary's new friend said that he and his older brothers sometimes swam in the river later in the summer, and maybe that was something he and Gary could do—although, as an afterthought, the river was running pretty high at the moment, and no one had tried it out yet. But OK! No problem! An old swimsuit, approximately Gary's size was found, the two pre-teen boys doffed their clothes and slipped into their trunks, then made their way down a steep dirt trail to the river bottom.

On the way down, Gary's new friend began having second thoughts about the wisdom of carrying out this proposed dip in the river. But, anxious to prove his mettle, Gary dismissed these concerns and instead continued elaborating on his swimming experience, pooh-poohing the potential problems of swimming in a river (which he had never done). Swimming was swimming, you just had to know the right way to do it, Gary said in self-reassurance.

The Boise River.

When they came into a clearing at the river's edge, Gary gave a little inaudible gasp. The distance between them and the opposite shore was wide—maybe fifty yards—a lot wider than he had thought it would be. Even more worrisome was how fast the deep looking water seemed to be moving past them. Too late now, though, to back off, as Gary heard his new friend saying, "Go ahead if you want, I'll walk down and meet you at the bridge below here."

Gary hesitated, then plunged in, and his new-found fears were immediately confirmed. The water *was* fast, *and* deep and, in addition was icy cold. Gary tried swimming in a straight beeline to the opposing shore, but the current was so strong he didn't seem to be making much progress at all except to move swiftly forward on an angle downstream. He exerted all the puny strength in his skinny arms and legs to fight the relentless push of the current, fighting hard to keep from being swept away. Slowly, slowly he approached the tantalizing safety of the opposite shore, albeit on an increasingly sharp diagonal from the point of his launch. But he was becoming exhausted and momentarily felt doomed. Gary closed his eyes and kept churning with what felt like his last remaining particle of energy when, *gracias a Dios*, he felt a toe brush against something solid and reflexively extended an arm out to grasp a slippery but angular shoreline rock. He pulled himself forward into a little shallow ebb pool, crawled onto dry ground, and lay there shivering on the shore, sides heaving, a goodly distance downstream from where he had started.

While gathering himself together before walking, with trembling, careful steps, further down the shoreline to meet his waiting new friend at the bridge, the lessons of this and previous follies finally did make a conscious appearance in Gary's thoughts: No more bragging, no more overestimating his abilities and underestimating the truth of other peoples' concerns, and no more careless dismissal of hard realities that he had not yet experienced for himself. Good lessons to learn, often heeded in the years ahead. But, regrettably, as with most of us mere mortals, not *always* heeded, as further youthful misadventures would affirm and to which Gary's wife, Lauren, will, on some occasions, dolefully attest in the present.

5.

JOUSTING WITH THE PHANTOM

There were two Phantoms. One was a cartoon character created and drawn by our older-artist brother, Don, and the other one was Don himself. This will require a bit of explaining.

Born four months after the Japanese struck Pearl Harbor, Don was roughly two years older than us. With the onset of war, our 30-year-old dad applied for and obtained a directorship position with the American Red Cross. Dad had played freshman football for Utah State University, was an amateur golfer of some ability, an avid fisherman, and had actively participated in a number of sports programs sponsored by the LDS Church throughout his youth and young adulthood. These athletic credentials seemed to be sufficient to win him the position as a sports and recreation director for men needing recreational distraction from the otherwise grim realities of war. As part of his schooling for the job he went through military basic training at Fort Ord, California and was then given the "equivalent rank" of a lieutenant colonel in the regular army, so he would be taken seriously when he was sent overseas to organize R & R programs for bolstering the morale of American troops in New Guinea. Back home in Salt Lake City, "Donnie" quickly became the apple of everyone's eye—especially in the eyes of our paternal grandmother, Ellen Brighton Shepherd. Donnie was her first grandchild (and a male to boot). Mom's sisters, Zelda and Alice, and her friend-girl neighbors were also thrilled and rallied around her to give much needed practical as well as moral support while Dad was gone.

Sixteen months later, when we came along, Don's cozy universe collapsed. (Apparently our dad got some leave time from training before shipping out for New Guinea, during which time we were undoubtedly conceived. When we were born, dad was far away in the South Pacific, not seeing us until we were almost a year old.) Suddenly, WE were the center of the universe—TWINS, no less. And we were "easy babies," Mom used to say. Unlike Don, we were a quick and relatively painless delivery (Mom almost died bearing Don). Unlike Don, we were not colicky or fussy as infants. We contentedly sucked each other's thumbs in our dual-sized baby carriage and slept peacefully when we were supposed to. Like greedy little sponges, we blissfully soaked up everyone's attention within smiling radius. We don't think Don ever quite forgave us for all of this; for displacing him from the ego-gratifying glow of the adult spotlight while serving as pointed examples of being good babies—and then good boys—in comparison to an increasingly sullen and resentful first-born older brother, who found himself suddenly and inexplicably dethroned as prince of the household.

**Gary, Gordon, our mom, Marjorie Coombs Shepherd, and Don,
circa December 1944.**

Our ongoing sibling relationship with Don as kids was rocky, to say the least. Growing up, Don did not deign to call us individually by our names. He would simply say to either one of us, "Hey, twin," thereby effectively identifying what he was up against: the attention-grabbing quality of seemingly duplicate little boy usurpers and the united, undifferentiated face we presented him as he struggled futilely to regain his anointed spot in the sun. It wasn't until young adulthood that we began to reconcile some of the smoldering animosities that hardened our childhood years together. We grew up harboring resentful rancor toward one another far more than mutual appreciation.

One of our earliest, shared memories, in fact, involves a two-against-one brawl in the living room while our mom was elsewhere in the house. The two of us were around three years- old at the time, which means Don was about five. And two-against-one meant us unitedly battling Don. On that particular occasion we were playing "jungle" with large, wooden pieces to a jigsaw puzzle of jungle animals. Gordon was supposed to be a lion and had one of the puzzle pieces in his mouth. We don't recall what animal Don was acting out, but he rammed Gordon hard into the leg of the living room couch and knocked a front tooth out. Seeing Gordon go down with Don on top, Gary instantly sprang on Don's back and wildly pummeled his head, neck, and ears with his little fists, while Gordon started yelling his head off. By the time our beleaguered mom arrived on the scene her three pint-sized sons were entangled in a tumultuous Gordian Knot of grabbing, kicking, punching, and flailing arms and legs. Gordon's mouth was bloody from the violent loss of a baby tooth, but Don's nose was also bloody from the subsequent mini-blows he had received from the two of us acting as one.

Since he was the big brother, and regardless of who was actually at fault, Don usually got into most of the trouble for these kinds of sibling donnybrooks. We see the injustice of it now, but at the time we naturally thought we were blameless, and that Don was a villainous tormenter who meant us harm. So the two of us perceived the need to righteously stick together in self-defense. To this day when people say we are so close because of our twin genetics, we say, naah, it's because at a very early age we had to learn the value of cooperative alliance against the depredations of our older brother. Together, we effectively resisted him; alone, we were at his mercy until a later age when we grew to be his physical equal. Don, we regret to say, is no longer around to give his side of the story.

**Don, Gary, Gordon, and our dad, Cowley, Wyoming,
circa December 1948.**

At any rate, Don's art ability was apparent from an early age. A little DNA was at work there, too. Our mother's mother, Estelle Taylor, had been a very good amateur artist, and our Dad's older brother, Robert L. Shepherd (Uncle Bob to us), was a locally-renowned, professional muralist and painter of western landscapes. His own father, Joseph Shepherd, and even more so, his paternal grandfather, William Shepherd, were both also talented artists. Uncle Bob was an especially important adult role model for Don as a boy. His successful career in art proved that, if you were talented enough, you could make a good living at it. Don determined that he, too, was going to be an artist. And that eventually led to the emergence of The Phantom. But first, a little more background.

In 1953 Uncle Bob was recruited by his friend, famous Utah illustrator, Arnold Friberg, to join him in Los Angeles, California, to assist in art-related production tasks in the making of Cecil B. DeMille's *The Ten Commandments*, starring Charlton Heston, Yul Brynner, Anne Baxter, and Edward G. Robinson. Bob was also commissioned to paint murals in the new LDS Los Angles Temple. Bob would be gone on these project s for over a year, and he asked our parents to move all of us to his modern, self-constructed home and large, beautifully landscaped property at 4300 South Highland Drive in order to keep a watchful eye on his estate, while he and his family were in Los Angeles. That meant our parents would temporarily rent out our old bungalow home on 312 Herbert Avenue, while we kids would be uprooted from our beloved Liberty Elementary School and neighborhood buddies for a half year in the fourth grade and another half year in the fifth grade. Our temporary new school was called William Penn Elementary. We thought that, relative to Liberty, it was a decidedly inferior name for a school.

**Views of Robert L. Shepherd's Los Angeles Temple World Room murals.
Images courtesy of Bridger Talbot.**

We were unhappy about having to leave all our friends in town. To us, Uncle Bob's home was virtually in the country, ten miles from downtown Salt Lake City. BUT we also thought his place was a palatial estate, especially in comparison to our modest little home on Herbert Avenue, a mere mile and a half from the famous, spired Mormon temple and tabernacle on Temple

Square. Today, of course, 4300 South Highland Drive is scarcely the country. The entire depth and breadth of the Salt Lake Valley are now brimming with suburbs, freeways, and shopping malls where our parents' parents tilled the desert soil and watered it from canals and irrigation ditches dug to channel water from melting winter snow captured in nearby mountain streams and reservoir lakes.

The yard and grounds around Bob's home were fabulous, covering over three acres of former farm and orchard land that he and our Aunt Olive had received as a wedding gift from Olive's parents in 1932. Possessing architectural drafting skills and handy with tools, Bob built a commodious home with a veranda style porch around the original, small brick house that stood on the property when he and Olive married. Shielding the property from car traffic on Highland Drive was a dense line of bushes and trees behind a concrete cinder block wall. A long, gracefully curving gravel drive descended from the street entrance to the garage. Both the front and back yards were landscaped and surrounded by fruit trees, walnut trees, and gooseberry and current berry bushes. There was even a sizeable fishpond outside the kitchen window, filled with gigantic carp and gold fish. Situated in the center of the pond, Bob had sculptured a little boy peeing into the water, which was actually part of the water recycling system that he installed to keep the pond from getting stagnant. But most wonderful of all to us city slickers was the swimming pool. On a slope descending from the back of the house, Bob had terraced a pathway and constructed a 20 by 40-foot swimming pool that was eight-feet at the deep end. Down the hill from the swimming pool was a grove of cottonwood trees and a swampy little pond ringed by cattails and pussy willows. Both the swimming pool and the swampy pond, not to mention the property's numerous fruit trees, were all to play a part in our jousting with The Phantom.

Robert L. Shepherd Home at 4300 Highland Drive, Winter 1955.

As a budding artist, and under the spell of full-length Walt Disney animated movies of the era ("Bambi," "Dumbo the Flying Elephant," "Cinderella," "Alice in Wonderland," "Peter Pan," "Lady and the Tramp," etc.), Don decided he should try his hand at cartooning. For Don, cartooning meant writing and drawing a cartoon strip, replete with narrative story lines. The hero or, actually, the anti-hero of his strip, was *The Phantom*. Don's art was excellent, although we remember very little about the creative quality of his story lines. Most of them seemed to involve the clever plotting of the villainous Phantom to frustrate his doltish adversaries. Don's Phantom was drawn in dark black ink, his face covered with a mask and his shoulders draped in a long, black cape. Interestingly enough, about that same time Don began taking on the identity of The Phantom himself—wearing a Zorro mask and cape, hiding in the bushes and springing out at us when we had friends over to visit, ransacking our bedroom drawers, and leaving little, menacing notes behind signed by "THE PHANTOM!" etc. We insisted to Don that we *knew* he was The Phantom and vowed to prove it.

A month or so after the contest of proving who The Phantom was got underway, we were having a cattail fight (the long cattails could be plucked and thrown at each other like spears) down by the swampy pond with Dave Lingwall—a Liberty school friend who had spent the night with us. Suddenly, on the brow of the hill above us, *The Phantom* made a dramatic appearance, yelling deprecations and challenging us to catch him. With a toreador's flourish of his black cape, he wheeled and disappeared from sight. We and Dave went charging up the hill determined to unmask The Phantom. When we got to the top of the hill we found ourselves at the edge of Uncle Bob's swimming pool. And there, at the bottom of the unfilled pool, lying stretched out flat on his back and moaning as dry leaves settled back down around him, was The Phantom. In his haste to escape from his doltish pursuers, and with his mask slipping down halfway over his eyes, Don had plunged headlong into the empty pool (fortunately, at the shallow end, lightly buffered by a layer of drifted leaves). As for us, what did we do when we arrived at the accident scene of a boyish prank gone painfully wrong? We jeered. Yes, we jeered and pointed and, without any brotherly sympathy, proclaimed our victory: "We *told* you we'd prove you were The Phantom!" we exulted.

Uncle Bob's pool filled with water several years before the Phantom incident (Gordon standing to Don's left).

After that fiasco, Don put a halt to drawing his Phantom cartoon strip. But in a manner of speaking, we, of course, continued jousting with The Phantom. That winter, for instance, we got a Flexible Flyer sled for Christmas and were testing it out from the edge of the swimming pool terrace and down the hill past the corner of the swampy pond, which by then was covered with a sheet of ice. Don appeared, sans Phantom attire, and decided he wanted to join in on the sledding. He hopped on the rear end of the sled, with Gary guiding and Gordon in the middle. Don's extra weight, however, made steering more difficult. In fact, instead of following our previous tracks skirting past the pond, we appeared to be heading straight for the middle of the pond! At the last second, Don yelled and bailed off the sled. That exertion, plus Gary pushing hard to the right on the sled's wooden cross-piece, shot us in an arc over the pond's edge, where we landed on icy ground beyond and kept sailing twenty more yards into the dead stumps of the surrounding cattails. Meanwhile, Don's own flight arc landed him *squarely in the middle of the pond*, where he crashed through the thin ice and found himself planted in frozen muck up to his armpits. When our little Flexible Flyer came to rest, we looked back to see Don struggling out of the pond and stomping back up the hill, crying with rage and issuing loud curses against his blankety-blank-conniving-blankety-blank-little-good-for-nothing-twin brothers. He was convinced that we purposely had steered the sled to dump him in the pond.

In the spring, the yard and grounds at 4300 South Highland Drive were a riot of blossoms produced by the many fruit trees Bob had planted. In the backyard there was a big apple tree with a fairly good-sized tree hut perched in its lower limbs. Don claimed it as his club house, and we were disinvited. As apples and other fruit on the property began to harden and grow, we deemed them perfect for throwing as make-believe baseballs and other missiles. Don had a bucket on a pulley-rope, which he filled with apples to stock his tree-hut fort with ammunition for throwing at us. He figured he would have the advantage of an enclosed cover and control of the apple supply. Unfortunately for Don, just out of range from the apple tree there was a *quince* tree. Quinces are very hard, tough skinned, pear-shaped little fruit whose flavor we hated, but which were even better for throwing than Don's apples. Since there were two of us, we deployed ourselves on opposite sides of Don's apple tree hut and began pelting him with a barrage of quinces through several large openings between the slats of the hut. Don was *trapped*. He yelled and tried to make a smaller target of himself by crouching down, but as soon as he concealed himself from one of us he exposed himself to the other. We were unrelenting in our missile attack. We had both just finished reading a junior reader's account of General Custer's Last Stand at the Battle of Little Big Horn, and it reminded us of that. We, of course, were the merciless Sioux warriors to Don's hapless Custer. In a panic to escape, Don lurched out of the tree hut to climb down but fell part way, from about six or seven feet above the fortunately fairly spongy ground below.

Later that evening at the dinner table, Don was covered with angry red welts. To his credit, Don made up some story and didn't rat us out to our parents. There were many other battles in the years ahead, including fistfights that produced more welts and black eyes, and even over-turned living room furniture and a broken window glass pane in our old Herbert Avenue kitchen door. All of this upset our mother considerably and caused our father to remonstrate with livid lectures. Maybe there was some particle of grudging admiration that we shared when the three of us united on rare occasions to keep our parents in the dark about some of the things we did to each other. But, as we got older, we mostly observed a sullen kind of truce in which we minded our own business. When our family moved to 1166 Denver Street near Liberty Park in the summer of 1957, the two of us shared a basement bedroom and focused on our school friends and sports. Across the hall, Don had his own little room in which, with the door closed, he focused on his art.

Pen and ink drawing by Don Shepherd in 1958 when he was 16 years-old.

One of Don's high school paintings of a Salt Lake City neighborhood scene in 1959.

Examples of Don's art as a freshman student in an illustration course at the University of Utah in 1961. The first, above, illustrates the famous death scene in Dostoyevsky's *The Brothers Karamazov*, and the second, below, is of a fatherless, refugee family landing at Ellis Island, New York in the 1930s.

We were actually quite proud of Don's artwork and occasionally snuck some of our friends into his room to show it off to them when he was out of the house. Don never seemed to take much interest in our sports. But two years after he had graduated from high school, as the co-editor of South High's yearbook, Don—by then an art major at the University of Utah—volunteered to make professional looking posters for Gary's campaign as a candidate for student body president at South High School. We think he took pride in that, and, in Gary's eventual victory as well. Gary himself recognized a turning point in our heretofore acrid relationship with Don and lauded our older brother's help in the course of his campaign assembly speech, which Don secretly attended, seated undetected in the large auditorium jammed with students.

There was, of course, much more beyond high school to the history of our mutual careers, sibling relationship with Don, and the larger family dynamics that unfolded with our parents—some of it bumpy and unhappy.

Recently, Gary uncovered an oddly shaped, folded and abused piece of canvas at the bottom of a chest of memorabilia belonging to Don. He contacted Kathy Carling Wilson, a respected professional artist and old friend from school days in Salt Lake City, who operated an art gallery located on Second East, five blocks north of our old Herbert Avenue home. The canvass had apparently been roughly cut out from an unfinished portrait of several art students at the University of Utah during the 1960s. The cut-out was filled with the face of only one young man: it was Don. Although the canvass piece is unsigned, Kathy suspects that it (and the larger work from which it was cut) may have been painted by well-known University of Utah art professor and portraitist, Alvin Gittins.

After her inspection of the canvass remnant featuring Don's face, Kathy asked if we would like her to stitch new canvass to the old, oddly-cut portion; paint-in matching background and a portion of Don's shirt and hair, where missing, onto this newly attached piece; stretch out the fold lines; clean up and restore the color of the old paint on the old canvass; frame and mount the repaired original; and then make additional canvass giclee copies (that are hard to discern from the original).

Absolutely! What a find. Though unfinished, we wonder what Don would say of the artisanship of his likeness?

Don Shepherd, portrait oil sketch attributed to Alvin Gittens, circa 1963.

Well, it's one of the oldest stories in the book—Cain and Abel—brothers who fight each other and take different paths in life. According to Freud, all history is family history; and to paraphrase the late Rabbi Lionel Blue, Mormons are just like everyone else, only more so. Even though Don died of a heart attack at the abbreviated age of 54, we regretfully think and talk of him often, acknowledging the unwitting role we played as kids in contributing to some of the demons he struggled with as an adult. In retrospect, we should have accelerated our belated efforts at reconciliation. Among other things, we would love to hear him tell his side of the story as our older brother—The Phantom of our youth.

6.

GETTING ACQUAINTED WITH
THE STOKERMATIC SALESMAN

We knew what most of our friends' dads did for a living when we were growing up. Ron Swenson's dad worked for the Rio Grande Railroad, and Lorin Larson's worked as a mechanic at Hill Field Airforce Base. Owen Wood's dad was a fireman, and Dave Lingwall's was a public schoolteacher. Phillip Starr's dad was an accountant, and Mike Mitchell's *grandfather* (who raised him) drove trucks for Salt Lake County. These were all solid, working class or middle class jobs. What did our dad—Alvin Brighton Shepherd—do for a living? Who did he work for? This wasn't always easy to say. If pressed at the time, we might have said, "well, our dad's a salesman, he sells real estate"—which wasn't always true, because, over the years, he shifted from one sales job to another. But these changes often involved working as a real estate agent for various realty companies. In our younger years we tended to equate sales with being in business and, frankly, that wasn't something that captured our boyhood interest. We were much more interested in our fantasies of playing baseball for a living than aspiring to become tycoons. We could never wrap our heads or hearts around the idea of trying to persuade people that they needed or wanted to buy goods or services from us rather than from other merchants in the marketplace. And the idea of making as much money in business as you possibly could as your occupational goal in life? Well, for some reason, that didn't appeal to us either.

The thing is, our dad seldom worked for a salary promising a monthly paycheck. Almost always he worked on commission, and that meant an uncertain livelihood of feast or famine. Maybe that's one of the reasons that business (especially business sales based on commissions) didn't appeal to us. It seemed more often like famine rather than feast in the Shepherd household when we were growing up.

During the year 1954-55, Dad was working as a sales representative for a company that produced a home heating unit called the "Stokermatic," which could be installed in a room of a modest-sized house. It was a compact heating system particularly appealing in rural communities where gas lines were not universally available, electrical heating options were too expensive, and basements for full-sized coal furnaces were not feasible. Most of Dad's work involved him making weekly sales and customer maintenance trips to Idaho. Dad was tuned into the fact that his weekly trips were putting unwanted distance between himself and his growing sons. So, when we were out of school, he would schedule one of us, taking turns, on separate weeks, to accompany him on his road trip through Southern Idaho in such towns as Pocatello, Idaho Falls, Twin Falls, Burley, Rexburg, and even as far north as Boise. The family car at the time was a reddish-brown Willys Jeep Wagon, of all things. Don't ask us how or why Dad had obtained this roughhewn vehicle—the progeny of World War II jeeps that had slogged through rivers and mudholes in both Europe and the South Pacific. In any event we loved these trips for several reasons, not all of which were directly connected to bonding with our dad.

We had never before stayed in a hotel. We had only rarely ever eaten in a restaurant. The Idaho hotels we stayed in were typically old, dingy, and smelled of stale cigarette smoke. But to us they were grown-up and exciting places where adults came in and out and were politely attended to by strangers, who sometimes wore uniforms. We usually ate in roadside diners rather than in more expensive hotel restaurants. But we loved those diners: Ground sirloin! Or meat loaf! Mashed potatoes and gravy! Cole Slaw! Dinner rolls and pats of real butter! An icy glass of root beer! Maybe a slice of apple pie! And juke boxes to serenade your dinner with five of the latest pop song selections for a quarter! Sometimes, after dinner, a movie in a real theater was thrown in before bedtime. And during the day, while dad would make his visits to mostly farmers in the countryside, engaging in what seemed interminable talking, we would contentedly curl up in the Willys Jeep with our comic books and other reading materials while happily nursing a nickel candy bar and patiently waiting for another dinner at the diner.

Don't get us wrong. We enjoyed some quality time with our dad, too. He was an athletic, handsome, and sociable man, and we felt proud to be with him as he navigated with seeming expertise the intimidating social ceremonies and business exchanges of the adult world. When we weren't sleeping on the front seat or up-chucking from car sickness at the side of the road, our best times to get to know our dad were during the long drives to and from Idaho.

Dad didn't have a child psychologist's orientation to ask his young sons questions about ourselves, what we thought, felt, and liked about our lives. But he would readily talk about himself, and we learned a lot from his stories. Dad told us mostly about the positive times of his life, for instance his early connection to golf as a youthful caddy at the Salt Lake Country Club, which led to his eventually being an informal golf instructor at Utah State University (USU) while he was an undergraduate student there. And speaking of college, he regularly told us stories about making the USU "Aggies" freshman football team as an end and "understudy" to the future All-American Aggie end, "Moose Mulleneaux," who went on to star for the Green Bay Packers in the 1930s and early 1940s. He related his LDS missionary experiences in South Carolina, Georgia, and Florida where he became a traveling assistant to the mission president—future Mormon Apostle, Legrand Richards (who encouraged him to try his hand at becoming a real estate salesman after his mission)—and how his mission led to his continuing association with Samuel Blue, a converted Mormon and Chief of the Catawba Indian Nation in South Carolina. He often rehearsed how he fulfilled his military obligation in World War II as a married man with one son (and two more on the way) by successfully applying to be a Red Cross field director, and he elaborated on his subsequent adventures serving in the South Pacific.

First Row—Mulleneaux, Christensen, L. Robertson, Lindsay, Christiansen, M. Warren, Mel. Warren, Houck, Andrus, Balls C. Lawrence.
Second Row—Clay, Burns, Jackson, White, Boam, Gold, Tolman, Dempsey, H. Callister, Smith, Stewart, Pratt, Robertson.
Third Row—E. Smith, Coach; Hansen, H. Barton, Ryan, E. Petersen, Wakley, Etzel, Spencer, Hogenson, Hansen, C. Petersen, Bunker, Stock, Aylworth, Teuscher, Shepherd, Bullen, Kowallis, Brown, Mitchell, Blanton, Swensen, I. Smith, Coach.

1933 Utah State freshman football team (Alvin Shepherd, third row, center-right, scowling with his teammates at the camera).

ALVIN B. SHEPHERD — American Red Cross field director characterizes the Mormon soldier.

1943 Feature story in the Deseret News on Dad's work as a Red Cross field director during World War II.

Dad didn't tell us much about other relevant but less upbeat aspects of his life on those Idaho trips. And we were too young or lacking in insight to ask more about the areas that he left blank. We did catch a few glimpses from Dad (and others later) that his own childhood had its share of dark undertones. For instance, Dad's father, our paternal grandfather, Joseph, was a man we never knew. He was born into a large extended family of English converts to Mormonism who had immigrated to Paris, Idaho in the latter half of the 19th century. Joseph was intelligent and artistically talented, but also apparently a bit cynical, quirky, and sometimes irascible. He did not fulfill his potential or fare especially well economically (like our dad, he shifted around in various sales jobs). He sheltered his family in a 19th century rock/adobe dwelling without much of a foundation and which, for a number of years, lacked indoor plumbing and electrical wiring. Dad always claimed that this structure, with gun portal openings in the side walls, had originally been one of Brigham Young's "summer homes" on what used to be Parley's Road (now Parley's Canyon Boulevard), overlooking the Salt Lake Country Club at the mouth of Parley's Canyon and Interstate 80. Dad did tell us once (but clammed up when we asked further questions) that his father had once cracked his head open with a fireplace poker in a rage over his teen-aged son's defiance, which had something to do with an incident on a motorcycle.

Watercolor rendering of "Brigham Young's Summer Home" on Parley's Road in Salt Lake City, by Robert L. Shepherd, our Uncle Bob.

Why didn't we ever know our grandfather, Joseph? Because he died long before we were born. As young boys, driving with our Dad to Idaho, we heard the sobering story of Joseph's murder by a neighbor, who was apparently even more irascible than Joseph, during a dispute over property water rights in the spring of 1934—just as Dad was finishing his first year of higher education at Utah State in Logan, Utah.

SALT LAKE CITY, May 22, 1934 (Associated Press)

TWO MEN DEAD IN SALT LAKE QUARREL OVER WATER RIGHTS. SIMON BARENDREGT SHOOTS JOSEPH SHEHERD AND THEM HIMSELF. BOYS FIND BODIES

Simon Barendregt, 63, and Joseph Shepherd, 54, are dead today, victims, Salt Lake City police said, of a murder and suicide—the outgrowth of a prolonged quarrel over irrigation water rights. The bodies were found in a field of the Barendregt farm near the Salt Lake City municipal limits shortly after six o'clock last night, approximately four hours, Dr. Henry Raile, city police surgeon, said, after Barendregt fired a bullet into Shepherd's abdomen and then sent a bullet crashing through his own brain. Neighbors said the two men had quarreled for months, Barendregt insisting that he was not being supplied with water in accordance with his rights, and threatening to resort to legal action to enforce his claim. The tragedy was discovered when Mrs. Barendregt, alarmed by failure of Barendregt to return to the family residence after several hours' absence, sent two boys. Guy Sundberg, 15, and his brother, George Sundberg, 12 to investigate. Police who were summoned said the men evidently had scuffled; Barendregt then had fired a bullet into the abdomen of Shepherd; the victim had walked some distance and then had fallen. Barendregt, they said, apparently had walked to Shepherd's side, and seeing him dying fired a bullet into his own head. The shooting occurred about 100 yards east of Twenty-second East street on Twenty-fourth South street. Shepherd was born near Paris, Idaho, and was active in the Latter-day Saints Church, having served on missions in Greece, Turkey and Egypt from 1906 to 1908. For several years he was the first counselor in the" Parley's ward bishopric and an instructor in the Young Men's Mutual Improvement Association. His widow, Mrs. Ellen B. Shepherd, two sons and a brother reside in Salt Lake City.

But left unsaid, and something we never learned until we were adults, was that, prior to marrying our Mom, Dad had briefly been married to another woman. That union lasted about a year and a half before being sundered by divorce and, most disconcertingly, had produced a baby son—our erstwhile stepbrother—who died during birth, and who never received a name or any other recognition of his brief sojourn on this earth beyond the cold clerical statement of his birth, sex, and simultaneous death that was typed on the official hospital record.

These later acquired insights into our dad and his life prior to our own births did not have the power to disturb our mostly positive perceptions of him that we had as young boys. He never revealed to us his inner insecurities or self-doubts. And it's true he was often absent from home on business trips and later on local LDS Church assignments (as a member of the Liberty Park Ward bishopric and as a member of the Liberty Stake High Council). Surprising as it might seem—given our early passion for sports—he didn't take us with him on fishing expeditions or on golf excursions to teach us how to play. These were relaxing retreats that he reserved for the exclusive company of his adult friends.

Nevertheless, Dad projected to us an outward image of an outgoing, self-confident man who was in charge and competent to deal with problems beyond our ken. When we misbehaved or disappointed him, he would deliver lectures in an angry tone. But he never spanked, hit, or employed any other form of physical punishment. We especially enjoyed those occasions when we watched baseball games on TV with him or the Friday Night Fights (sponsored by Gillette Blue Blades and Pabst Blue Ribbon Beer). He was then relaxed and knowledgeable, and we could ask him questions about Mickey Mantle, or Ted Williams, Sugar Ray Robinson, Gene Fulmer, or even the boxing hero of his own youth, Jack Dempsey.

Dad was not a bigoted man and conveyed to us an attitude of racial and ethnic equality (as did our mother) that was a bit rare for the time and place of 1950s Salt Lake City. He wasn't cynical, in spite of his struggles to make a living, and didn't cuss or rant angrily about people he didn't like. Our dad made us feel somehow safe, notwithstanding the financial difficulties that often confronted our family. We saw him as a leader among his contemporaries, not in a professional, career sense, but in the self-possessed way he interacted with his adult friends and colleagues. He didn't push us in any particular directions, and, although his own career aspirations were never realized, we nevertheless somehow acquired a degree of his outward optimism and grew up believing that someday, perhaps, we could amount to something.

7.

THE AVON LADY

To us growing up, Marjorie Coombs Shepherd—the mother of three sons and a daughter—was a model, 1950s-era stay-at-home wife and homemaker. She was a skilled cook who planned three meal-a-day-weekly menus; bottled fruit, pickles, and preserves; baked bread, pies, and cookies from scratch; washed, ironed, sewed, and mended our clothes; cut our hair; kept an immaculately clean house; scrupulously supervised our Saturday morning chores; and, in her spare time, read the *Reader's Digest*, played hymns on a small upright piano in the living room, and, without fail on Sunday mornings, turned on KSL radio for us to listen to the Mormon Tabernacle Choir and the Spoken Word before we all left the house for Sunday services at the Liberty/Liberty Park Ward chapel.

Marjorie Coombs's missionary farewell portrait, 1939.

Mom was devout in her LDS faith. In 1939-40 she served an LDS proselyting mission to the East Central States Mission (which included the states of Kentucky, North Carolina, Tennessee, Virginia, and West Virginia). In 1941 she married our dad, "Shep,"—who also had served a church mission in the same region a few years previously. After the Second World War, she moved uncomplainingly with her salesman husband and growing family from her home in Salt Lake to Provo, and from Provo to Billings, Montana to Cowley, Wyoming and back to Salt Lake, all within a span of four years while Shep was trying to make his mark in business. Finally settling down within the neighborhood boundaries of Salt Lake City's Liberty Elementary School (a 16-square block central city area defined by the intersections of State Street and Ninth South and Fifth East and 1300 South), Mom taught Sunday school and Mutual Improvement Association classes (MIA was an organization for youths between the ages of 12 and 17) and served as Liberty Park Ward Relief Society president under two different bishops. She also sold Avon.

By the late 1960s, "Ding, Dong, Avon Calling!" was a punch line for television comics. But in the years following WWII, Avon Products Inc. successfully recruited a large workforce of married women in every state of the country who wanted to make a little extra income by selling Avon home and beauty products to their friends and neighbors without upsetting their culturally defined roles as mothers and homemakers. Our Mom—"Marge" as she was known to friends and as "Sister Shepherd" to Liberty Stake and Ward members—saw a chance to help her family's often shaky finances by becoming an Avon sales representative. Over the years she cultivated a loyal Avon customer base, consisting of middle-aged and older women who lived on nearby streets in our Liberty School neighborhood.

Mom never went door to door doing Avon cold-calls. She accumulated regular customers by word of mouth and maintained their loyalty through friendly service, accurate account keeping, prompt delivery of their orders, and by staying abreast of the growing line of family health products (like "Smokers Toothpaste"), as well as women's cosmetics which were displayed in what seemed to us as extravagant Avon catalogues. We can remember occasionally accompanying our mother as she made her deliveries when we were early elementary-age kids, walking alongside her on the neighborhood streets that marked the overlapping boundaries of our Liberty Ward and Liberty Elementary School world and trudging up the steps of customer's small cement porches to ring their doorbells. Each customer's purchases were itemized and placed in a separate paper sack, which Mom had neatly organized in boxes according to the order of delivery. Mom would often be invited in by her customers to chat and visit while browsing the most recent Avon catalogue with them to update their next purchases. As a veteran Avon lady, her sales commissions probably never exceeded a few hundred dollars every month. We remember one year in particular when mom worked extra hard to win bonus points from Avon toward claiming a complete set of porcelain nativity figures, which she proudly displayed at Christmas every year thereafter. There were many times when Mom's few hundred dollars kept us in groceries and paid for other necessities.

So our mother, like our dad, helped to materially support us kids by selling other people's products. They were both good at customer relations. Less gregarious than dad, who was more spontaneous in his decisions, mom was better organized and benefitted from a modest customer base that could be counted on to make regular, small purchases. In contrast, our dad hoped for and intermittently achieved some "big sales," which would stave off his creditors for a while and permit the luxury of an occasional family trip. But Dad was not an aggressive closer. When push came to shove, his friendly appeal to both friends and strangers was not accompanied by a relentless willingness to do whatever was required to close a deal. In retrospect, his sociable personality was probably better suited for an occupation in social services or public relations than in sales. When we were older, Mom would occasionally lament to us that Dad should have kept his American Red Cross position that he had for a year or so after the end of WWII—a respectable job with a reliable income—but Dad didn't like the humdrum of office work, not to mention that Red Cross began downsizing its local operations after the war.

One other important side of our mother's family commitments was displayed in her loyal ties to all three of her siblings—her older sisters, Alice and Zelda, and their younger brother Melvin. As boys growing up, we strongly identified as being Shepherds and not Coombs. Retrospectively, this strikes us as unjustly prejudicial. As kids, we concluded that the surname Shepherd was cool while Coombs sounded funny. To us, our Uncle Bob's renown as an artist and his beautiful home and expansive property on the outskirts of Salt Lake seemed glamorous and appropriately aspirational, whereas our Coombs relatives' ordinary occupations and conventional, small houses in middle class neighborhoods of the city seemed humdrum and lacking in imagination.

But the reality was, we had far more association with Mom's side of the family than with dad's. The only Shepherds with whom we had semi-regular contact were Uncle Bob's family, which included his wife Olive, their two adopted children, Larry and Sandra, and our paternal grandmother, Ellen, who resided with Bob during the last 20 years of her life. At most, we may have seen or visited with Bob's family a half-dozen times a year— that is, until Bob decided, in 1955, to stay in California to work for an art decoration firm after completing his wall murals for the Los Angeles Temple. Thereafter, beyond a yearly car drive for a few day's visit with Bob's family in the greater Las Angeles area, our Shepherd family in-person contacts effectively evaporated. The rest of the Shepherd clan—as far as we knew—resided in the vicinity of Bear Lake and Paris, Idaho, and we kids didn't know or associate with any of them.

In contrast, on our mother's side of the family, there were numerous adult relatives and dozens of cousin peers who lived in Salt Lake City whom we saw regularly on holidays and almost weekly Sunday gatherings at Aunt Zelda's house at 1405 South Hollywood Avenue, two streets north of Sugar House Park. Zelda's house was modest sized and crammed to the brim when the extended family assembled. Constrained by the spatial limits, house rules, and close proximity to adults discussing topics of little interest to us, we were often bored at these gatherings. However, Aunt Zelda—Mom's oldest sister—made superlative layer cakes with satiny frostings. In complementary fashion, our mom made superlative from-scratch pies (lemon meringue was a particular specialty). The promise of these sweet treats at family get-togethers compensated for the absence of more appealing activities for young boys.

The three sisters—Marjorie, Zelda, and Alice—spoke frequently on the phone, sustained an active interest in one another's lives, and always pitched in to support each other in whatever ways they could. Aunt Alice couldn't bake a lick, but she encouraged our reading habits and quietly chipped in with needed aid when our family slipped into perilous financial waters. The sisters' concern for one another included their younger brother Melvin, his wife Margaret and their five children, with whom they stayed in close touch even after he moved his family to El Cajon, California, for a better paying job. Consciously underappreciated by us growing up, we would like to think our mother's staunch loyalty to her siblings was something that sunk in and attached itself to the subconscious development of our better selves as we matured.

To summarize the obvious, Marjorie Coombs Shepherd—Alvin Shepherd's hard working wife, our attentive and conscientious mother, model homemaker, loyal sister, Women's Relief Society president, and the neighborhood's Avon Lady—demonstrated in all her roles the virtues of selfless organized service and, hand in hand with persistence and resilience in the face of life's many problems, a dutiful commitment to her responsibilities. We are indebted and grateful for her quiet, unassuming example. Thanks Mom. Even though we never learned to play the piano—and frustrated you to no end when we rebuffed your efforts to teach us—we like to believe we absorbed at least some of your valued attributes that consequently have helped shape our own fortunes in life for the better.

8.

LEARNING COMMUNITY AND DEMOCRACY FROM FREDDY THE PIG

In retrospect we gotta admit, one of our important boyhood role models was a pig—a fictional pig, to be sure—a thinking, talking pig with a keen sense of loyalty, duty, and higher purpose; a pig whose admirable qualities of character stand in glaring contrast to those of an infamous reality show huckster who, once upon a terrible time, claimed 1600 Pennsylvania Avenue as his temporary mailing address. The fictional pig's name is Freddy.

Freddy the Pig was the creation of Walter R. Brooks, who, from 1927 to 1958, wrote a total of twenty-six "children's novels" about the adventures of Freddy the Pig and his farm animal compatriots on the Bean Farm in upstate New York. These books featured titles like: *Freddy Goes to Florida, Freddy the Detective, Freddy and the Clockwork Twin, Freddy the Politician, Freddy and the Ignormus, Freddy and the Bean Home News, Freddy the Pied Piper, Freddy the Magician, Freddy the Cowboy, Freddy the Pilot, Freddy and the Men From Mars, Freddy and Simon the Dictator*, etc.

Calling the Freddy books *mere* children's novels, however, would constitute a mean injustice both to Freddy and Walter R. We were very pleased recently to discover that actual *literary* critics (e.g., Anthony Boucher, J.

Francis McComas, Adam Hochschild, Roger Sale, Stuart Mitchner, AND Lionel Trilling) have praised the superb writing and effortless exposition of fundamental moral values that Brooks wove into the adventuresome plots of Freddy and his Bean Farm companions. And Nikolas Kristoff, columnist for the New York Times, proclaimed that Freddy books rank among the best children's books ever produced, saying they were "funny, beautifully written gems." These professional encomiums, we modestly agree, retrospectively validate our shared boyhood taste in good literature. While Freddy books were written for young readers, Brooks never talked down to his audience and resisted the temptation of utilizing a minimalist vocabulary in the composition of his anthropomorphic tales of talking animals. If nothing else, from reading Freddy we both learned the importance of selectively caring about the right words to use in good writing.

Exactly how we became acquainted with Freddy and his friends escapes us now. It probably happened serendipitously when we first began the practice of making regular visits to the old Salt Lake City public library on 15 South State Street around the age of nine or ten. Our Aunt Alice was a fifth grade schoolteacher who encouraged us to read by giving us books for Christmas or as birthday gifts. Reading Aunt Alice's gift books whetted our appetites for more and consequently we discovered THE LIBRARY. Analogous to the pithy answer attributed to bank robber Willie Sutton when asked why he robbed banks—"because that's where the money is"—we began frequenting the library because *that's where the books were.*

Old Salt Lake City public library at 15 South State Street.

Neither of us recalls going with a list of books to find; it was pure random searching in the fiction section for Young Readers. We both remember simply pulling books off the shelves that had catchy covers or interesting titles as we strolled down an aisle and then browsing through them to see if we thought they'd be worth our time to read. What we DO remember attracting us to the Freddy books at the beginning were the terrific pen and ink illustrations by Kurt Wiese, which included succinct captions that captured highlight-moments in each story. We were hooked.

If we remember right, the check-out limit was seven books per week per library patron. Naturally, Gary checked out his limit of seven, Gordon did the same, and then we shared all fourteen books before returning to the library the following week to get another set of fourteen. We checked out other books besides Freddy, of course, including all of the books in Frank Baum's Oz series, some science fiction, sports books, and American history biographies for young readers. But without question, our favorite reading was the adventures of Freddy the Pig. We re-read the entire canon multiple times throughout the years of our childhood and early adolescence. The particulars of our other youthful readings have mostly faded from recollection.

But we still remember Freddy with clarity and a combination of fondness and genuine appreciation.

It was especially in the summer when we indulged in library reading binges. As our age approached double-digits in the mid-1950s, little league baseball and library book reading gradually replaced swimming at Liberty Park as our daily pastimes. With lazy fondness we recall sprawling out on the cushioned porch swing at our Herbert Avenue house with a stack of books. We would finish a chapter of Freddy, doze a little, and then regain cognizance to stare blissfully at a soft, cotton-seed shower wafting on gentle breezes coming from the row of immense cottonwood trees lined up across the street on Third East. Is this what the celestial heaven vaguely envisioned by prophetic mystics might be like? If so, we could buy into it—especially as an escape fantasy from today's ugly age of growing authoritarianism. But let's not get too far ahead of the story.

One of the charming strengths of the Freddy books is the wide range of barnyard characters—representing a fair moral sample of the human menagerie—that play significant roles in the realization of Brooks' compelling fables. In addition to Freddy, other principal characters include Jinx the Cat (*especially* Jinx), Mrs. Wiggins (a cow), and Charles the Rooster. None of these, or any other of the characters in Brooks' stories, is a perfect paragon. They all have their "human" weaknesses, as well as strengths. It is their allegiance to one another as part of a diverse community of political equals that gives them their collective strength. Important issues that arise are debated at proto townhall meetings in the Bean barn, and democratic voting is conducted when momentous community decisions need to be made.

Without compelling characters, though, you can't have a compelling novel. Even we, who have never written a novel, know that much about novels.

Freddy is clever, multi-talented, a day-dreamer poet, imaginative, and idealistic. He's also a little vain, slovenly in his housekeeping habits, and has definite lazy tendencies during tranquil times. But when confronted by problems that provoke his lively curiosity or especially by ones that threaten the peacefulness or integrity of the farm or portend harm to his friends, he is an ingenious and energetic pig of action who is undaunted by obstacles in his path. In confronting life's challenges, Freddy is a renaissance pig who alternately is a detective and master of disguise, a newspaper publisher and editor (of the *Bean Home News*), a magician, a political campaign manager, an artist, a pilot and adventurer, as well as a compulsive poet of doggerel verse.

Jinx the cat is Freddy's improbable best friend and counterpart. Jinx is the realist to Freddy's romantic idealism; he is fearless, blunt, disdains cant and hypocrisy, can be impetuous and fierce, but is a friend you depend on for getting results when the chips are down. A good natured Holstein cow, Mrs. Wiggins is a combination of tender-heartedness, stubborn commitment to her old-fashioned yet humane values, and a font of common sense wisdom that often serve as a corrective to some of Freddy's more flamboyant ideas. But when it comes to personal flamboyance, Charles the Rooster is the personification of flashy showiness. Much more vain than Freddy, Charles is an eloquent public speaker in love with the sound of his own voice. He lacks good sense and judgement, however, and talks a much bigger game than he plays. He is self-centered and irritatingly complains too often about the indignities of his life. But he, like Jinx, can also be a loyal friend when the chips are down—even if occasionally he has to be kept in line by his impatient and practical wife, Henrietta. Henrietta and Mrs. Wiggins, we should point out, both act as effective female counterpoints to the male presumptuousness of Freddy, Jinx, and Charles.

Other important Bean Farm residents, whose distinctive personal qualities are woven into virtually all of the stories, include Hank the horse, a stoic, strong, and reliable comrade when situations require both muscle and integrity; Alice and Emma, timorous sister ducks who fawn and fuss over their fraudulent Uncle Wesley, but who also demonstrate pluck and rectitude when pushed too far; and Whibley, the sardonic great horned owl, who delights in puncturing the various pretensions and follies of the other animals but always offers words of wisdom and guidance in times of crisis.

We should also point out that the Bean Farm animals do not merely interact with one another. Rather, their stories routinely implicate them in the affairs of the larger human society beyond the boundaries of the farm. The literary device Brooks employs to make this plausible is to portray the Bean animals as being capable of human speech in a way that initially *surprises* human actors and consequently bestows great notoriety upon them as the "talking animals." *How* they acquired speech is never explicated, and it doesn't need to be. It's simply introduced as a fact and thereafter satisfies the fundamental premise of all fantasy stories and most science fiction, which require the suspension of readers' disbelief.

Freddy the Pig stories are mystery/adventure yarns and therefore require villains. In the adventures of Freddy there are two types of villains: barn rats and human rats. The barn rats are led by the oily and sinister Simon, who exercises tyrannical control over the rat clan. Simon and his unprincipled progeny do not share the other animals' commitment to community and fair play. They ceaselessly attempt to plunder the Bean animals' food and possessions and engage in a variety of other criminal depredations, which challenge the civic order of the Bean Farm's citizens. Given the chance, Simon would like to become dictator over all the animals.

The *human* rats are people who are offended by the Bean animal's presumptions of equality, look down upon them, and/or attempt to exploit them for personal gain. While the majority of humans are both decent and accepting of the animals and collaborate with them in various ways, the *rats* among them are mean and remorseless. They stupidly think the animals are pushovers and can be taken advantage of with impunity. Some of the latter, by the way, are local plutocrats who flaunt their money and pettiness toward others with narrow convictions of inherent superiority. In many of Brooks' stories, the community good will and democracy of Freddy and his friends are ultimately at stake and must be sustained by their concerted efforts to overcome the villainous plots perpetuated against them or their friends by human adversaries.

So why did all of this appeal so strongly to us at our age and circumstances as elementary school kids in central Salt Lake City in the 1950s? The answer is both simple and subtle. We were reasonably bright kids whose reading proclivities had already been reinforced by our mother (who read stories to us as preschoolers) and our book-gifting, public school teacher, Aunt Alice. And, as we recounted earlier, random chance played its part in our discovery of Freddy books in the public library. But as far as the appeal of these books to us is concerned, we don't think they were stunningly revelatory or somehow *caused* us to embrace the principles of community and democracy that were part and parcel of the stories' adventurous plots. Rather, these principles were bracingly congruent with what we matter-of-factly had come to accept and value already in our own youthful experience with neighborhood friends at Liberty Elementary school and the local Liberty/Liberty Park Ward of the LDS Church (values which later were strongly reinforced at our public junior and senior high schools).

In some analogous way, our childhood associations in those primary institutions were manifest in fictional form as Freddy and his friends living on the Bean Farm in upstate New York. When we read about the adventures of Freddy the Pig and his Bean Farm associates, we thought, "Of course! They're just like us and our friends at school and church." We experienced an affinity with Brooks' animal characters and their stories, because they seemed to resonate with our own emerging values and friendship priorities. We even identified different Bean animal characters with many of our friends and adult guardians, whose personalities seemed roughly equivalent—whether endearing or obnoxious—including candid depictions of their various shortcomings along with their personal virtues.

Having said this, we must also say that whatever our rudimentary ideas about friendships and democratic loyalties might have been at that age, they were not coherently defined or articulated in any clear way. Looking in retrospect at the stories of Freddy the Pig, we both appreciate how they clarified, consolidated, and strengthened a tolerance of diversity, sense of unity, and concern for the welfare of others beyond our own egos, which perhaps we first began gravitating toward as identical twins when we were children. These kinds of reflections, of course, may sound pompously self-serving, and we don't mean to portray us in our innocent dumbness to have been democratic child prodigies. We were pretty ethnocentric about a lot of things for a lot of years beyond our childhood. All we're saying is that, however imperfectly acquired, understood, and practiced, these were values that resonated with many of our most important experiences growing up. And may we add that one of the important functions of great literature is to inspire and reinforce a vision of humane values for imperfect humanity. For us as young readers, the adventures of Freddy the Pig probably served this function far more effectively than the scriptural readings of Christianity and the LDS Church, to which we were regularly exposed during that same period of our lives.

As for dictator demagogues who disparage the community and democratic values exhibited by Freddy and the Bean Farm animals, most of our political history attests that, sooner or later, their villainy and personal pettiness is upended. The nakedness of a fake emperor who wears no clothes is not pretty. When this is belatedly acknowledged by a deceived people, self-serving autocrats are predictably deserted by their toady lieutenants and opportunistic supporters, who abandon ship like Simon the Rat and his treacherous offspring.

To bring full circle our reflections concerning the influence that Brooks' stories had on our thinking about community and democracy while growing up, let us offer these fond hopes for our country's future: May the community values and democratic principles of Freddy the Pig and the Bean Farm Animals live long in American society—even in—and especially in—today's disturbing political climate of fearmongering and authoritarian appeals to the darker angels of our nature.

9.

REGRETFUL REMINISCENCE
OF A DOOMED KID

S ometimes Gordon's Arkansas-born wife tells him he grew up in a bubble: the bubble of Salt Lake City—the City of the Saints—in 1950s Utah. But then he reminds her of the story of Morris—Morris Hulse. Somehow his name seemed apt to us at the time we first met him; it sounded menacing.

Midway through the fifth grade at Liberty Elementary School our aging but elegantly coiffed principal, Miss Robey, marched Morris into our homeroom and announced we had a new classmate. Morris stood at the front of the room and said nothing. But he didn't smile shyly either, he glowered. He glowered in blue jeans and a white tee-shirt, with the short sleeves rolled tightly past his biceps—standard prepubescent and adolescent attire for the time: it was the spring of 1955.

Did we say biceps? Yes, his biceps were a lot bigger than most of ours, and he was barrel-chested. He stood defiantly with his arms folded and his feet spread apart while we obeyed Mrs. Robey's instruction to say hello. He had thick, dark hair that was a little unruly. But he didn't sport a fussy ducktail, and he wasn't buzzed crew-cut short, either. He had a broad, flat forehead, a nose that looked a little flattened too, and dark eyes that didn't twinkle. At the tender age of eleven, his face looked like a boxer's. (His older, juvenile delinquent brother had in fact been a golden gloves fighter, and he had taught Morris plenty.)

At recess, a mere hour or so after his introduction to us, he got directly to the point: "Who's the toughest kid in the class?!" he demanded to know. His demand didn't convey any hint of horseplay or boyish fun, and we were forced to take his intensity seriously.

"Not us," the two of us stammered, "Rhue Webster's a lot tougher than we are," we speculated. Poor Rhue. Rhue Webster had been held back a grade and was a year older than the rest of us. Maybe he could fight the new kid, if that's what he wanted.

Morris Hulse, 1955.

It turned out that Rhue was not the toughest kid in our fifth grade class, and Morris quickly bloodied his nose to prove it. It also turned out that the toughest guy in the school was actually Steve Kemp, another older kid—the son of German immigrant parents—who had been held back a grade or two. Unlike Rhue, Kemp *was* tough. He was also the class clown, who aggravated teachers with his immaturity. He was big and strong and a head taller than the rest of us, with hair under his armpits, an adolescent Adam's-apple above the base of his throat, and what seemed like adult-sized biceps, bigger, even, than Morris's. He looked like a 12 or 13 year-old version of Jim Thorpe, the early 20th century Olympic hero from the old Carlisle Indian School. Kemp didn't look for fights but he didn't run away from them either. This time it was Morris who went down. But that was fine with Morris; he just wanted to know his place in the playground pecking order. "I'm the second toughest kid in the school," he declared, with cool equanimity. Nobody disputed him.

After that was all settled, we obeyed our Shepherding instincts and befriended Morris.

Morris wasn't like us and most of our middle-to lower-class Mormon friends at Liberty Elementary. And he wasn't like Leo Sotiriou, our pint-sized Greek Orthodox friend, or even Rhue Webster, our Syrian-American Catholic friend, who Morris had pounded on the playground his first day of school. Morris Hulse wasn't like any of us. But he wanted to join us.

First, we taught him how to play marbles—the schoolyard rage for boys our age (until the authorities outlawed playing for keeps on school property). We loaned him a portion of our cache of marbles, until he could win some for himself. And we schooled him how to shoot his taw properly with power and precision from the knuckle of his thumb—not weak fudge-knuckle from his fingernail.

That summer we got him on our little league baseball team—we don't remember how we negotiated that—and decided he was a third base-man, because he could throw hard. Morris loved to pull his green Hafers Incorporated ball cap low over his brow, with the brim radically bent, and hoarsely yell: "Hey battabatta, SWING!" when an enemy player was at the plate. He had never played ball before, but he loved being on the team, and he exulted when we won the league championship.

We even taught him not to swear. Or, more precisely, he insisted that we *prevent him* from swearing by "kicking me in the *ass* every time I say a cuss word."

"But Morris," we objected, "you just swore! Ass is a swear word!"

"Then kick me in the ass, *Goddamn it!*" he insisted, forcefully. So, of course we had to oblige him.

In the sixth grade we wrote him into the script of our student-produced class play on Julius Caesar. His role was to stand as Caesar's guard on the Ides of March in the senate forum the fateful day of the dictator's assassination. Both the senatorial assassins and Morris were armed with stout Roman swords that David Lingwall helped us make by swiping some small boards and wood rasps from his father's workshop to sculpt them into reasonable facsimiles of those formidable weapons. Bam, bam, BAM! Morris sorely bruised the knuckles of every one of Caesar's would-be assassins and sent their wooden swords clattering to the floor at the dress rehearsal. "No, NO!" we exclaimed, "Caesar is *supposed* to be killed!"

"Not when *I'm the guard*," Morris replied uncomprehendingly; "you told me that was my job!"

Earlier that year, we had inveigled Morris to attend a few Sunday school classes with us at the old Liberty Ward chapel, just a half block west of Salt Lake City's Liberty Park. But his interest quickly waned. Shortly after Morris stopped coming to church with us, we were shocked to discover that he had apparently joined the Jehovah's Witnesses. The JW's little Kingdom Hall church was situated on the corner of 400 East and Williams Avenue, a couple of blocks from where Morris and his mom lived in a little rental apartment on the north side of 900 South and 400 East.

One Saturday we saw him standing on the corner in front of the Kingdom Hall in an ill-fitting brown suit and purple tie, black hair slicked back—incongruously decked out for a Witness bible-study meeting in the heart of our LDS neighborhood. We stopped our bikes for a quick chat and said we were glad. Silently, however, we were disappointed he hadn't decided to become a Mormon. But we didn't ask why, and we never found out the reason. Maybe his mom was behind it, simply doing her best to follow-up on Morris' avowed efforts to stop swearing and be a good kid by directing him to her own church. Whatever the case, Morris' flirtation with religion turned out to be brief.

And then there was another schoolyard fight. A biggie. It was Steve Kemp again, but this time his scrappy adversary was Guy Snarr. Guy Snarr, it so happened, was Morris' cousin, but for some reason we didn't know that at the time. Guy too was a tough kid: blonde, bantam sized but wiry, and absolutely fearless. He lived in an old, 19th century, red brick house directly across the street on 300 East from Carolyn Olson. But Carolyn's mother wouldn't let him come to Carolyn's birthday party, because she thought Guy was a trouble-maker.

We never knew exactly how the fight got started. All we could see at first was a rapidly expanding crowd of dozens of kids encircling the combatants. And there, in the center, was Guy Snarr, leaping back to his feet from the asphalt playground, his fists swinging wildly, blood in his mouth, and his left eye already bulging and swollen shut. Steve Kemp, unmarked and efficient, sent him crashing back to the asphalt with another brutal blow.

Steve Kemp and Guy Snarr, 1956.

As Guy struggled to get up and fly at Kemp again, out of nowhere, Lisle Brown entered the ring. Lisle? Lisle Brown?! Lisle Brown was a classic "nerd" from Happy Days: bony, studious, polite, artistic, uninterested in sports, but actually pretty funny when you got to know him. Lisle was also a "traffic cop," a singular honor bestowed upon a dozen sixth grade boys who did reasonably well in their studies and didn't cause trouble in class. We were traffic cops too. But Guy Snarr was not, and neither were Steve Kemp or Morris Hulse. Boy traffic cops got to wear red garrison caps and bandolier belts with badges on them to signal their authority when they were stationed at crosswalks before and after school to stop traffic for their fellow students. And, in the absence of adults, some arrogated authority to patrol the schoolgrounds for petty rule infractions committed by their schoolmates.

Liberty Elementary Traffic Patrol, 1955-56.
Front, L-R: Owen Wood, Ernie Jager, Leo Sotiriou, Udell Stones. **Middle, L-R:** Gary Shepherd, Gordon Shepherd, Clyde Jensen, Lisle Brown, Steve Hardy. **Back, L-R:** John McClain, Lorin Larsen, Larry Swanger, John Anderson.

Lisle was on duty. He displayed his traffic cop insignia and held up his hand: "No fighting on the schoolgrounds," he said in a quavering voice.

"What?! What did he say?!" Morris was standing in the inner ring of the densely packed circle, cheering on his spunky cousin.

His cousin was in a savage fight with approximately zero chance of winning. But it was fair, in a way, since Guy had apparently provoked it. And by Morris's logic, it had to be settled the right way: not by talking, but with fists. Deeply incensed by Lisle's puny righteousness, Morris lunged forward and grabbed his spindly neck. He slapped Lisle, and, with a thunderstorm look on his face, raised his right hand to do more.

According to Gordon, "That's when Gary, my do-gooder twin brother, decided he should be next to step into the ring."

Gary gently rested his hand on Morris' stocky shoulder: "C'mon Morris, don't hurt Lisle; he didn't mean anything. He was just trying to do his job."

Morris dropped his punching hand, released his grip from Lisle's neck, shook off Gary's restraining fingers, and turned menacingly around: "Do you wanna fight me instead, Gary, is that it?"

"No, no Morris, nobody wants to fight," Gary soothed, "let's just break it up."

"No, I don't think so," Morris answered with icy deliberateness. "You don't break up a fight; that's a rule. If it ain't Lisle, then *you'll* have to fight me."

Morris took a step forward and jabbed Gary in the chest with the flat heel of his hand. "C'mon, man, c'mon! You have to fight me! Put up your fists!" Morris kept advancing and jabbing Gary in the chest, pushing him back: He slapped his face, soft. Then again, hard. It stung, and Gary's cheek burned red. Slowly, Gary raised his fists. His nostrils now flaring, Morris' taunts gathered intensity: "Go on! Hit me! I dare you! Throw the first punch! Fuck'n chicken shit! Hit me first!

So much for the anti-swearing campaign.

Gary, who had never been in a serious fight in his life, lobbed a tentative round-house right in the general direction of Morris' head. Easily deflecting the errant blow with his left forearm, Morris snapped Gary's head back with his own quick, smashing right hand punch to the mouth.

A little spew of crimson speckled starkly on Morris's white tee-shirt. Gary bent over and, cupping his hands to his mouth, tasted salty blood, and felt one of his teeth poking through his lower lip. He tried to stanch welling tears of pain and shame.

Morris was immediately transformed, bending over with Gary, his arm around Gary's slender shoulders; "You okay? Sorry man. I had to do that. I didn't want to hurt you, but you can't break up a fight. That's a rule."

All the fighting was done for the day as the recess bell rang. The boggled and buzzing crowd of our elementary school mates dispersed, and we all trudged back to class. Morris draped his arm around Gary as they walked. He reiterated why he had to punch him, and why they could still go on being friends. Business is business, Alfredo, a concept that we didn't quite grasp until we saw *The Godfather* 25 years later.

Where was Mrs. Robey? Where were the real cops? Well, lest we forget, it was the Salt Lake City bubble of the 1950s.

But Morris wasn't on our baseball team that summer, and we saw less of him in the fall of 1956 as he advanced with us and the rest of our Liberty Elementary School classmates to the seventh grade at Lincoln Junior High. We remember this now because, standing on the third row next to Ray Kaleel, Rhue Webster's cousin, Morris' picture appears in the 1956-57 Lincoln Junior High annual. We checked the picture just to make sure. Morris was in the "other" seventh grade class—Mrs. Buck's class, who tutored the kids deemed academically less gifted, in contrast to Mrs. Carlyle's class, who taught the supposedly more advanced kids introductory algebra.

But the rest of our shared memory about Morris from then on is a little fuzzy. We don't remember him, for example, in our gym class or competing in intramural wrestling, at which, undoubtedly, he would have excelled. At some point, he mysteriously disappeared from school. His mother, a single mom whose oldest son was serving time for armed robbery (in what we used to call "reform school"), apparently withdrew Morris from Lincoln while she looked for another job and a different place to live, in parts of the city unknown to us.

Two years later we saw Morris again at Lincoln in the ninth grade. He had been re-admitted halfway through the school year. How much had he changed in those two years? How much had the rest of us changed? He greeted Gordon in shop class and right away, affirming his loyalty from days gone by, assured him he would happily "beat the living shit" out of anybody who was bothering him at school. Gordon expressed gratitude but hastily assured Morris that he was rarely bothered.

Granted, his belligerence didn't sound radically different to us but, even then, we could tell that something had been snuffed out. What was it? Was there ever a small ember of hope for his life lodged somewhere in his boyhood soul when he eagerly aspired to play marbles at Liberty Elementary and trash-talked the other team at third base on our little league team? Have you forgotten that, once upon a time, *he* was the one who insisted he was going to stop swearing? That he was the one who decided to try going to church? Why would he do that when he was 11 and 12 years-old?

Now he conspicuously displayed a black widow spider tattoo on his right shoulder, in plain sight below the sleeve of the rolled up tee-shirt he still wore. That meant he had joined the Black Widows, Salt Lake City's most notorious gang of delinquent hoods. Sadly, his banty-rooster cousin, Guy Snarr, also had joined the Black Widows. Now when Morris spoke belligerently, there was no righteous claim to fairness and street justice to excuse his aggressive intentions. He was no longer looking for acceptance and a place to belong with the "good kids" of Salt Lake's saintly civic culture, whose parents tried to protect them from the likes of Morris Hulse. It wasn't long before he was expelled from Lincoln, another fossil educational practice from the 1950s.

Morris never attended high school. He never experienced the democratic fervor that his old Liberty/Lincoln schoolmates felt in 1962 when we finally graduated, having gratefully learned to sing, "On South High, we stand behind you forever!" Would Morris have been proud to know that South's 2,000 students had elected Gary as their student body president? Liberty, Lincoln, democracy and equality at Salt Lake City's South High—to us it was a providentially seamless transition to the adult side of the civic bubble.

Sometime after our high school senior year we read in the city section of the *Salt Lake Tribune* that there had been a shooting in a downtown bar: a man had been killed in a dispute over a woman. The shooter was Morris. Later, as students at the University of Utah, we learned from Fred VanderVeur, a former South High friend who was working part-time as a guard at the Utah State Penitentiary (and later became warden of the Central Utah Correctional Facility in Gunnison, Utah), that Morris had bulked up a lot by spending all his spare time in the prison gym lifting weights. And, then, a few more years down the road—after we both returned home from our Mormon missions to make Latter-day Saints out of Mexicans—we belatedly learned that Morris was dead. Somehow he had managed to kill himself in a lonely cell at the Point of the Mountain, where the Utah State Penitentiary was surrounded by acres of gates and concertina razor wire at the southern edge of the Happy Valley of the Great Salt Lake.

We still think about Morris from time to time. He's even in our dreams occasionally. This isn't the case with all our old friends from childhood. There are many we never think about, much less encounter again in our dreams. Why do we still remember him, with both fondness and much regret?

Morris. Morris Hulse. A troubling name from our childhood past. He was a damaged boy who grew up in 1950s Salt Lake and, for a time, tried to associate with the likes of us. But we never got him to live inside our bubble. Might we have? Was there a brief turning-point moment in time when his life might have been tenderly altered by something or someone, so that he could be remembered differently today? Maybe, probably not. But we can't help wondering. Gary can still feel with his tongue the scar tissue on the right inside of his lower lip.

10.

JUST THROW TO MY MITT!
When Baseball Was Our Passion, Season I

Baseball eventually became our passion as kids, supplanting our interest in daily summer swimming excursions to Liberty Park. When and how did baseball wedge its way to the top tier of our boyhood priorities? For what now are mostly foggy reasons, the game apparently began percolating in our heads at a fairly early age.

In the summer of 1951, not long after beginning school at Liberty Elementary, we have a clearly etched memory of our 39 year-old father slugging a long drive into left center field during a men's softball game for the Liberty Ward softball team. Most of the players on the team were fathers of our neighborhood friends. The wives and children of these men—including us—were cheering excitedly on the sidelines as our dad rounded the bases and slid safely into third. As the dust settled, Dad stood, looked behind him, and quickly threw his hands back around the seat of his pants to close the center portion of an embarrassing rip in the gaberdine slacks he was wearing that ran from his rear belt loop to the back of his knee. In a flash, the ever-resourceful Maureen McLean—the wife of our future next-door neighbor and ward bishop, and a registered nurse—materialized at Dad's side, whipped out needle and thread from her purse, and quickly sewed up the offending tear with a half dozen Frankenstein style stiches.

Later that year, our second grade teacher, Miss Nelson, assigned an art project for which we were supposed to draw a picture of what we wanted to be when we grew up. Gary carefully drew an awkward image of what he purported to be a baseball player, costumed in a crayon-colored white uniform with a blue number on the back and a blue hat on the player's head.

At that age, we had no actual experience playing ball, beyond a few simple throw and catch moments with our father. But we did watch occasional big league games on television as kids, especially world series games. Gordon remembers coming home one summer afternoon in 1953—shortly after our parents had made an extravagant purchase of a modest black and white TV set—to discover our dad watching a game in the living room. "Who's playing?" queried Gordon.

"The New York Yankees and the Cleveland Indians," Dad responded.

"The *Yankees*?! Wow. Alright. I want the Yankees to win," Gordon enthused. The two of us had begun cultivating a boyhood interest in the Civil War, as well as the usual cowboy and Indian Hollywood fare that dominated both television and movie screens at the time. We quickly equated the Yankees with the good guys of the U. S. Cavalry and became devoted fans. Coincidentally, our dad also liked the Yankees, and we instantly absorbed his comments about the game and its star performers—especially Phil Rizzuto, Yogi Berra, Whitey Ford, and Mickey Mantle, not to mention the Yankee's eccentric but crafty manager, Casey Stengel. The fact that the Yankees routinely won the American League pennant and then the World Series almost every year convinced us of the righteousness of our decision to be loyal fans, even when everyone else seemed to hate them for winning so much.

By the fourth grade, we began to fancy ourselves as good ball players, even though we had yet to actually do anything much more than play catch between ourselves. In the summer before fifth grade, when we were living at and taking care of Uncle Bob's home in Holladay, our skill levels escalated after we fashioned a bat from a piece of scrap wood and began having batting practice by taking turns pitching and hitting black walnuts—still encased in their tough, green outer skin—that had fallen on the ground from several large trees on the outskirts of Bob's spacious property. When the walnuts were exhausted, we discovered that fallen quinces were even better ball substitutes due to their larger size and harder surface. That Christmas, Mom and Dad gave us an old fashioned fielders' glove with thick fingers, no webbing, and not much of a pocket, plus a big old catcher's mitt. Now we could really start throwing hard and not just lob a ball (or quince) back and forth.

After we moved from Bob's back to our old Herbert Avenue home in Salt Lake, we employed the same basic scheme for our batting practice but substituted homemade tinfoil balls for walnuts and quinces. We were alert to snatch tinfoil wraps—after they were discarded—that our Mom had used to cover baked foods or protect leftovers in the fridge. When these used scraps were not available, we furtively snitched a swath of new tinfoil straight from the Reynolds Aluminum dispenser box.

We folded and mashed the tinfoil into a sphere that could be used for our batting games. After sufficient pounding, our homemade tinfoil balls became as hard as small rocks and would sting like the dickens when we occasionally threw a wild pitch at each other at bat behind the house. Our backyard was a narrow rectangle of grass and a small garden, maybe 20 yards in length and 15 yards in width. It was bordered in the back by a wobbly wire fence, about three feet high, and anchored by several old wooden two-by-fours. The batter would stand on the small square of concrete that fronted the back of our house, and the wooden door immediately behind served as the backstop. The pitcher stood about ten yards back in the grass and would throw with reasonable force towards the door. When the tinfoil ball was new and somewhat puffy, it was relatively easy to hit with our little homemade bat. After multiple blows the ball compacted and hardened and correspondingly could be thrown faster and was much harder to hit. At that point it was time to scrounge more tinfoil for a new ball.

We had been devotees of the library for a couple of years, eagerly combing the shelves for every available volume of the adventures of Freddy the Pig and his talking farm animal friends. But now we began to branch out a bit more and particularly looked for baseball books, both fiction and non-fiction. By that point, the two of us were confirmed baseball addicts. In addition to library books, we acquired pocket copies of the *Gillette Blue Blades Baseball Encyclopedia* and devoured its statistics. Oddly, we were drawn to the history of baseball's early days and became more knowledgeable about the game's great players from 1900-1940 than we were about contemporary heroes. To this day you can ask us what Ty Cobb's lifetime batting average was, how many games Walter Johnson won in his big league career, what Christy Mathewson's famous pitch was called, how many homeruns Babe Ruth hit in his first season for the New York Yankees in 1920, or what Ted Williams' batting average was in 1941. You wouldn't want to bet against us.

In the mid-1950s, an immensely popular TV show called the $64,000 Dollar Question, had sprung up and lured large audiences to watch con-testants attempt to answer questions of increasing difficulty for increasing amounts of cash prizes. One contestant had chosen baseball as his subject and worked his way up to the $64,000 question, which he then flubbed. The two of us, watching at home, shouted out the answers to most of the questions before the contestant did, including the winning answer that the chagrinned, sweaty faced contestant missed.

We started playing Little League baseball at the age of twelve for a team sponsored by Hafers Incorporated, a used motor vehicle parts company on the west side of Salt Lake. We played all of our games at Municipal ballpark, kitty corner from Liberty Park at the intersection of 1300 South and Seventh East. We were a pretty rag-tag collection of kids, coached by an emaciated looking adult smoker who was intense but didn't appear to know much about the finer points of the game. We persuaded him to allow three of our friends onto the team after formal try-outs were done—Ron Swenson, Morris Hulse, and Lorin Larsen, none of whom had much previous experience playing baseball—to help beef up the team's prospects.

Gordon, Lorin Larsen, and Gary gearing up to practice for Hafers, Inc.

Surprisingly, Hafers Inc. did well. In spite of our thin physiques, both of us had mysteriously developed some modest muscles in our arms. We had practiced pitching to each other for several years, and we could throw pretty hard for our age. So we became the team's pitcher and catcher, alternating between these two positions every other game. We had never before donned catcher's gear (head mask, chest protector, knee and shin guards) and squatted directly behind a swinging batter prior to our first game. But we both quickly adapted to the strange requirements of this ungainly position and even became fairly good at it. And we were both decent pitchers who could consistently zip a fastball into the strike zone.

**"Mysteriously developed . . . muscles." Gordon showing off
his modest bicep at age sixteen.**

Our team was undefeated up to the last game of the season and played for the
league championship against the only other undefeated team. Gary started
as pitcher and had given up only one run to our opponents prior to the last
inning. The other team's pitcher—Richard Turnbull—was a big chunky kid
who threw hard, and we were lucky to have eked out a solitary run off him.
After two were out in our half of the last inning, Gary managed to draw a
walk, advanced to second on a passed ball by the catcher, and then Gordon
sliced a soft blooper into right center field for a lucky double that brought
Gary home and broke the 1-1 tie.

In their at-bat in their half of the last inning, Gary struck out the first
two batters—the weak tail-end of their batting order. But then our worthy
opponents proceeded to fill the bases with an infield error, a walk, and a hit
batsman. The next batter was our old neighborhood buddy, Dave Lingwall.
Gary was tired and tense, and he was losing control of his pitches. On Gary's
first throw, Dave swung at a bad pitch but nevertheless hit a long, high fly
down the right field line, well beyond the reach of our little right fielder.

"Foul ball!" the umpire declared. Dave took another impulsive swing on the next pitch—one that was wide of the plate and almost in the dirt. Strike two. Then Gary, by now almost shaking, threw three more pitches that were also off the mark, and this time Dave let them all go by without swinging, all of them called-balls. Full count. Gordon trotted out to the mound from behind the plate, dirt mixed with sweat streaked on his face: "Just throw to my mitt! You can get him!"

"Yeah, sure, I know." Gary wound up one more time and threw wide and low of the plate again on his final pitch, only to watch in disbelief as the umpire jerked his right thumb upward and dramatically called, "Strike three!" Hafers Inc. was league champ, and we righteously celebrated our victory despite the umpire's bad call and Gordon's lucky hit. Such are the inequities of life we were beginning to learn—only this time, the capricious Fates had come down on our side.

Nevertheless, playing star roles on a winning Little League team made us feel pretty cocky. We were talking with our new LDS ward deacon quorum instructor at church one Sunday morning just after our team had played in the championship game. He was a young guy, and, after listening to us brag a bit, revealed that he was the coach of a Little League team that played in a different area of town, and that they were undefeated in their own league. We thought we knew some of the kids who played in that league and didn't believe his team could be any better than ours. So we boldly asserted that we could probably put together a team made up of Liberty Park Ward deacon quorum kids, plus a few other buddies who didn't go to our church (like Ron and Morris), and beat his team in a practice game. He called us on this boast, and we whirled into action, recruiting players from all our ward buddies and other friends, and even organized a practice session so we could get our positions and batting order set.

On the appointed Saturday morning our collection of hastily drafted misfits joined our instructor's team at Liberty Park and set up a makeshift ball diamond on a grassy expanse in the middle of the park. His team was in fact pretty polished. We didn't know many of their players after all, but could see from their warmups that they were well coached and had several solid athletes who looked pretty good. Our instructor had no doubt sized us up as a little bit too full of ourselves and saw an opportunity to teach us a lesson in humility, as well as get in a little helpful practice for his team before their final game. We could tell he didn't take us too seriously, because instead of starting his star pitcher and most of his first string players in other positions, he put in younger, second string players to give them some game experience.

The game was set up as a standard (Little League) six inning contest with our instructor serving as behind-the-plate umpire. Gary pitched for our side, and Gordon was catcher. We took advantage of their young pitcher, who couldn't throw very hard, and knocked out a bunch of hits and walks in the first three innings, scoring six runs. Meanwhile, Gary held the other team's second stringers to a couple of dinky, groundball singles and no runs. Our quorum advisor was visibly surprised. In the fourth inning, he put in his first team, including his best pitcher, who was definitely good for kids our age. Our team's hitting withered immediately. And their first-string batters were good, too. Gary was shocked when they started hitting him pretty hard—no easy outs now. In the end, our initial six score advantage proved just enough for us to eke out a 6-5 win. It began to dawn on us that maybe we weren't as good as we had puffed ourselves up to be. There would be several more baseball summers ahead to confirm that suspicion but, for the time being, we were on top of the world.

II.

WILLFUL DISOBEDIENCE AND
THE LAST FOXTROT

In retrospect, one of the most willfully dumb things Gordon did as a kid (there were many) was to defy Miss Jensen, Liberty Elementary School's veteran sixth grade teacher. To 11 and 12 year-old boys in 1955-56, Miss Jensen—who was close to retirement age—looked like a relic from the roaring twenties. She wore her hair bobbed short, with curling iron waves parted on the side, and she dressed in 1920s style, mid-heel oxfords with support hose.

But Miss Jensen was not a doddering push-over. To the contrary; she was firm, authoritatively decisive in her teaching methods, and knew how to manage pre-pubescent boys. Nobody talked back to Miss Jensen. She was in charge of choosing and supervising the school's boy traffic cops, and she made sure during activity periods that her students learned how to square dance, waltz, and especially how to do the Foxtrot (her favorite). "Foxtrot *one*, Foxtrot *two*, Foxtrot *three*!" she would call out in a strong, clear cadence as she glided around the room making sure that everyone was in proper step. Miss Jensen insisted on respectful manners, reading comprehension, the importance of clear writing (including good penmanship), and loyal citizenship. For what it's worth, the first poems we ever composed—and the first original writing that we can remember ever taking ownership of or pride in—were for Miss Jensen's sixth grade Christmas assignment. Gordon called his poem "Once Within a Stable Lay," and Gary's was entitled "The

Christmas Bells"—both poems revealing our taken-for-granted, boyhood understanding of Christianity's origin story.

ONCE WITHIN A STABLE LAY

Once within a stable lay, a little child upon the hay

Up above him from afar, brightly shone a glowing star

It led the wisemen from the East, who came in search of love and peace

Mary lifted her head and smiled, "This is Christ the Holy Child"

He was born in Bethlehem on Christmas Day, over the ocean far away

*He was kind and gentle from his birth to bring love
and peace to men on earth*

For men who stole, killed, and lied, he was put upon the cross and died

THE CHRISTMAS BELLS

The Christmas bells always remind me

Of the Christ who was born in Galilee

How he taught the people to live a good life

In a world of darkness and toil and strife

And when upon the cross he died

The angels all were by his side

To comfort him to bear the pain

Until at last the Christ was slain

And so the bells ring on and on

To tell the story of Christ in song

Gary's illustration for his Sixth Grade Christmas poem.

At the end of the 1956 school year at Liberty Elementary, Miss Jensen organized a graduation event. The following year we would be moving on to Lincoln Junior High as seventh graders. So, at noon on the last day of class, we were all excused to go home, change into our Sunday best, and return to school for a dance (where we would display our recently acquired waltz and Foxtrot skills) and the awarding of graduation certificates. The day before, Miss Jensen had given us a free period to circulate around the classroom and fill out our dance-cards. There were ten dances listed on the card, and Miss Jensen expected every girl to be asked and every boy to do the asking for all ten dances.

This is when Gordon became willfully disobedient. He was old enough to actually like girls for being girls, but he was afraid of them. Afraid of what? Oh, he wasn't afraid to tease them and talk scornfully about them for not being able to shoot marbles the right way or throw a baseball properly. No, that wasn't it. He was uncomfortably shy and simultaneously proud around girls. He was proudly afraid to talk to them, afraid he wouldn't know what to say, afraid he would seem foolish and gauche (which, of course, was not a word he knew at the time), and he was unwilling to try for fear of failure.

What if the girls he really liked had already filled out their dance-cards or were saving their dances for someone else who *they* really liked? Gordon was envious of Owen Wood, one of his and Gary's classmates, whom they had known since kindergarten. Owen seemed self-confident and sophisticated around girls—able to communicate with them and win their confidence. He was already beginning to ask girls *on dates*, for heaven's sake. This was far beyond Gordon's highly constricted repertoire for interacting with the opposite sex.

Owen Wood, 1956.

What about Gary? He too was suddenly shy around girls. We say suddenly because up until the sixth grade neither of us really considered girls to be objects of particular fascination; they were just additional friends and class-mates we had grown up with. But by the sixth grade, most of the girls had already hit the early stages of puberty and, although lagging slightly behind, so had we. Girls began looking and talking differently. They now seemed increasingly alien and mysterious to us, but somehow they also had become desirable creatures, which required of us wholly new and unfamiliar ways of interacting. And this ballroom dancing business—no longer square dancing that involved only the occasional clutching of sweaty hands, but boys and girl's arms around each other—seemed enticingly contrary to our boyhood lessons of Sunday school virtue. Nevertheless it was sanctioned, required even, by Miss Jensen, who insisted on teaching boys the polite but manly way to hold their partners while leading them around the dance floor. Most of the girls seemed to be less nervous than we were about all of this. But for us, the forbidden sensuality of actually holding a girl was accompanied by mixed feelings of immature longing, confusion, and embarrassment.

Gary's confusion and embarrassment were, for some unexamined reason, not as overpowering as Gordon's (a point of differentiation in the identical twin stereotype of perfect alikeness). He had harboured a secret crush on Carol Jean Christensen for several years previously. But Carol Jean's family had moved away at the end of the fifth grade. Not finding it too hard to do, Gary overcame his awkwardness and, adhering to Miss Jensen's instructions, he approached and asked the requisite number of girls to fill out his dance card (oblivious to their undoubtedly much greater anxiety over the humiliating prospect of not being asked and then having boys compelled by Miss Jensen to return and mumble an insincere request). It should be noted, however, that Gary made sure that the first girl he approached—as fast as he could maneuver himself to her side before any other boy in the room could preempt him—was Katheryn Keat. Katheryn was a new girl in our class for whom Gary had developed an instant liking, and who, contrary to the rules, he inveigled to sign up with him for both the first and last graduation dances.

Kathryn Keat, 1956.

In contrast, Gordon, in his dumb, inarticulate pride, sat at his desk and refused to fill out his dance card. At the end of the allotted hour Miss Jensen checked everyone's card, discovered Gordon's intransigence, and—taking matters into her own hands—commenced to fill it out with the names of girls who still didn't have their dance cards completed. She even penciled *herself* in as Gordon's dance partner for the last dance on his card. Criminy! The ultimate humiliation!

What to do? What to do? Gordon knew one thing for sure. He liked and respected Miss Jenson a lot, but he determined he wasn't going back to school that afternoon. When the twins arrived home for lunch, their mother greeted them with a cheerful smile and their Sunday clothes all laid out and neatly pressed for the dance and graduation activities. As they were changing clothes, Gordon informed Gary of his improvisational plan of defiance: He would leave with Gary to go back to the school, but once they turned the corner at Third East and Herbert Avenue, out of sight from their waving mother, he would double back and head for "the field"—the vacant, weed-filled lot behind Ron Swenson's house. Before leaving the house he had managed to conceal a couple of comic books and a Freddy the Pig adventure book. His plan was to fashion a kind of bowery shelter in a corner of the field to shade himself from the sun, keep his clothes neat, read his books, and wait for the dreaded dance to be done. Gary's part in the plot was to simply go on to school, tell Miss Jenson that Gordon had skipped out, but he didn't know where he was (the one falsehood Gordon allowed), and then come back to the field after the graduation festivities to fetch Gordon so they could go home together and greet their mom with certificates in hand as though nothing untoward had happened.

**Dressed for Miss Jensen's sixth grade graduation dance,
Gordon ducked out.**

And that's exactly what happened. Gary reported to Gordon that Miss Jensen had been mad as a hornet and initially said she would refuse to sign his graduation certificate; that his parents would have to come for it with him in tow after he confessed his stunningly disobedient behavior. But then, in a surprising moment of pure grace, Miss Jensen relented. She signed Gordon's certificate while telling Gary to tell his brother that she was disappointed in him, that she thought he would be braver than that, and that he had let her down. Ouch. Gordon was vastly relieved and simultaneously guilt-stricken. In his petty smallness, however, the relief temporarily outweighed his guilt.

Gordon: I never had the courage to go back to Liberty School to apologize to Miss Jensen and ask for her forgiveness. I never saw her again. I regret that to this day.

Well, needless to say, both of us had a lot of maturing to do. And, as with most adolescents, there was still a fair amount of stumbling for us in the years ahead as we pursued our secondary education is Salt Lake City's public schools. But as we reflect on our elementary school experience, we are grateful for the strong women teachers of that era (there was not a single male teacher or administrator at Liberty Elementary during the seven years we attended). To us, they were proof positive that educated women were just as capable as men in their knowledge and mastery of academic subjects, as well as in their ability to provide lasting character lessons and civic guidance for the development of their youthful charges. In a very essential way, our first public role models for what it meant to be adults and contributing citizens to the community in which we lived were our women elementary grade schoolteachers.

Gordon Postscript: Dear Miss Jenson, if I were magically permitted to do it over, would you be my dance card partner for the last Foxtrot? Thanks!

12.

FREE RANGE KIDS AND BOYHOOD BRUSHES WITH THE GRIM REAPER

Waiting in long car lines to drop off and pick up their children from school has become normative for many parents, even though there are dependable school busses with assigned routes for this purpose. And let's not forget to mention the old fashioned option of *walking*, for kids who live reasonably close to the schools they attend. That so many parents consider it their responsibility to personally drive their kids to school is symptomatic of a child-centered culture in which middle class adults have increasingly become actively involved in organizing and supervising their children's daily lives and activities. Is this a bad thing? What ever happened to the good old days of growing up as "free-range" kids? Well, let's just say that like most normative changes, it's a complicated question with both positive and negative sides to debate. What follows, for better or worse, is a sampling of some of our own free-range experiences growing up in 1950s Salt Lake City. Feel free to draw your own conclusions.

One of our first childhood memories involves a free-range incident *predating* our boyhoods growing up in Salt Lake City. As pre-schoolers we lived for a short time in Provo, Utah. It was 1947, we were around three years of age, and our dad was home from the Second World War trying to make a civilian living to support his young family. We lived temporarily in a big, yellow brick rental house on Fourth West and Third South, three blocks north of Provo's railroad tracks. Our backyard was surrounded by a picket fence, which kept us corralled while we played in a corner sandpile. By the way, we're stretching definitions a little here by labelling this story as a "free-range" incident because, technically, we definitely had not been given parental permission to roam. But, since it was prescient of later misadventures, let's tell this story first.

It was summertime, and the two of were in the backyard as usual. We have no idea where our older brother Don was at the time. Our Mom had gone into the house to take a telephone call. One of us noticed that the back gate had been carelessly left unlatched. Eureka! The outside world beckoned to us and, with immense curiosity and zero trepidation, we slipped through the gate, wandered through a neighbor's yard, and then headed south, down Fourth West. Our exploratory journey took us past three blocks of modest homes, straight to the railroad yards on Sixth South.

Gary and Gordon, circa 1947, in their Provo backyard.

We can only image our mother's panic when, having finished answering the phone, she returned to the backyard to discover we were gone. We're a little fuzzy on how she found us so quickly. She spotted us several blocks away, as we stood raptly gazing at a large warehouse across from the freight-busy railroad tracks. What fascinated us was a sliding door on the side of the building that kept opening and closing. Every time it did, men with lunch pails would appear and disappear. As we ventured forward to get closer to the mysterious door, Mom yelled loudly from behind and came running toward us, with her arms frantically waving. It was a little confusing. We sensed we must be in some kind of trouble but only recall being hugged and covered with kisses like prodigal sons when mom reached us at the edge of the tracks.

Fast-forward five years and we were back in Salt Lake City after short residencies in Billings, Montana and Cowley, Wyoming, where our dad had attempted to jump-start a business in ice cream and candy sales. The two of us were racing each other home for lunch. The Liberty Elementary School where we attended third grade was a half block around the corner from our home at 312 Herbert Avenue. But there was also a driveway shortcut on Third East, which we always took by hopping a fence and squeezing past the adjacent garages that separated our parents' property from the next-door neighbors. Gordon got over the fence first and forged ahead through the narrow opening between the two garages.

"OOWWW! OOOWWWW!" Gary suddenly began howling as an excruciating pain inexplicably stabbed through his right foot. Gordon whirled around and saw Gary hopping behind him on one foot. Stuck to the bottom of the PF Flyer on his other foot was a long board. For a dazed moment, Gordon didn't understand what was happening: Why was his brother hopping around with a board stuck to the bottom of his shoe? Within seconds, however, the problem became crystal clear: Jumping the fence, Gary's foot had landed on a large nail sticking up from a discarded board, and it had been driven into the lower sole of his foot. Gary was now crying for help with increasing anguish as he too realized what had happened. Without the slightest hesitation or forethought, Gordon rushed to Gary's side, grasped the sides of the attached board with both hands, and yanked it free from his foot. The two of us hobbled into the house together, presenting ourselves on the back-porch stairs to our frantic mother, who, while fixing our lunch, had heard us shouting.

After an emergency visit to see our family doctor, who administered an uncomfortable tetanus shot, Gary survived the ordeal and returned to school the next day, navigating awkwardly on a discarded crutch from Grandma Shepherd. What cautionary lesson did we learn from this painful occasion? Not much, apparently, as demonstrated by future misadventures, but at least from then on, we always looked to see what we were going to land on before taking shortcuts and hopping over neighborhood fences. And we knew we had each other's backs no matter what.

A year later, we conspired with our older brother Don (which we seldom did) and one of his neighborhood buddies, John Jennings, to make an unsanctioned trip to Memory Grove and the State Capitol Building at the top of State Street, overlooking the Salt Lake valley. We talked two of *our* friends, Ron Swenson and Eddie Stover (who lived next door to Jennings on Williams Avenue, one street north of our Herbert Avenue home) into joining us. The plan was to tell Mom that we were going to play at Liberty Park on Fifth East and ask her to make some sandwiches for us and our friends to take along. Sure, why not? Mom saw no good reason to turn down our modest request. As it was, we went almost every day with friends to Liberty Park in the summer to go swimming anyway. But we didn't go to Liberty Park. Instead, we stashed our swimsuits and boarded a city bus, whose route took passengers three and a half miles north to the grounds of the state capitol building. Upon arriving, Don and Jennings left us to our own devices, so we slid down a forested hillside to play army with Ron and Eddie in Memory Grove, climbed back up the hill to tour the basement exhibits in the capitol building (which included Ab Jenkins' famous "Mormon Meteor" race car), and ate our sandwiches. We were thirsty and put our nickels in a vintage soda machine to share a couple of little green bottles of icy Coca-Cola—a drink forbidden by the LDS health code. We were overcome by temptation, however, and sipped those Cokes frugally to make them last. Our delinquency was instantly rewarded—man, did they taste good! We would, however, soon have to pay the piper for our extravagance.

It was mid-afternoon and time to catch the bus for home before our Mom started to worry about us. But that's when we realized we had a problem. We had spent our nickels on cokes and didn't have enough money for bus fares. More accurately said, Ron and Eddie didn't have any money, and we two only had a dime between us (bus fare was five cents). But Don and Jennings had a couple of quarters each. When we approached Don for a "loan," to get home, we regret to say he sneered at us and said, "Tough! You shoulda saved your money. You can find your own way home." He and Jennings boarded the bus and left us standing on the capitol steps underneath the roaring lion statues. There was no way *we* were going to abandon Ron and Eddie just because we had a dime to ride the bus and they didn't. We had two other options: walk home four miles through downtown Salt Lake City or use our dime to call our parents from the pay phone booth to explain where we were. We called our parents.

Dad was steaming mad when he arrived to pick us up twenty minutes later. "Dang kids, you give'm an inch and they take a mile!" he expostulated. As we recall, Ron and Eddie got off scot-free. But the two of us were sentenced for fibbing to our Mom (and for "turning her hair grey with worry over your shenanigans!") to confinement in the backyard for a week. Since we were more or less compelled to rat Don out to Dad, he was grounded too, which only served to reinforce his conviction that we were the bane of his existence.

Later that same summer, not long before Liberty Elementary would usher us into the fourth grade, Gary was pumping hard on the little second hand, red and yellow bicycle that Dad had purchased for the two of us as compensation for the new, big, silver and blue bike that Don had received for his birthday that April. Gary had built up a head of steam blowing out of the tiny side street (425 East Grace Court) that ran only one block in length and dead-ended at the back of the Sudbury Maxwell grocery store on Ninth South. Immediately in Gary's field of vision loomed Fourth East—a busy north-south thoroughfare. A small Jehovah's Witnesses Kingdom Hall—improbably situated in the middle of our Mormon neighborhood—stood on the other side of Fourth East. Houses and trees on Williams Avenue blocked the view of everything north or south of Kingdom Hall until one was practically at the intersection. Gary knew he should at least slow down and survey for oncoming traffic, but he was pelting forward at top speed, and no cars could be seen traversing his limited field of vision. Go for it! That impulse easily overrode the modicum of cautionary good sense that, for a nano second, had whispered inside Gary's head.

Contemporary view of intersection of Williams and Fourth East with the Former Kingdom Hall in background.

Well, of course a car was directly on track to meet Gary. It suddenly zapped into the periphery of his left eye as he shot across Fourth East, a late 1940s dark blue Chevrolet. SCREECH! BLAM! The Chevy's left bumper smashed through the little red bike's rear tire. Gary was propelled headfirst, over the handlebars, into the gutter that was flowing with run-off water right in front of Kingdom Hall. Saturday service congregants had just emerged from their worship services and were milling about on the sidewalk adjacent to the curb. They stood stunned as Gary landed with a splash before their feet. Gary lay stunned too, stupidly wondering if he was dead. The only person in action was the car driver—a young adult with floppy blonde hair and blue tattoos on his sinewy forearms, who was chauffeuring his mother. He immediately jumped out of the Chevy and was at Gary's side in a flash. Without hesitation, he scooped Gary up and laid him in the back seat of the car while his mother cried, "Oh no, oh no!" Gary remembers only two questions from the young man: "Are you hurt?" Gary: "I don't think so." Young man: "Where do you live?" Gary: "312 Herbert Avenue; it's just the next street down the block from here."

One of our neighborhood friends, who coincidentally witnessed the accident, sped through a nearby alley to alert our parents. By the time Gary and his broken bike were delivered to the house, Mom was already in the front yard, wringing her hands with an anguished look on her face. Dad bounded down the porch steps accompanied by Gordon, who had been reading a book on the front porch swing. Just then, a black Ford police car roared around the corner and pulled up behind the Chevy in the driveway. The cop jumped out, assumed command, lifted Gary out of the seat and carried him up the porch steps into our house, as neighbours began bunching around. "Can you stand, son?" Yes, I think so." The officer stood Gary on the floor. "Where are you hurt, son?" "I don't know; I don't think I am." "Well, we better take a look." The officer pulled and off came Gary's damp, dirt-smudged t-shirt. Then he tugged and down came Gary's torn Levi jeans and droopy little boy underpants—huge embarrassment! But all that the disrobing revealed were scrapes on Gary's right knee and right elbow and a few scratches on his stomach and the palm of his left hand. "Looks like a damn miracle," concluded the cop.

Halfway through the school year of the fourth grade, Dad moved our family to Uncle Bob's home and spacious property on Highland Drive, on the south-eastern outskirts of Salt Lake City, as one-year caretakers. Bob had been commissioned by the LDS Church to paint a large mural in the new Los Angeles Temple. Simultaneously, famous artist Arnold Frieberg had asked Bob to be a production unit artist for Cecil B. Demille's "The Ten Commandments" in Hollywood. Bob, his wife, Olive, and their two children moved temporarily to L.A. to accomplish these tasks, while our family occupied and cared for the Highland Drive home in their absence.

While living for a year at Bob's house, we attended William Penn Elementary school on Siggard Drive in East Millcreek, a little over a mile away. We were supposed to take a designated bus to school, but, hey! we were free-range kids from the city, accustomed to walking places and finding short-cuts to wherever we needed to go. So, naturally, we prevailed upon our parents to get the school's permission to allow us to walk the mile and a half from Bob's house to William Penn along Highland Drive instead of taking the bus. Subsequently, we took unrighteous pride in the fact that we always beat the bus to school in the morning by leaving early, running every other block, and cutting through a wooded area on the edge of the school.

A year later we were back in Salt Lake City proper, attending the fifth and sixth grades at Liberty Elementary again. At the outset of our sixth grade year, Liberty was undergoing some major renovations and the addition of a new auditorium, so a sharing arrangement was made with the Whittier School—located east of South High on Third East— for their students to occupy Whittier's classrooms in the morning, while Liberty's students would replace them for classes in the afternoon. Whittier students attended school from 7:00 a.m. to 1:00 p.m. and we attended ours from 1:00 to 6:00 p.m.

The Whittier School was almost exactly one mile from our home on Herbert Avenue, so, once again, we were expected to take a bus to school. Once again, we objected. We insisted that as veteran walkers to William Penn Elementary—an even longer walk along busy Highland Drive, we could certainly manage to walk a shorter distance on safe, city sidewalks. Both our parents and school officials granted our petition without a fuss. We also convinced our new buddy, Lorin Larson (who lived at the corner of Fourth East and 1300 South) to join with us. Every day we walked to Lorin's and then, unitedly distinguished from our peers by our unorthodox independence, walked on to Whittier while the rest of our classmates rode. Once more, of course, we took unrighteous pride in beating the bus and, in the process, strengthened a strong friendship with our walking buddy, Lorin.

By the time we were sixth graders we had real bikes for transportation, and our territorial boundaries were exponentially enlarged. Lorin Larson had become one of our best friends, whose own bike we admired because of its ram's horn shaped handlebars. With Lorin we rode our bikes all over town, including the bench-like hills of the Lower Avenues that overlook the downtown business and spiritual center of Mormon Salt Lake City, about a mile and a half north from our homes near Liberty Park. On one memorable occasion, Lorin and Gordon were parked at the elevated intersection of B Street and First Avenue. Their gaze was fixed downward on the steep sidewalk that paralleled B Street and terminated at South Temple—one of Salt Lake's busiest thoroughfares—directly in front of the magnificent Roman Catholic Cathedral of the Madeleine. They had heard rumors about kids racing their bikes down this very hill. Gordon and Lorin looked at each other: "Let's go for it!" they agreed in unison. First Lorin, then Gordon wheeled their bikes and accelerated down the sidewalk, gaining locomotive speed as they went. The challenge, of course, was to *brake* and *turn sharply* at the corner so as NOT to sail into the middle of thick car traffic on South Temple. Both Lorin and Gordon succeeded brilliantly in doing this and were intoxicated by the thrill of it all.

Salt Lake City's Cathedral of the Madeline on B Street and South Temple.

Naturally, they bragged about their exploits to Gary who, in turn, was determined to try it for himself. The next day Gary and Lorin peddled all the way back to downtown Salt Lake. This time, however, Lorin suggested that Gary try riding down A Street, one block west of where he and Gordon had made their runs. Descending from First Avenue, A Street is significantly steeper than B—in fact, it is one of the most precipitous paved hills in the City. At the bottom of the sidewalk there is a slim slope of grass, about 15 feet in width, that buffers the sidewalk from the intersection of A Street with South Temple. A spark of doubt pierced Gary's enthusiasm: "So tell me again how I'm supposed to keep from flying out into South Temple?" "Just brake and slide your bike on its side when you get to the grass," Lorin confidently explained.

OK, easy. With a gulp of breath, Gary was off. Halfway down he lightly tested his brakes; the bike frame shuttered and wobbled, and Gary quickly stopped applying pressure to the peddle. He had never travelled this fast on a bike before. Suddenly, the grassy slope and South Temple were rushing to meet him. Ok, nothing to it, just hit the brakes again and tip the bike into a slide on the grass. What could go wrong? A sprinkler head, sticking up about an inch from the edge of the lawn and sidewalk provided a quick answer to that question. BAM! The front tire hit the sprinkler head with full center force, and Gary experienced an almost slow-motion sense of floating in the air, separated from his bike (which was rotating gracefully just below him). The bike hit the pavement first, and the rear tire assembly partially cushioned Gary's side-way landing on top.

The Buckingham Apartments at the intersection of A Street and South Temple.

SCREECH! SCREECH! Gary had heard that sound before. Car drivers going in both directions on South Temple frantically stomped their brakes to avoid plowing into the young boy and his bike that had suddenly dropped from the sky right in front of them. A very large, pink 1956 Lincoln had come to a jarring halt within three feet of Gary's head as he gingerly lifted it up to survey the scene. People were jumping out of their cars, rushing to help or gawk. Lorin was solemnly slow-walking down the A Street sidewalk, his face stricken with fear and guilt while an old lady watching from her porch at the Adjacent Buckingham Apartments screamed at him, "Shame on you! Why did you let him do it? You've killed him!"

But Gary didn't feel dead. He felt nothing but relief, because every part of his body was telling him that, apart from a stinging cut on the backside of his left knee, he had no injuries. Gary extricated himself from the twisted wheel assembly, picked up his damaged bike, and began pushing his way through the circle of astonished adults while answering their expressions of shock and concern with "I'm fine, I'm fine." Lorin met him on the stone steps leading down from the grassy slope above South Temple with an awed expression on his face that looked like he had just witnessed a cadaver being raised from the dead.

But this wasn't a tale either Gary or Lorin were going to repeat as a faith promoting testimony miracle at church on Sunday. No. What they were going to do was tell Gordon and then keep quiet about this little incident. We were certainly not going to confess to our parents how close Gary (and all of us, really) had come to the Grim Reaper's scythe because of our foolish stunt-riding down A and B Streets. Some story would have to be concocted to account for the wrecked bike. We don't recall the details of our explanation, only that our dad was piping mad again about our habitual carelessness and habit of breaking and losing things. There would be no more Christmas bikes for us! we were angrily informed. "Oh well, fair enough" we said to ourselves; our misadventure on South Temple could have turned out a lot worse than losing our bikes.

By the seventh grade, and at the onset of adolescence, riding boy-bikes for transportation no longer seemed as cool to us anyway, so Gary's bike-loss and the dysfunctional disrepair of Gordon's didn't seem like the end of our free-range world. We started walking again, including to the campus of

Lincoln Junior High, our new school which was located on the corner of State Street and 1300 South.

Among other things at Lincoln, we were introduced to an actual gym class, whose instructors were actual male gym teachers (Hal Hardcastle and Dean Papadakis). We were assigned gym lockers, given a list of necessary apparel items (white gym shorts, white t-shirts, gym shoes, sweat socks, and our first jock straps) and informed that we were expected to take said items home every week to be washed. Hardcastle and Papadakis also told all of us that we needed to start using underarm deodorant on a regular basis. All of this meant no more random, unsupervised marble matches for us at recess on the school playground. At Lincoln we had entered the big time of boy's organized athletic competition.

One of the organized sports activities we were introduced to at Lincoln was track and field. We remember in particular watching a film about the summer Olympic Games, which included a segment on throwing the javelin, an event we knew nothing about, but which excited our interest: the javelin! You get to throw a spear in competition as far as you can! Since the two of us had played little league baseball and thought we had good throwing arms, we speculated that javelin throwing might be something we could do as well. Javelin throwing wasn't an event sponsored for young adolescents, however, and javelins were not issued for us to practice with at Lincoln Junior. However wise this policy was from a responsible, adult perspective, from our perspective it merely represented a challenge to our creative imaginations as free-range kids. After all, we weren't *restricted* to playing sports or practicing them only in our gym classes at school. We could walk over to Lincoln's playing field after school hours or on the weekend any time we wanted. As for throwing the javelin, we hatched an idea: Why not make our *own* javelin and practice with it on our own, free time? That, of course, is exactly what we did.

Fortunately for us, Lorin's dad had mechanical skills and tools, including, of all things, a small blow-torch device that could be used to weld metals. We're not sure how he did it, but Lorin somehow soldered a heavy piece of lead into a kind of dull point attached to the end of a broom handle. A little sharpening of the point with a file and voila!—we had our homemade javelin.

That Saturday, Ron Swenson joined with us, and the four of us walked over to Lincoln's athletic field to try out Lorin's javelin. It was awkward at first, but we began getting the hang of it and started launching a few decent throws, which we measured by pacing off steps from a line we had dug in the grass with a stick. Eventually tiring of our new sport, Lorin, Ron, and Gordon strolled off the field and started heading for home. Meanwhile, Gary was still practicing throws on the other side of the field, 50 to 60 yards away. On his last throw he heaved the primitive spear just right; it caught a nice breeze blowing across the field and climbed the sky, the way we had seen javelins properly thrown in the film shown to us in gym class, before arcing back to earth. Gary was mesmerized by his own achievement. Not one of us previously had come close to making such a long, elegant throw as this one. Gary gazed at the spear's flight path until it began breaking downward. Suddenly, Lorin, Ron, and Gordon appeared in his line of vision. LOOK OUT! Gary yelled urgently from across the field. Too late.

Gordon heard Gary yell and turned to see what the matter was. *Thunk!* Lorin's javelin pierced him in the groin. Yes, it pierced. But Gordon didn't know that at first. He instantly grabbed the spear's broom handle when it struck, and it fell to the ground as though it had bounced off him. His groin stung, but Gordon was madder at Gary than worried about any possible injury. "Blankety-blank-blank! He bellowed through gritted teeth as he hopped around on the sidewalk, "Why didn't you look where you were throwing that blankety-blank broomstick!" Gary, of course, was abjectly apologetic and wanted to know how badly his brother was hurt. Gordon looked at the small, entry hole in his jeans and said, no he didn't think it was bad, it just smarted a little. He'd be okay, he said, with practiced nonchalance.

Lorin and Ron collectively issued a sigh of relief, and the four of us headed back to Lorin's house, which was closest to the school (and besides, Lorin's parents weren't home). By the time we got to Lorin's, Gordon was limping badly and thought it best to take a closer look at himself. Lorin went with him into the bathroom and Gordon dropped his pants. There was hardly any blood, but he could see a small, bluish puncture wound near the intersection of his crotch and right thigh. He bent over for a closer look. That's when he lost consciousness. All Gordon can remember is groggily coming to on Lorin's bunkbed, where he had been dragged and laid prone by Lorin, Gary, and Ron. At that point we knew we would have to bring our parents into the picture.

What resulted was another emergency visit to the family doctor, who happened to be a relative on our mother's side: Maurice Taylor. Dad took the two of us in the family car, while mom stayed home with our little sister Sue to fret and say a prayer. Laid out on an examining gurney, Dr. Taylor probed Gordon's puncture wound with a blunt, steel instrument. "Look at this, Shep," he said to the twins' father as he raised and twisted his instrument high enough to show the length of the wound. "Another quarter inch to the right and it would have severed his femoral artery." Gary watched grimly as Gordon grimaced in pain at Dr. Taylor's rude poking. And this time it was our dad who fainted, flat onto the tiled floor of the examining room.

As with Gary's earlier brush with the Grim Reaper on his bike, our parents never learned the true story of what had happened that day. To protect his brother and buddies from any blame for the accident, Gordon devised an implausible story about awkwardly tripping on a mysterious spike while running laps at Lincoln in preparation for the school's annual track meet at the end of the year. Lorin, by the way, thought it best to destroy and dispose of his homemade spear. No more javelin throwing for us! But we're not sure we learned any sober, adult wisdom from the experience. For us, the corollary outcome of another brush with the Reaper and our subsequent cover story was not a lesson in the avoidance of risky behavior as we were growing into adolescence. Rather, what primarily resulted, once again, was greater reinforcement of our brotherhood bonds and boyhood friendships, which we had forged and valued most highly in the intoxicating world of free-range kids of the 1950s.

13.

WHAT ABOUT GIRLS?

What about girls? Outside of Gordon's boycott of Miss Jensen's sixth grade graduation dance, we haven't made much mention of girls in our youthful chronicles beyond mostly generic statements of admiration and retrospective advocation of equality, made long after the facts pertaining to the experiences we narrate have settled in the mists of memory. Did we think much about girls—not just as classmates and neighborhood friends—but as opposite sex attractions who accelerated our heart rates upon thought or sight? Well, of course we did, certainly by the time we were in high school. But reciting tales of our increasingly separate romantic encounters with girls in later adolescence and young adulthood would take us a bit far afield from our focus on boyhood adventures growing up together. During our preteen and early adolescence, however, when hormones first began stirring, there were a couple of girl-related experiences that we shared and now recall with a mixture of innocent fun, chagrin, and nostalgic bemusement.

On the threshold of puberty at approximately age eleven, both of us suddenly became shy around girls. This was especially true of Gordon, who, more so than Gary, stubbornly asserted his opposition to perceiving girls in a new light that required acting differently. Secretly, however, Gordon was smitten by Janice Yano and ineptly endeavored to conceal his attraction by showing off and annoying her. At roughly the same time, Gary developed a full blown crush on Carol Jean Christensen.

Carol Jean (never just Carol) was the smartest kid in our age group at Liberty Elementary, even smarter, we thought, than Philip Starr, Janice Yano, Annette Bowman, or Kathy McClure. And, of course, smarter than either one of us. Carol Jean was also a very good artist, better, we thought, than Lorin Larsen or Lisle Brown. In fact, we conceitedly conceded that her artistic talent was on par with our own. She was cute, also very shy, and she lived just around the corner from us in a small, white frame house at the intersection of Blair Street and Harvard Avenue, directly across from David Lingwall's house. Even at a young age, Gary felt a little leap in his heart whenever Carol Jean came into view.

Carol Jean Christensen, Fifth Grade at Liberty Elementary.

Homemade Valentine card from Carol Jean to Gary, Fifth Grade.

At the end of the fifth grade, Carol Jean's father received a job promotion with the Social Security Administration. Now the Christensen family could afford a new home, but while it was being built in Holladay (a Salt Lake suburb) they temporarily moved to Provo—40 miles south of Salt Lake City—and her family was suddenly gone from our neighborhood. The jolt of this unhappy surprise for Gary was slightly mitigated by vague hopes of seeing Carol Jean again when our parents made periodic trips to Provo to visit some of the friends they had made while briefly living there after the Second World War.

This is a story to which we will later return, but at this juncture in the narrative, let us recount the first time we asked girls as our dates to a dance—the 1956 Liberty Stake Gold and Green Ball. In those days, the Gold and Green Ball was an annual, formal dance sponsored by the LDS Church's Mutual Improvement Association (MIA)—an organization for youths between the ages of twelve and seventeen. At the age of twelve, both boys and girls commenced attending gender segregated, once a week "Mutual" classes and were consequently eligible to attend the yearly Gold and Green Ball dances in their stakes and wards, as well as participate in sporting activities (softball, basketball, volleyball) that the MIA also sponsored. Typically featured at the Gold and Green Ball were a live band, an elected Queen and King, and extravagant floor decorations. It was considered a big deal.

Oddly, our introduction to the now antiquated tradition of the Gold and Green Ball occurred much earlier, when we were just 5 years-old. By that time, our father's post-World War II business ambition in sales had taken us to Cowley, Wyoming, a small Mormon community that lies just west of the Big Horn Mountains in northern Wyoming. The two of us—sporting Mom's home-made gold and green elf costumes—were designated as the "crown bearers" for an inauguration ceremony of the Gold and Green Ball's Queen and King at the old log stake center on Cowley's main street. We thought the costumes were cool but, because we had misunderstood our mother to say that we were going to be "the crown *bears*," we couldn't understand why we ended up as elves instead of bears.

Gary and Gordon as Crown Bearers for the 1949 Gold and Green Ball in Cowley, Wyoming.

In any case, the 1956 Liberty Stake Gold and Green Ball was held at the Harvard Ward amusement hall, located smack in the middle of the Liberty Elementary School boundaries. Our buddy Lorin Larsen was agitating for the three of us to go. We were now of age, he argued, and should be taking active part in what the older kids were doing. "Besides, man, a real band! Maybe we could learn how to do the bop! Maybe we could even ask some girls to go!"

Gary was okay with this last thought. Since Carol Jean was gone, he had developed another crush on Kathryn Keat, a cute, petite new girl with shining dark eyes whose family had just moved into the Liberty Elementary School district. But Gordon? He wasn't so hot on the idea: "Ask a girl to go to a dance? Learn the 'bop?' Are you kidding?"

Gary pleaded: "Come on, we'll all be together, it'll be fun. Don't be such a chicken."

Gordon finally relented. He would ask one girl, and if she said no, that was it. Egged on by Gary and Lorin, Gordon asked Kathryn Keat's best friend, Lynell Ipsen—a pretty but ultra-shy girl who was even more socially reticent than Gordon. Lynell said yes.

Lynell Ipsen, 1956,
Sixth Grade at Liberty Elementary.

The Liberty Stake Gold and Green Ball was held on a cold, mid-March night with thin, frozen patches of snow still on the ground. In spite of having promoted the whole idea, Lorin had abruptly fizzled out when the deadline arrived for actually asking a girl for a date. But he still wanted to go. We were annoyed, but also wanted his company to bolster our confidence. So the two of us, with light zipper jackets over our Sunday best shirts, trudged over to Lorin's house on 1300 South and Fourth East to pick him up. Then the three of us walked back to the little duplex on the corner of Third East and Hampton Avenue where Lynell lived. Gordon walked up to the door, knocked, and disappeared inside, while Gary and Lorin stood back like security guards at the edge of the sidewalk. After a few minutes, Gordon emerged with Lynell, accompanied by a parting call from Mrs. Ipsen, "Have a nice time!" Lorin trailed behind the three of us, making wisecracks as we marched four more blocks to Kathy Keat's house, another tiny duplex on Williams Avenue, bordering State Street. This time Gary walked up the steps and knocked while Gordon, Lynell, and Lorin waited on the sidewalk. As soon as Gary was ushered into the cozy living room by her mom, Kathy popped out of a side bedroom with a radiant smile that made Gary feel maybe that evening's adventure might turn out all right after all.

The final leg of our nine-block stroll was the Harvard Ward chapel, just a block away from where we had started out at our home on Herbert Avenue. Things were already well underway by the time we arrived, with the little dance band blaring and the gym floor (where on many Saturdays to come we would learn to dribble basketballs and shoot jump shots with neighborhood friends) was jam-packed with dancers. Like Lorin, a number of young people had showed up solo, and then waited on the sidelines for a prospective dance partner to make their interest known. Helen Moody, a tall, cheerful girl we had known at Liberty Elementary since we were five years old, spotted Lorin and quickly whisked him onto the crowded dance floor. As for us, we didn't try to learn how to do the bop. Instead we hugged the sidelines until the band played a slow tune, and then clumsily tried to execute the foxtrot lessons that Miss Jensen had been drilling into us at school. One thing we quickly learned was that foxtrots didn't turn out well in a crowded gymnasium at a youth dance with a swing band playing mostly pop music tunes of the day.

An hour or so later, we had another decision to make: Where should we go after a closing prayer had concluded the dance? Lorin, who Helen had returned to us unharmed, proposed Cumming's, an ice cream and soda fountain venue on Main Street and 1100 South. This meant another four block walk from the Harvard Ward chapel in the freezing night air. During summer months, Lorin, the two of us and other friends would make excursions to Cumming's whenever we could scrounge a dime or two for pint-sized glasses of iron port—a soft beverage concoction that blended cola, crème soda, and cherry flavors into what we thought was the best tasting drink in the world. But that night we had quarters to pay for high topped root beer floats—the first time we were inducted into the iron-clad custom in those days of boys paying for girls on a date. At least Lorin earned our forgiveness for his failure to get his own date by keeping conversation alive with jokes and amusing banter. As the clock ticked down to 11:00 p.m., and with cold root beer and ice cream swirling in our stomachs, it was time for Cummings to close and for us to embark on another chilly jaunt to escort Kathy and Lynell home. Hasty good nights were exchanged with chattering teeth on the girls' brightly lit doorsteps, and our first, honest-to-Jupiter dates were history.

Fast forward five or six months: Our parents had been friends with Carol Jean's parents through shared church activities in the Liberty and Liberty Park Wards, and when the Christensens moved they kept in touch. About a year after their move, Mr. and Mrs. Christensen invited Mom and Dad for a visit to their new home in Provo, and Gary—only Gary—was invited to come too. Gary was excited but wary: How come only he, but not Gordon, had been invited? Gary sat awkwardly with his parents on a sofa facing Carol Jean and her parents arranged on an opposite sofa. Small talk ensued between the adults and averted eyes between Gary and Carol Jean. Then Mrs. Christensen brightly suggested, "Why don't Carol Jean and Gary walk downtown to see a movie matinee while we visit?"

Gary never knew for sure if Carol Jean liked him the way he liked her. There was that encouraging homemade valentine she put on his desk the year before. But there also was her subsequent pointed correction of his spelling mistakes on a writing assignment in front of the class to Mrs. Anderton, and the time he made her cry in the third grade with some thoughtless remark. But for now, as they walked together through the neighborhood streets toward downtown Provo, what to talk about? was the only question pounding inside Gary's paralyzed brain. Carol Jean broke the self-conscious silence: "I wish I were a boy," she declared, apropos to none of the frozen thoughts inside Gary's head.

There was a confused pause, then a clueless, "How come?" from Gary.

"You guys get to go almost anywhere you want, do almost anything you want. Girls can't do this, and we can't do that. It's not fair," Carol Jean had to explain.

"Oh," Gary stupidly said, but with a glimmer of comprehension that had never really struck him before and never thereafter escaped his awareness. " I guess you're right."

As promising as this conversation started out, it quickly evaporated as they approached the theater marquee and ticket booth. Emblazoned above their heads in block letters were the words: PICNIC, starring WILLIAM HOLDEN AND KIM NOVAK. This was a pretty risqué mainstream movie for 1956—just the thing for two shy pre-teens sitting next to each other alone in the dark, uncomfortably thrown together by well-meaning Mormon parents who hadn't checked to see what was playing. Both Gary and Carol Jean shrank down into their seats when Kim Novak, in a clinging, scoop-neck summer dress, started slowly clapping her hands at the side of her head and then sensuously swayed her way down a long set of steps towards an arms-out waiting Bill Holden. Another scene involving Kim Novak and her younger sister changing into swimsuits at a public swimming pool, barely concealed behind half doors, caused Gary and Carol Jean to slink even further down into their seat cushions. The walk back to Carol Jean's home was strained and virtually mute.

Kim Novak and William Holden dance scene in PICNIC © 1955, renewed 1983 Columbia Pictures Industries, Inc. All Rights Reserved. Courtesy of Columbia Pictures.

Gary didn't see Carol Jean again until the eighth grade, when, once more through mediating parents, Carol Jean invited Gary to be her partner at a girl's choice dance at Olympus Junior High School, located ten miles away in Southeast Salt Lake where her family had moved after leaving Provo. This time, Gordon was also invited, as a blind date for Sharon Anderson, Carol

Jean's new best friend at Olympus Jr. Despite his recalcitrance to participate in Miss Jensen's sixth grade graduation dance at Liberty Elementary two years earlier, Gordon was now intrigued but also ambivalent: It was hard enough talking to girls we had known most of our lives, let alone strangers! But, well, "Okay, let's give it a try," Gordon thought, "the worst that can happen is that I'll hate it for a couple of hours, but so what?"

Dad drove us to Carol Jean and Sharon's homes, respectively, to pick them up and then dropped us off at Olympus Jr. To Gordon's immense relief, Sharon Anderson was cute, outgoing, and talkative. Initially flummoxed, his bashful self-consciousness quickly dissolved. At the same time, while Carol Jean was still quiet and observant as an owl, she had grown up quite a lot and now complemented her unpretentious intelligence with a winsome smile and a biting sense of humor. Gary was still smitten.

Although we had learned some rudimentary ballroom dancing under the watchful tutelage of Miss Jensen, we had also learned two years previously that the waltz and Foxtrot were not exactly the order of the day at 1950s youth dances. Elvis Presley had made his Ed Sullivan debut a year earlier, and rock'n roll was the new dance beat, even in Salt Lake City. But at least we knew how to properly hold a partner and shuffled around to the intermittent, slow tempo tunes, while sitting out the fast ones. Sadly, our dancing skills had not perceptibly advanced since our Gold and Green Ball initiation two years earlier.

Dad reappeared at end of the Olympus Junior High dance and chauffeured us to a near-by ice cream parlor, then vanished for a half hour while we nibbled at fudge sundaes and smiled in response to the amusing chatter generated by the charming Sharon, who single-handedly kept the conversation going all evening. Nothing remotely romantic ensued during doorstep goodbyes while Dad sat behind the wheel of the family car with the engine running, gasoline vapor puffing out the tailpipe, and porchlights shining.

In retrospect it may seem strange that at our age—going on 14 at the time—our parents encouraged and facilitated "dates" for us to attend an elaborate dance event. And needless to say, from our viewpoint, it was more than a little awkward having Dad doing the driving and hovering in the background. But it's also fair to say that we were too obtuse to realize that Carol Jean and Sharon had exercised their own agency in helping to plan the event and inviting us to join them. Gordon had actually enjoyed the evening and liked Sharon. He thought of her occasionally afterward but never phoned her back, nor in any other way tried to follow up. Gary remained in sporadic contact with Carol Jean over the years, but, like Gordon, took no active steps to effectively reciprocate her tentative overtures. In an era that still idealized male chivalry, our inaugural dating experiences did not prove to be shining, Sir Galahad moments for the Shepherd brothers.

14.

SHOWDOWN AT HIGH NOON
The Last Fist Fight

Gordon and his best buddy, Lorin Larson, pulled into the Shepherd's carport on Denver Street, hot and thirsty. They had just finished biking to and from Fairmont Park in Sugar House, a roundtrip distance of approximately six miles. It was the summer of 1957. They, and Gordon's twin brother Gary, would be commencing the eighth grade at Lincoln Junior high in September. All three boys were 14 years of age—old enough to begin shaving the peach fuzz off their cheeks but not old enough to drive the family car, let alone buy one for themselves. On their ride to Sugar House, Lorin and Gordon had been discussing how this embarrassing handicap was probably one of the reasons why girls their age seemed to prefer older boys.

Oh well, their most pressing concern at the moment was to quench their thirst, and they barged into the kitchen to get a drink of water, banging the screen door behind them. Gary was inside, looking at the latest issue of *Life Magazine*. He looked up in greeting just as their older brother Don came storming up from the basement. "Damn it!" yelled Don at Gordon, "You just woke up Susan (their 2year-old sister) from her nap! So, now, *you're* going to tend her!" Don had been assigned to tend Sue that morning by our parents, who had gone to spend the day visiting some old friends in Provo, 40 miles south of Salt Lake. Lorin glanced at Gordon and began edging out of the kitchen. He was a little bit afraid of Don, who was two years older. Gordon put down his glass of water, looked defiantly at Don and said, "Oh yeah? Try and make me!" And with that, he and Lorin bolted for the door, jumped on their bikes, and sped back down Denver Street toward the Liberty Ward chapel, where they made a ninety-degree turn on Harvard Avenue, and then another ninety on Fourth East.

Gordon and Lorin were laughing and showing off by peddling their bikes with no hands, as they continued riding to Lorin's house on 1300 South. That was their intended destination, anyway, but suddenly, in his peripheral vision, Gordon saw a blurry figure hurdling toward him on a diagonal from across the street. It was Don! In a furious rage at Gordon's impertinent refusal to accept responsibility for waking their little sister, Don had jumped the backyard fence behind their Denver Street house, cut though the long driveway separating the two apartment buildings on the east side of Fourth East, and intercepted Gordon and Lorin as they passed by on their bikes.

Apartment complex on Fourth East from where Don charged to tackle Gordon off his bike.

SMACK! Gordon went down with Don and his bike on top of him. Don pulled Gordon up roughly and ordered him to go back home to watch Sue for the rest of the day. But Gordon had already decided his course. "No. No way," he said.

Don was bigger and stronger, and he had always been able to physically overpower his younger brothers when dealing with only one of them alone rather than both together. Now, though, Gary wasn't there, and Gordon knew he would have to fight by himself. Don kept trying to get Gordon in a headlock, so he could take full advantage of his superior size, but Gordon slipped away. This time, however, he didn't run. Instead, he raised his fists. Gordon had never hit Don in the face before but only hesitated a second: POP! Gordon's knuckles bounced off Don's forehead above his left eye, as Don tried to duck the blow. Gordon's knuckles hurt, but so did Don's forehead.

Warily, they circled one another, both throwing punches, some of which landed and left their evidence in shades of black and blue the following day. Gordon could taste blood in his mouth, but he was giving back as much as he was absorbing. Their fisticuffs had drawn them off the street and onto the front lawn of an old Victorian house that was being remodeled. Gordon could hear one of the painters exclaim to his buddies, who were all watching the brotherly brawl from their ladders, "Hey, look at the little one fight back!" Suddenly, Don charged and tried to tackle Gordon in order to get him in a headlock again. Gordon sidestepped and somehow ended up on top of Don. Without thinking, he shoved his knee hard into Don's groin and held it there. He could immediately feel the fight go out of his older brother who stopped struggling. Gordon held his knee down for a couple of seconds and then stood up. Don slowly got to his feet, gave Gordon a baleful glare, shoved him as though he was getting in the last punch, and limped back across Fourth East toward the apartment complex and our backyard fence. It was the last physical fight they ever had.

House and front lawn on Fourth East where the last fistfight occurred.

For the briefest of moments Gordon experienced a stab of remorse. His older brother's public humiliation was palpable, but Lorin was quickly at his side, slapping him on the back and excitedly rehearsing some of the details of the fight he had just witnessed. Gordon grinned in acknowledgment, and the two got back on their bikes and rode off.

Where was Gary during all of this? Sue, our little sister, had been upset by the yelling that occurred in the kitchen; somebody had to stay with her when Don went charging over the backyard fence to tackle Gordon off his bike. But Gary also benefitted from the brawl, in that Don never threatened either one of us again. As a team we had finally prevailed over our older brother in the most primitive sort of way. But as a team we also had lost something we increasingly came to regret as we got older. Brothers fighting brothers is not a novel fact of human experience. But if brothers are lucky, and if they live long enough, they may transcend their boyhood rivalries to achieve a genuine affection and respect for each other that mutually enriches their lives. We had always had this between the two of us, but, in a fundamental way, our solidarity was also enjoyed at the expense of our older brother's sense of self-worth. As young adults we became friendlier with Don without becoming true friends, kinder without sharing genuine warmth.

We reconciled many of our differences, but neither we nor Don ever quite succeeded in shedding our remembered animosities and resentments of the past. This has never been a proud or inspiring chapter in our history. Gordon's High Noon showdown with Don on Fourth East in Salt Lake City was, in many ways, not a triumph, but the low point of our fraternal lives together.

15.

THROWING PAPERS FOR *THE SALT LAKE TRIBUNE* AND OTHER BOYHOOD JOBS

Gordon recalls that "I never had a full-time, salary-paying job with benefits until I was 30 years-old—on the verge of *middle age*, for crying out loud. I was still researching and writing my Ph.D. dissertation when I accepted an adjunct position to teach sociology at Wheaton College, in Norton, Massachusetts in order to support my growing little family. I have to admit, when I was a kid growing up in Salt Lake City, I couldn't fathom the likelihood of ever having a real, adult occupation and, if so, what that could possibly be. Thank God for the ivory towers of academia. If there was no such institution in our world, and with no practical skills to speak of, I'd be dead. But I digress. Other than getting 50 cents and a glass of lemonade once a week for mowing the widow Carter's lawn next door to our home on Herbert Avenue, my first paying job at the age of thirteen was throwing papers for the *Salt Lake Tribune*. More accurately said, my brother Gary and I got a job together throwing papers for the *Trib*."

You see, our Uncle Melvin, who lived four or five blocks south of us on Emerson Avenue, between Fourth and Fifth East, had been throwing a neighborhood *Tribune* route for several years as a way to make a little extra money supporting his family. We liked Uncle Melvin. He was our mother's younger brother, and he always called her "Sis." He had an easy going sense of humor and seemed more comfortable around adolescent boys than some of our stiffer relatives. He had been a young lieutenant in the Second World War, fought grimly amidst death and destruction in the Battle of the Bulge (which he thereafter never spoke about to anyone except once to us when we were adults), married a British bride, and commenced working for the Utah National Guard as a civilian after the war. In 1957 he got a promotion that required him to move his family to Dugway Proving Ground. Dugway was a military facility established in 1942 to test biological and chemical weapons and was located in the desert mountains about 85 miles southwest of Salt Lake City. So, his paper route would have to go.

**Uncle Melvin and Aunt Margaret
on their wedding day, July 5, 1944.**

We seemed like half-way responsible kids, so he asked us if we wanted to make a little money by taking over his route. Neither of us recalls if we were elated by the prospects of becoming paperboys, or if we stoically agreed to do it because Uncle Melvin asked us with the obvious collusion of our parents. Our older brother Don previously had had a *Deseret News* route for a year or two, and subbing for him on occasion had not been a particularly thrilling experience for the two of us. We had become accustomed to spending our leisurely summer days reading library books on the front porch swing, going swimming at Liberty Park, and playing baseball with our buddies. Throwing papers so we could take over the expense of paying for new school clothes in the fall at first had only a limited appeal.

It was the summer of 1957. Earlier that summer we had moved a few blocks from our old home on Herbert Avenue to a new house on Denver Street Circle—a half block down the street from the Liberty/Liberty Park Ward chapel—and we were getting ready to go back to school as eighth graders at Lincoln Junior High. This also was when we commenced getting up at 4:30 in the morning for two days of on-the-job training with Uncle Melvin to learn the paper delivery business. We say business, because, as Uncle Melvin informed us, we were considered by the newspaper to be *contractors*. That, of course, meant that the paper owed no benefits to us or its other carriers. The very first financial obligation we had to meet each month was to pay "our bill" to the *Tribune* for the cost of the papers they gave to us, which, theoretically, *we* sold to customers. More on the problem of paying "the bill" a little later, but, first, let's get back to on-the-job training with Uncle Melvin.

His route consisted of approximately 150 *Tribune* customers within an eight-square block area, bounded north and south between 1300 South and Kensington Avenue, and west and east between Fifth East and Seventh East. Uncle Melvin handed over to us his records book binder with the names and addresses of all of his customers, which we were supposed to carefully keep up-to-date. But, of course, our first task was to memorize the houses and streets where customers actually lived. The first morning we followed Uncle Melvin and took mental notes. The second morning Uncle Melvin followed *us* to make sure we didn't miss any houses or break any glass milk bottles that had been put out on porches for pick-up. The third day we were on our own (after being properly admonished by Uncle Melvin not to tarnish his good name with his customers by failing to be conscientious in delivering their papers dry, unripped, and on time every morning before they went to work).

We should also report that Uncle Melvin customarily delivered the route on his five-speed racing bike, but walked the route with us so we could more easily soak it all in. His practice was to fold all of his papers *first*, before stuffing them in big canvass shoulder bags and hopping on his bike to make deliveries. When we took over the route, we deviated from both of these practices. For one thing, we didn't have bikes—at least bikes in working condition. Gary had mangled his in a perilous stunt-riding incident two years previously and Gordon's was in need of new tires, new gears, and new brakes. Presumably, as budding entrepreneur "paper-contractors," our first order of business should have been to invest in some new bikes. But we didn't. To us they seemed prohibitively expensive, and we needed money right away to pay for our school clothes. Furthermore, Uncle Melvin's practice of carefully folding papers before delivery seemed, to our impatient minds, to take too much time. Also, if papers weren't folded exactly right, there was a good chance they'd fly apart when flung from a speeding bike, and that blunder would take even more time to correct. Finally, Uncle Melvin's method for carefully folding papers was arcanely intricate (akin to folding an American flag into a neatly packaged triangle), and we never got the hang of it.

So here's what we did instead. We acquired an inexpensive, hand-wound and noisy (TIC-TOCK, TIC-TOCK) alarm clock to wake us up in the morning, *and* we requisitioned our little sister Sue's red wagon, that featured a long pulling handle. Every morning at 4:30 we trudged through the vacant lot across from our home on Denver Street Circle and on through a long driveway separating a set of two-story apartments on Fifth East across from Liberty Park's Tracey Aviary. We cut a diagonal path through the park's southern end, crossed at Sixth East, and continued pulling Sue's rattling, little red wagon all the way to 1700 South to pick up our papers where they were dumped in two, big bundles by the *Salt Lake Tribune*. These papers were now ours, and we would have to pay for them every month before counting our profits, if any (again, more on this later). The corner of Sixth East and 1700 South, where we picked up our papers, was also the corner of the old

Hawthorn Elementary School's playground, where many of the kids who would join us later at South High had attended.

Salt Lake City streets that defined the borders of our *Tribune* route.

We pulled Sue's little red wagon precisely for the purpose of loading our heavy, bundled bales of newspapers to carry back to a little mom and pop grocery store on Sixth East between Roosevelt and Emerson Aves. There, we divvied them up between the two of us. We had split Uncle Melvin's paper route in half, with Gary throwing papers on 1300 South, Sherman and Harrison Avenues and the small, intersecting streets of Park, Tyler, and Green, while Gordon did the same on Kensington, Roosevelt, Cleveland, and Browning Aves. After throwing our papers we would meet again at the little store and trudge back home, retracing our steps through Liberty Park while listening to the strange mating calls of the peacocks in the Tracy Aviary as we crossed Fifth East.

As for our method of throwing papers, we stuck them into our shoulder bags *unfolded* and commenced walking the streets to our customers' houses, pulling out one newspaper at a time as we walked, folding it in a quick, three-step process that produced a rectangular shaped paper, edges tucked in, for reasonably accurate throwing. Instead of throwing overhand the way Uncle Melvin did with his compact triangle papers, we threw ours backhand, across the body, as if throwing a frisbee. We rarely used rubber bands (those too had to be purchased at our expense from the *Tribune*), except on Sundays when the paper was too big for our customary folding practice. We always threw for the porch, aiming so the paper would slide to a stop in front of the door—never in the driveway. We modestly admit we got pretty good at it, only on rare occasion hitting some obstructive bushes instead of the porch, or, in fact, knocking over an occasional milk bottle carelessly placed by a customer in front of the door on small porches.

Gordon can recollect virtually sleepwalking down a street, suddenly regaining cognizance with no recollection of having thrown any papers, and running back to check his customers' porches only to discover that, yes indeed, their papers had all been delivered. Gary occasionally supplemented his walking reveries by creating school writing assignments in his head—like a poem or short story—that he would memorize and write down when we got home from doing our route. Curiously less diligent about his schoolwork, Gordon typically walked his half of the route daydreaming about being the hero on our summer baseball team or starring in our junior high, intramural sports programs.

But let us now review the least agreeable thing about our paper route— even less agreeable than getting up every morning at 4:30 to queasy feelings of "paper route stomach"—and that was "collecting." As independent contractors, collecting was *our* job, not the *Tribune's*. If you didn't collect, you didn't get paid, but you still had to pay your bill to the *Tribune*. Collecting required us to knock on our customers' doors every month to get their payments for subscribing to the paper. We're a little hazy now on how much a monthly subscription cost back then. Let's guestimate on the high-end and say 25 cents a day for weekdays and Saturdays and 50 cents for the Sunday paper. If our math is accurate, those amounts would total to $8.00 a month. Retrospectively, that sounds too high—the monthly charge might have been closer to $5.00—but let's go with the higher figure. Either way, it wasn't a Trumpian fortune.

Many customers were home when we came knocking at their doors in the evening, and many cordially invited us inside while they fished out their wallets or check books. But, of course, some customers were not home (or *never* home), and, not infrequently, we would be asked by others "to come back some other time," because they didn't have the money for it the night we had called. (As Mormon missionaries a decade later in Mexico, we disliked door-to-door tracting, looking for potential investigators, for many of the same reasons we hated collecting for the *Salt Lake Tribune*.) If we had been better novice businessmen, we would have carried calendars with us, made specific return dates with those who didn't have the money for us, and extracted promises from them to pay up with the explicit threat of stopping delivery of their paper if they didn't. But we didn't do any of that. To late-paying customers who told us to come back we would simply say, "Okay, thanks," and walk away. They were "adults," we were kids, and at the time we didn't fully realize that not all adults were adults. Maybe that was one of the basic lessons we eventually learned from our paper-route experience.

In any case, there was nothing more demoralizing than having to return a second or third time to collect from deadbeat customers, and then have to start all over again, collecting for the next month's bill, *ad infinitum*. As it turned out, we were not dedicated collectors. If we didn't get our money on the first attempt, we often didn't go back. And, of course, this meant that we lost money. Our financial needs at the time were relatively modest. If we shared fifty-bucks profit by the end of the month (with another fifty left uncollected and a certain amount handed over to parents as our small contribution to the family's fragile finances), well, okay. Fifty was better than nothing, and we could get by on that much. Clearly, the Shepherd brothers were not motivated to *maximize* their financial profits. Successfully maximizing profits by relentless collecting ran counter to our "let's-just-try-to-get-along" personalities and, most importantly, it would take away too much of our precious free time, which was devoted to activities with our boyhood friends. We would never have made it in the collection agency business, let alone the career realms of higher finance, investment, and venture capitalism.

Speaking of the importance we placed on boyhood friendships, indulge us a small anecdote from our newspaper days. For some strange reason, some of our neighborhood buddies thought it would be fun to sleep over at our house and get up with us in the morning to deliver papers. On one such occasion we plotted with Ron Swenson, Al Ebert, and Udell Stones to sneak our dad's 1956, two-tone, blue-green Mercury Monterey out of the carport and take it for a spin around town while he, our mom, and sister Sue were gone from the house on the morning of the 24th of July.

The 24th of July is, of course, a very big deal in Salt Lake City. It's an official state holiday for commemorating the arrival of Brigham Young and the Mormon pioneers into the valley of the Great Salt Lake in 1847. Celebrated now as "Pioneer Day" and the "Days of '47," July 24 features Utah's biggest parade. The parade commences at South Temple and State Street at 9:00 a.m. sharp, proceeding East to Second East, turning south to Ninth South, then east again to Sixth East where it terminates at the northern entrance to Liberty Park—a route covering a distance of approximately two and a half miles. Our home at 1166 Denver Street, you see, was only three blocks south of Ninth South and a scant half block west of Liberty park. That was in easy walking distance of a choice spot on Ninth South to watch the parade with its zillion pioneer decorated floats, uncounted high school bands, sheriff posses with their prancing "apple-dropping" steeds, and convertible limos for elderly LDS Apostles positioned in the back seats to wave to the faithful throngs.

But to claim a good, curbside spot on Ninth South, you had to get there early and patiently wait for the parade to begin and slowly wend its way to Liberty Park. *That* meant our parents and little sister would be out of the house by 7:30 a.m., not long after we had returned from throwing our paper route with Swenson, Ebert, and Stones tagging along. And in turn, *that* meant we would have unfettered access to our dad's Mercury until almost noon when the parade would be over. The only problem was getting the car started, because, unfortunately, we didn't have an ignition key. Solution: Dave Wunderlich, another neighborhood kid who lived a few doors down the street, had taught us how to hotwire 1940s-50s vintage cars by connecting a couple of wires under the dashboard. Eureka! It worked! The Mercury was ours for three hours, the plan being that we would return it before our parents got back from the parade.

Approximate likeness of our Dad's 1956 Mercury Monterey.

Why all the skullduggery? Why didn't we just ask permission to take the car? We didn't ask because, a year after taking over the paper route from Uncle Melvin, we were still only 14 years-old, and we didn't have drivers' permits, let alone licenses. Furthermore, our dad was pretty touchy about his insurance rates going up if he had to report teen-age boy drivers, living at home.

So, even though keyless, we got the car going and eagerly piled in with Swenson, Ebert, and Stones who occupied the back seat. The two of us swapped turns in the driver's seat. That Mercury had a 220 horsepower V8 engine that really pressed you back into the seat if you goosed the accelerator. But, we didn't do anything outlandish or crazy with the car that morning. We drove at reasonably conservative speeds in neighborhoods south of the parade area, where the streets weren't clogged with parked cars and late stragglers trying to get to the parade before it was over. We don't remember everything we did. We might have stopped at Dee's Hamburger Drive-in on 2100 South in Sugarhouse for 20-cent burgers and dime-cokes. But if we did, we would have had to leave the engine running. We wouldn't have wanted to draw suspicion to ourselves by re-hotwiring a car in a fast-food parking lot. Mainly, what we craved was the exhilarating sense of grownup freedom and mobility that being in control of a car gave us.

So that part was great. BUT, when we returned home just ahead of our parents and sister Sue, UNCLE MELVIN'S CAR WAS PARKED IN THE DRIVEWAY, blocking us from restoring our dad's Mercury in its customary place under the carport. Shit! Uncle Melvin and his family had come back to Salt Lake from Dugway to celebrate the holiday with us, and, arriving late, he had taken the only parking space available on the street, namely our driveway. What the heck were we going to do now?

Gary, in the role of older brother (he was born seven minutes before Gordon), assumed the lead and stoically concluded, "We'll just have to face the music."

Swenson, Ebert, and Stones said "Adios," and scattered for home.

After parking the Mercury behind Uncle Melvin's car in the driveway, we walked into the house and THERE WAS UNCLE MELVIN sitting in the living room.

"Hi boys," he called out, "What's up?" His wife and three young sons (two daughters would come along later) had gone on to the parade while he stayed behind to read that morning's *Tribune*. (It turned out that Uncle Melvin wasn't that crazy about watching parades either.)

"Well, the thing is" . . . Gary began explaining what we had done.

Uncle Melvin listened in solemn silence and then, quickly flashing a comprehending smile, said, "Would you like me to back my car out of the driveway so you can pull your dad's in?"

Why yes, that's *exactly* what we wanted him to do. Not many minutes later, our parents and sister Sue arrived home from the parade with Melvin's family and began making preparations for a picnic later that afternoon at Liberty park. Winning our eternal gratitude, Uncle Melvin never breathed a word about the car heist.

After three years of throwing papers for the *Salt Lake Tribune*, we gave up Uncle Melvin's old route to a new carrier and engaged in other forms of part-time employment while still going to school. These other odd jobs included sweeping the grandstands after baseball games at Derk's Field on 1300 South and West Temple (Smith's Ball Park today); peeling potatoes and washing dishes at the Morrison Meat Pies Diner on State Street, just north of 1300 South (long gone); bagging groceries at the Sudbury and Maxwell Food Town on Ninth South (today the home of Southeast Market), where traditionally we watched the Days of '47 parade; and summer life-guarding at the old Hotel Utah Motor Lodge (Gary) on West Temple, where the LDS Church History Museum now stands, and at the Deseret Inn (Gordon) on 50 West and Fifth South, right around the corner from Salt Lake's old dance venue, the Rainbow Rendezvous (later named the Terrace Ballroom, which today is a parking lot). None of these jobs paid more than minimum wage, if there was such a thing at the time.

So what did we acquire, if anything, from our paper-throwing gig and other odd jobs growing up in Salt Lake City in the 1950s? It's tempting for self-satisfied people retrospectively to entertain loving images of their not always realized aspirations. And it's easy for all of us to project our egos in ways that coincide with how we imagine ourselves to be. Fair enough. What we can say with a combination of chagrin and perverse pride is that we did not acquire much business acumen or any real interest in or aptitude for making money. It's also accurate to say that we acquired an appreciation for Uncle Melvin's tolerance of us and, as we said earlier, we learned that not all adults were actually adults. In that regard, we think we *did* acquire a keener sense of personal responsibility, which has characterized most of our adult work. One thing we worked hard at as paper carriers was to avoid getting dinged by customer complaints, which would then be added as fines to our monthly bill by the *Tribune*. We may not have been motivated to maximize our financial returns through assiduous collecting, but we *were* motivated to maintain self-respect by earning the respect of the people we worked for.

As paperboys, our motto was "Zero Complaints"—an ideal Gordon tried to pass on to his own children when they took turns inheriting a paper route in Conway, Arkansas, where he retired from teaching sociology at the University of Central Arkansas in 2016. We should mention that Gary also retired as a sociology professor from Oakland University, Michigan a year or two before Gordon. Did our shared experiences growing up in Salt Lake City and working for the *Salt Lake Tribune* at an impressionable age in our lives turn us both away from money-making enterprises and toward academic sociology? . . . Nah, it must have all been due to our shared DNA.

One other thing, though: Before going to work as paperboys for the *Tribune*, our parents had always subscribed to the state's dominant paper, the LDS Church owned *Deseret News*. The *Tribune* had begun its history in the 19th century as a critical and oft times vitriolic counterweight to the media influence of the LDS Church. Priding itself as an "independent voice," the *Tribune* gained a reputation as the state's "liberal" paper, in contradistinction to the *News*' dependably conservative orientation. Since we always came home from throwing our route with a few extra copies of the *Trib*, we both started reading it. When we say reading, we mean we would glance at the headlines, skim some of the lead news stories, and then go directly to the sports page for sports news on our favorite local teams (the

South High Cubs and the University of Utah Utes, and our national sports idols like heavyweight boxing champion Floyd Patterson and the Yankee's Mickey Mantle).

But in glancing at headlines and skimming news stories every day while throwing papers, we also acquired a modest sense of connection to world and national events beyond our boyhood bubble—events that were dominated by Cold War stories of the nefarious Soviet Union and equally nefarious Southern sheriffs, who were unleashing attack dogs and water cannon on negro civil rights demonstrators in Southern cities. To us these latter stories had a certain far-away quality, but we also began to experience righteous, youthful anger at the unjust violation of American citizen's rights because of their race. At the time, we were only dimly aware of the racial discrimination practiced every day in our own city and neighborhoods. News events, however, were beginning to cast a few shadows on the ideals of American democracy that we were being taught in history and civics classes at school.

Is it too much of a leap at this late date in time to surmise that regular exposure to news stories, while throwing the *Salt Lake Tribune* when we were 13 to 15 years of age, might have influenced the ultimate direction of our academic careers in social science? Probably not—there were other far more important influences. But we're not going to say absolutely not. At a minimum, we learned that a free press was an important part of the world and of adult consciousness in a democratic society. We have been devout newspaper readers ever since. We've both appreciatively read our share of fiction too, but have never confused the latter with the essential civic function of professional journalism, so often slandered by authoritarian tyrants as "fake news" and "the enemy of the people." We've no way of knowing now, but we trust that Uncle Melvin—who died in 2015 at the age of 95—would agree with us about the value of American newspapers as a vital source of information concerning both global and local events and as a critical check on the potential abuses of power in a democratic society. Even if paper, ink, and newspaper carriers all become extinct artifacts of a bygone era, may the principles and practices of a free press long endure in a globalized world in which people, now more than ever, must think and care about current events outside the boundaries of their own family and tribal bubbles—even in the happy valley of the City of the Saints.

16.

ARE YOU IN OUR DREAMS?
Role Model Apparitions From our Youth

Are you in our dreams? Sometimes we tell people about our dreams, especially our wives who counterclaim that they rarely dream, or that if they do, they can't remember them, or if they can remember them, they weren't very clear or detailed. When we were kids growing up, before getting out of bed in the morning, the two of us would query one another: "What did you dream about last night?" And then we proceeded to take turns narrating what we had dreamed about. So, if you're going to remember what you dreamed, maybe you have to get in the practice of *telling* your dreams.

Some people keep a record of their dreams by writing them down for their analysts to interpret. We do no such thing. And, by the way, neither of our dreams are religious, either. They're not visions or revelations from God. They're not instructions to other people about how to live or what to believe. Whatever their crazy narratives might entail, almost always our dreams are populated with various family members or friends, both old and new (especially including old friends and significant adults, like omnipresent apparitions, from our childhood and youth).

The point is, the people we dream about are the people, both living and dead, who have meant the most to us, or they're people who in some way, for better or worse, have had an enduring influence on our lives. So, if you're in our dreams, you're somebody who is important to us, and, from our egocentric points of view, that's what 's important to understand. Often we both dream about being in Mexico again, and in those dreams we can still speak fluent Spanish. But more often, we dream about being back in school—the schools of our childhood and youth.

Do we ever dream about our old *teachers*, you ask? Yes, sometimes, but strangely enough, not that often, given the important role that many of them played in our lives—especially the dedicated women teachers whom we still remember with fondness and appreciation at Liberty Elementary (whose administrative and instructional staff did not include a single male): Teachers like Mrs. Madron, Nelson, Poulson, Lawrence, Murphy, McDermaid, Anderton, Taylor, and Jensen, among others. To an unsung degree, these women helped impetuously energetic and curious boys like us acquire a basic sense of fairness and responsibility toward others in a socializing context of learning how to read, write, and do arithmetic in the public school system. God bless our underpaid, women public school teachers. Saying this in perfect sincerity about the many women teachers we admired, we must also admit that the teachers from our youth who are most likely to make appearances in our dreams today are men, two in particular: Hal Hardcastle and Dean Papadakis. Hardcastle and Papadakis were the boys' P. E. teachers at Lincoln Junior High.

When it came to directing adolescent boys—capturing their attention, channeling their underdeveloped potential and inchoate aspirations, while simultaneously imposing elementary discipline on their behavior—it wasn't the school principal (whose name we can barely remember—Richards, maybe?), or any of the academic faculty: It was Hardcastle and Papadakis. Hardcastle and Papadakis. Their names went together. They were a tag-team, complementing and supplementing each another in organizing and running Lincoln's elaborate boys' P.E. program. Their authority and over-sight of the school's young men were unquestioned. And, to the extent that the predictably intemperate behavior of teenage boys between the ages of thirteen and fifteen can be disruptive of institutional order, it may be said, practically speaking, that Hardcastle and Papadakis virtually ran the school.

Lincoln Junior High, 1300 South State Street, circa 1957.

Is that an overstatement? Undoubtedly it is. But we want to emphasize the critical role played by Hardcastle and Papadakis in nurturing a budding sense of educational community and therefore increasing awareness of civil norms of mutual respect and reciprocity among their adolescent male charges. In doing this, they became our most important adult role models at Lincoln Junior High.

Salt Lake City Junior high schools in the 1950s did not, as a rule, sponsor competitive athletic programs with other schools. For that, one had to wait for high school. Instead, there were intramural sports that pitted different gym classes in competition against one another throughout the school year. At Lincoln there were traditional team sports (flag football, basketball, and track and field events), but in between these there were numerous other competitions as well, including wrestling, the sit-up contest, the rope climbing contest, the free-throw shooting contest, the weightlifting contest, and the softball throwing contest. Not only were individual winners recognized in these events for their achievements, but points were allocated to different gym classes over the year to determine which class was the overall grade-level champion. And, of great motivational importance to aspiring boy athletes, school records were kept, updated, and posted yearly.

We both disliked wrestling (sweaty, smelly, exhausting, and we always hated getting pinned by huskier kids), so we'll skip past that to highlight some of the school's other individual sports. The sit up contest, for instance, was pretty basic: How many sit ups could you do in 20 minutes? As seventh graders, we recall the school record was over 500. The next year, Dennis Madsen, a slight, wiry kid, obliterated the old record by doing over 1,000. We remember watching him for 20 minutes in mesmerized amazement as he popped up and down like a well-oiled metronome. In the ninth grade, Gordon tried competing in the sit-up contest as the rep from his gym class, and painfully squeezed out approximately 500—not enough that year, sad to say, for even an honorable mention. Gary pulled a stomach muscle and didn't even qualify for the contest.

The rope climbing contest was a timed event to see how fast you could scale a 50-foot rope from the gym floor to a beam in the ceiling. We had been given instruction on the proper techniques for climbing, which involved coordinating "foot wraps" with one's arms systematically hoisting one's body, hand over hand, to the top of the rope. A good climb would take less than ten seconds. Johnny Grego, a handsome, broad-shouldered Mexican American kid, disregarded the foot wrap part of the technique and simply scrambled up the rope by pulling himself with agility and sheer upper body strength to set a new school record of a little over five seconds. (We only mention that he was handsome because all the girls seemed to be cheering for him to win.)

Free-throw shooting was a test of consistent basketball shooting accuracy: How many free-throws could you shoot in a row without missing? If we remember right, the record before our ninth grade year was somewhere in the low twenties. Alan Owens, better known for his math and slide-rule skills, proceeded to swish *fifty* in a row. Fifty. We kid you not.

In weightlifting, our neighborhood hero was Larry Swanger. Swanger was one of those kids who matured early and inherited big biceps from his gregarious, blue collar dad. To most of us, Larry Swanger looked like Sampson. He was tall, ruggedly handsome, and girls liked his 1950s Elvis-style hairdo. In the finals he was opposed by . . . by . . . well, hell, we can't remember the other kid's name (he didn't continue on with us to high school). In any event, he was squat, had a crewcut, and short, thick arms. Unlike Swanger, you couldn't *see* his muscles. Neither of us recalls how many standing, overhead presses it took, but eventually Swanger couldn't lift anymore, but *the squat kid kept going*. He won and set a new school record! Our champion Swanger had gone down to gallant defeat. But such is life, we were beginning to learn.

Finally, in the softball throw, a contestant would stand behind a line at one end of the playing field, run forward a few steps for momentum up to another line, and heave the ball as far as he could. In our eighth grade year the school record was shattered by Dennis Borup, the ninth grade student body president. Borup, like Larry Swanger had matured early and was a head taller than everyone else. When he threw the ball, *it hit the side of the auditorium* that stood twenty yards past the end of the field. Thereafter, we suppose, a new record would have to be measured by how far up the auditorium wall the ball hit.

Well, as we said, these (and others) were the individualized sports and the corollary prospects they offered for individuals to set new school records; they were a big part of the socializing allure of sports competition for sports-addled boys at Lincoln Junior High. The big team sports in the intramural program—flag ball and basketball—were seasonal sports that bestowed bragging rights and class points to the accumulating totals, but for which no statistical records were kept. Arguably, however, the biggest sports event at Lincoln was the annual track and field meet, again pitting different gym classes against each other in the late spring, toward the end of the school year. For this track meet, all classes were dismissed, and the entire student body became an audience to what transpired. (Yes, in the long decades of public school education prior to Title IX, girls were expected—if not required—to attend and support boy's sporting events, and many did so with what appeared to be more interest in the boys themselves than whatever it was they were doing on the gym court or athletic field). And because track and field events feature individual contests that can be quantified by measures of time and distance, school records were also made and broken, and the results posted for subsequent student cohorts to admiringly contemplate on the walls of Hal Hardcastle's and Dean Papadakis' gym offices.

David Triptow and Daley Oliver in the boys track meet at Lincoln Junior High, Spring, 1957.

Which brings us back to reflect on the dynamic duo of Hardcastle and Papadakis and what they meant to most of the boys at Lincoln Junior High. We're perfectly confident that every Salt Lake City junior high school in those days had intramural programs similar to Lincoln's. But in blissful ethnocentrism, we're also confident in asserting that no other school's intra-mural programs were managed as effectively and inspirationally as they were at Lincoln by Hardcastle and Papadakis. If you think we're wrong, prove it.

Both men, of course, were athletes themselves, so that was good. They had somewhat contrasting personalities, but that was also good, because, as we already said, they complemented and supplemented each other. Hardcastle was a little more intense; Papadakis was a little more relaxed. Most importantly, they were respectful friends who agreed on how best to co-manage the many sports programs that involved every boy at all three grade levels at Lincoln Junior High. They were like conscientious parents who presented a united front to their kids. And what they were united on was what was most important for the kids they taught: honest effort, fair play, and mutual respect for your classmates, regardless of their presumed natural abilities in sports.

Hardcastle was ruddy, blonde, crewcut, broad shouldered, and thick-chested. He was a football player who threw the hammer at the University of Utah (an ancient, esoteric field event still included in the Olympic Games) that requires agility, speed, and significant upper body strength. Papadakis—an exemplary specimen of Salt Lake's Greek community—was a couple of inches taller than Hardcastle, with dark hair combed in a modest pompadour, an easy smile, and Mediterranean features. Papadakis was a basketball player with a deft, lefthanded shot. He was also an artist, who applied his skill to the production of first-rate posters and charts to promote and record the sporting events of Lincoln's unparalleled intramural programs.

Lincoln Junior High School Green Team, 1959.
Front Row, L-R: Bill Gehrke, John Telford, Gary Shepherd, Cornell Griffin.
Back Row, L-R: **Coach Hal Hardcastle,** Russ Newren, Mike Mitchell, Dave
Strong, Kent Cammack, Alma Mansell.

Lincoln Junior High School White Team, 1959.
Front Row: Alan Owens, Johnny McGowan, Ivan Einzinger, Fred Vander Veur.
Back Row: **Coach Dean Papadakis**, Owen Wood, Richard Ablehouzen, Wayne
Miller, Tim Christensen, Leo Sotiriou.

But, as adult role models for boys, it wasn't just sports that they were good at. We looked up to Hardcastle and Papadakis for guidance, and they didn't disappoint. One of the other activities we were exposed to in our junior high gym classes was a week of learning how to dance with girls from the girls' gym class that met the same period we did. When we say dance, we mean old fashioned ballroom dancing. The jitterbug, bop, and later the twist and other popular dance styles, presumably were dance moves that kids would pick up on their own. In retrospect, the main thing about our gym class get-togethers with girls was not so much to teach us how to dance the minuet, but how to act properly around girls. We can remember both Hardcastle and Papadakis lecturing us ahead of time to mind our manners and also reminding us that they would be chaperoning the dances. Even though both men had a good sense of humor and were well aware of the smart-aleckyness and arrogance of some of the boys under their charge, the bashfulness of others, and the immaturity of almost all of us at that age, they insisted that we be respectful to the girls at school.

We remember one occasion in particular. An African American girl was a new student at Lincoln and, Hardcastle informed us, she would be dancing with the boys in our class like everyone else. There would be no refusing, no eye-rolling, no smirky quips or comments. We would be friendly, politely take our turns, and we would damn well like it. We respected that then, and we still do.

On another vividly remembered occasion, a fairly large group of kids showed up on the steps of the school at lunch time for a fight (some of them were Lincoln students, some of them were not). A dozen fist fights and brawling quickly erupted. For a moment it looked like all hell was breaking loose. But suddenly, Hardcastle and Papadakis came flying out of the building—not the school principal or anybody from the administrative office. When someone ran into the school for help, to report what was going on outside, they went straight to the gym offices of Hardcastle and Papadakis. The insurgent fighting was over in a matter of seconds. Hardcastle and Papadakis each grabbed two kids apiece, knocked their heads together, and angrily ordered everybody off the steps. The sizable crowd that had formed because of the fight quickly dispersed. Nobody else at Lincoln could have done that. No other adult authority on the school premises could have acted so quickly and so effectively to snuff out a potentially dangerous moment of harm to the school and its students. No other adults on campus would have been obeyed with such alacrity by a pack of overheated juvenile boys. We respected that then, and we still do.

Hardcastle and Papadakis. Two adult role models from our youth, who continue to inhabit our dreams at night. Are you too in our dreams? Feel free to ask us some time.

17.

MORE THAN A GAME
When Baseball Was Our Passion, Season II

When we weren't playing organized team ball during our junior high and early high school years, we often scrounged up neighborhood friends to join us in simplified, oddball versions of baseball—work-ups, over-the-line, or over-the-fence—that didn't require a full complement of players. Over-the-line, for instance, could be played with as few as three members on a team. The team in the field (on a regular ball diamond) could consist of three outfielders, while the three-man team at bat would take turn swinging at slow pitches from one of their own teammates. Ground balls and infield pop-ups were counted as outs (hence no need for infielders). Any ball hit in the air "over the line" between bases was in-play. If the ball was caught by one of the three outfielders before hitting the ground, it was, of course, an out. If it was not caught, the batsman would run as many bases as he could until the ball was retrieved and thrown-in to the diamond by an outfielder. If the throw crossed the infield "line" before the runner reached a base, he was out. As in regular baseball, batters would continue hitting until there were three outs and then take their turn in the outfield while the other three players had their turn at bat.

We often played over-the-line on the Lincoln Junior High playing field until one Saturday in early mid-September when we were just beginning eighth grade. Besides the two of us, other players that day included Owen

Wood, Leo Sotiriou, John Anderson, Dave Lingwall, and Ron Swenson. Gordon tried showing off by hitting left-handed, but instead of connecting with Gary's first pitch he hit a pop fly foul ball to the right of first base where a small pickup truck was parked alongside the auditorium building. Splat! right in the center of the windshield, leaving a crater impression in the glass that radiated outward in a multitude of cracks. There was instant consensus that the game was over and, unheroically, we all scattered for home. The next morning during home room hour at Lincoln, an ominous sounding directive came over the classroom intercoms for each of us, named in alphabetical order, to appear immediately in the office of the school principal, Mr. Richards. Yes, someone apparently had ratted us out—plenty of people who knew some of us culprits lived around the school and could have spotted us scramming from the ballfield. But the evidence was weak, we were only suspects. The two of us, however, had felt guilty running away, and now we had a chance for moral redemption. Everyone else stared down at the floor, so we said yes, it was the two of us. No one else said anything. Mr. Richards gave everyone a hard look, then said, "Okay, luckily the owner's insurance will cover most of it. Gary and Gordon, your parents will have to cover the rest."

Gordon and Leo Sotiriou teaming up for a game of over-the-line.

Needless to say, our moral bravado dissolved when we arrived home to face our parents, who rejected our protests of innocent victimhood: "Just because *we* were the ones who happened to be pitching and batting when it happened doesn't mean it was *all* our fault. All of us were playing there. It's a schoolground *ball field*, not a parking lot. Why was a truck parked right next to where we were playing? Shouldn't the driver be in trouble too?"

"Nope. You ran away and that was wrong," we were told. "We don't care what your friends did or didn't do, and you're going to pay back the insurance costs with your paper route money." Our self-righteousness deflated, we knew they were right: We shouldn't have run.

It was a beautiful morning in early June, eight months after the broken windshield incident. Both of us were recovering from summer colds and had a lot of overnight congestion in our throats and chests. But we suppressed our normal inclination to cough and hack. It was an important day for us. Tryouts were being held at Municipal Ball Park that morning for Cops League—an organized baseball program for 13-14 year-old boys, whose teams were sponsored by prominent Salt Lake City businesses and coached by members of the Salt Lake City Police Department. We had not known about tryouts for this league the previous summer, and we were fearful our mom would now tell us we couldn't go this time if we appeared to still be sick from several days of low fever, runny noses, and coughing around the house. We silently got dressed, grabbed our baseball gloves, and surreptitiously slunk out the backdoor without having breakfast.

"Wait a minute, boys!" our mom called out from the front door as we were speed-walking down Herbert Avenue. "Where are you going so early? How are you feeling? Are you still sick?"

"No, Mom. We're fine. Not sick at all. They said we had to be there early. Bye!"

The main thing we remember about the tryouts was being told to go either to a spot on the infield, if we thought we were going to be infielders, or to the outfield, if we thought we were going to be outfielders. Then coaches would hit groundballs to the wannbe infielders and flyballs to presumptive outfielders. Fielding and throwing skills were presumably noted by the coaches as a basis for making choices. Gordon chose infield, and Gary picked outfield. Among the outfield candidates was a standout kid who was faster than all of us, bigger than most of us, and was already well advanced into puberty, with a hint of beard and a prominent patch of dark hair on his chest that was revealed when he took off his shirt in the hot sun. One of the coaches—a wise guy—hit a long flyball that only this kid was fast enough to chase down and snag with a leaping catch. "Sign up the kid in the black t-shirt!," the coach yelled out. The kid was Fred Richeda, future baseball star at South High School, one of Gary's competitors for student body president four years later, Sterling Award Scholar, and all-around good guy.

Fred Richeda, all-around athlete and outstanding student at South High.

Everyone at the tryout was picked by coaches, each in his turn, as they went down their lists of names. The choosing was done out of sight and hearing of kids trying out. All we knew was that both of us had been picked to be on the same team. However, so many kids had tried out that there was not going to be space on the rosters for all the kids chosen (among other things, each team had been allocated a fixed number of uniforms). This meant further evaluation and selection by team coaches to winnow the numbers.

The designated coach for our team—Sandy Carson—was a twenty-something Salt Lake City cop who had only been on the force a few years. He arranged with another coach to play a practice game between their two teams as a means to finalize team rosters. Kids were shifted in and out of the lineups for the coaches to observe. It was pretty chaotic. Waiting on the sidelines, Gary was finally told to grab a bat and go to the plate with two outs in that inning. The pitcher threw him a big, slow round-house curve, and Gary smacked what he thought must have been the longest hit of his life, maybe even a homerun! He was already rounding first base, sprinting for second with his head down, when he noticed that the other team players were running in from the field. Gary's imagined homerun turned out not to be even a hit—just a long flyball out, routinely gloved by the left fielder. "Oh well," Gary exulted to himself. "At least I hit a curveball hard and showed I'm a good batter." Gary turned back to the dugout to get his glove. He wanted to share his pride with Gordon. But where was Gordon? Gary anxiously scanned the field. No Gordon. He felt a sharp pang in his chest as he asked would-be teammates and then the coach: "Where's my brother?"

"We had to make some choices," he was told. "Maybe he can come to practices to help out if he wants to."

Gary had never felt so empty and lost as he slowly walked back home through Liberty Park. "This isn't right," he thought to himself. "Gord is good enough to make this team, better than a lot of the others, better than me. They didn't give him a fair chance."

Gordon did go with Gary to the first regular team practice. One of the kids who had made the team didn't show up, and Gordon filled in for him at shortstop. He snagged hard grounders and thew accurately to first base. He stepped into batting practice pitches thrown by the coach and cracked some hard line drives. By practice end, coach Carson said, "I made a mistake; you're on the team."

Our final team line-up, now including Gordon, consisted of 17 boys, a dozen who were 14 years-old, and another five who were 13. Only one of the 13year-olds was a starter—our hustling little right fielder, Teddy Lay. Most of our teammates would end up attending East High in a few years. The two of us, plus Kenny Caputo and David Shurtleff, were the only ones who would be going to South. Shurtleff was our first baseman, Caputo played second, Gary was in left field, and Gordon had won the shortstop position. None of us were star players (except maybe Kenny Caputo). Both of us were decent fielders, with average speed, and good throwing arms. We were also fair hitters but, like most normal human beings, cringed at getting hit by inside fastballs, which made us too tentative instead of aggressive at the plate.

Our 1958 Cops League Team and starting nine.
First row, fourth from left: *Teddy Lay* (right field); fifth from left: *Neil Maxfield* (center field); sixth from left: John Griffith (third base). **Second row**, first from left: Ray Nichols (pitcher); second from left, *Kenny Caputo* (second base); fourth and fifth from left, *Gordon shepherd* (shortstop) and *Gary Shepherd* (left field). **Third row** left to right: *Sandy Carson* (coach); *Bob Hinckley* (pitcher); *Jay Leishman* (Pitcher), *Tony Frost* (catcher); *Phil Purcell* (pitcher); *David Shurtleff* (first base).

Truth be told, our team was lucky to make it as far as we did that year. Coach Carson was tall, a little flabby, kept his strawberry blond hair cut short, used profanity around young boys, sipped beers in the dugout when we were taking batting practice, and—although he projected a cocky mix of assurance and toughness—didn't seem to know a lot about baseball. Our team floundered at the beginning of the season, and we lost our first three games. Our coach's older cousin (who was also a cop and voluntarily attended practices as an "assistant") determined that our problem was a lack of exemplary adult leadership and conducted a private interview with his cousin across the street from the playing field. Beer cans subsequently disappeared from the dugout, cussing was replaced by conventional baseball chatter and encouragement ("Atta boy!" "Everybody hit!" "Alright now!" "Let's go get'm!" etc.), and our coach started learning players' names, patting our backsides when we scored, and paying attention when a game got underway and we were up to bat. Coincidentally, we started winning some games. It also helped that we had three, hard throwing pitchers (Hinckley, Purcell, and Nichols) who started pitching strikes, and a tough, smart catcher—Tony Frost—who had just barely made the age cut-off for Cop's League and was actually a year ahead of everybody in school. It was Tony who emerged as our captain on the field. Most of the 1958 season is now a blur but here are a few random recollections.

Kenny Caputo and Gordon would routinely rehearse making double plays when warming up before a game. It never happened in an actual game, though—except once. The opposing team had a runner on first base with one out. "Take two," Gordon called to Kenny, who nodded his head. The batter swung on a low pitch and hit the ball hard on one bounce, right at Gordon, who didn't even have to move. Gordon fielded the ball, threw sidearm to second base which—at the crack of the bat—Kenny had quickly run to cover exactly the way they had practiced. He grabbed Gordon's throw, pivoted, and threw around the sliding runner to Shurtleff at first: Double play! Inning over!

Kenny Caputo taking a cut at Municipal Ball Park.

But Gordon also made his share of errors in the field, including occasional wild throws to first base. His most embarrassing error was muffing a simple pop-up, that almost hit him in the head. It was a late morning game, with a bright, July sun directly overhead. The batter swung hard under a rising fast-ball and popped it high over the infield. Gordon followed its steep ascent and gauged that it would come back to earth somewhere in his vicinity. "Mine!" he called out. Then, suddenly, as the ball reached its apex, it disappeared in a blinding glare of light. "Where the hell is it!" Gordon yelled in panic, stumbling backward and blindly holding his mitt in front of his face. When the ball dropped in front of him, and he scrambled to pick it up, everybody was yelling, and the runner on third took off for home. Gordon could see nothing but sunspots and almost threw the ball over the backstop trying to keep the runner from scoring. We were lucky that the guy whose pop-up Gordon missed didn't also score on the play.

Gary had a few bad moments of his own out in left field. One in par-ticular is embarrassingly memorable. A cinder topped utility-vehicle-trail ran on a straight diagonal several yards beyond the curve of infield dirt, violating the outfield grass. An opposing batter hit a sharp twisting line drive between third and shortstop that kicked up a puff of cinder dust on the trail, then bounded straight towards Gary. Instead of charging the ball so he could throw to catch base runners who were sprinting to third and home, Gary stayed frozen in his tracks and awaited. Suddenly the ball took an erratic hop and squirted right between his stationary legs. Before Gary could turn and chase down the errant ball and heave it towards the infield, two runs had scored for the other team. Ouch. "Can't let the team down like that again!" Gary uselessly berated himself in humiliation, as he pounded his glove with his fist and heard the disappointed murmurs from teammates and spectators in the stands.

As for hitting, Gordon batted second in the order behind Kenny, who was the fastest runner on the team and was the leadoff hitter. There weren't many left-handed pitchers in the league (who we actually preferred hitting against, because we could see the ball better coming at us from that angle of delivery). Hard throwing right-handed pitchers—especially if they threw sidearm—worried Gordon more about hitting him with an inside pitch. (One such pitcher in the league was Dallas Farrimond, who went on to star for South High and even pitched a few years of minor league baseball after we graduated.) But not many 14 year-old boys could throw a good curve ball. One exception was a Mexican American kid by the name of Lawrence Gallegos. Gallegos threw a nifty curve with uncanny accuracy, pitching no-hitters and routinely striking out the side when he was on the mound. Oddly, curve balls didn't seem to scare Gordon the way they did most kids our age. Gordon knew Gallegos would throw mostly curves when he pitched, so instead of ducking or jumping back before his curve broke over the plate, Gordon would just wait for one and step into it.

Gary usually batted fifth or sixth in the order and had an opposite take on pitches. Side-arm fastballs didn't bother him much, but sharp breaking curveballs did. When Gallegos pitched against us during regular league play, Gary was typically an easy out. But when someone like Farrimond was pitching, he kept his stance in the batter's box and swung away with confidence.

It was Gallegos who pitched against us in the second game of the 1958 championship round robin tournament. (In the first game we had finally disposed of an evenly matched team from Toole, 7-6, in a game that went 13 innings.) We were underdogs against Gallegos' team, but in the next-to-last inning, Gary managed a walk when a Gallegos curveball barely nicked him, Gord got a crucial line drive hit to left field that knocked in a run in the last inning, and our team won an upset victory by a score of 4-2. As luck would have it, Dallas Farrimond pitched for the team we played in the quarter-final game. This time it was Gordon who managed a walk, and Gary tagged a soft flyball double to left-center that barely fell beyond the outstretched grasp of the racing center fielder. Gordon came all the way home to score. Our teammates also hit surprisingly well in clutch moments of that game, knocking in insurance runs, and we wound up with another unexpected win. But our Cinderella season came to a dead end in the semifinal game against the undefeated regular season champ. They were loaded with players who went on to star at both East High and West High. They didn't exactly pulverize us, but we were soundly beaten.

We share a distinct memory of our mother attempting to console us after our team was eliminated from the tournament, saying to us when we came disconsolately home to report our defeat, "Don't be upset boys. *It's only a game.*"

"You don't understand!" we vehemently protested. "It's not just a game! Our season is *over* and now we won't get to play for the championship!"

Monopoly is a game. Checkers is a game. Trivial Pursuit is a game. Even over-the-line is a game. But for us, organized baseball was not just a game. Every baseball summer was a season of our lives. You had a brief moment in youth to strive for it, to be part of it—part of its unfolding local history, its abiding rules and standards of excellence, its records, its championships, and, in our young minds, if you were good enough, to partake of its mythical promise of immortality. When we were 14, baseball was more than a game.

18.

NATIONALITY AMERICAN

In late January 2018, Gordon got an email from Gary, with the sadly shocking news that Janice Yano—one of our earliest childhood and adolescent classmates from Liberty Elementary through Lincoln Junior and South High schools in Salt Lake City—had passed away unexpectedly of natural causes. Janice Yano?! Of *natural causes*? Jesus. At our 55th high school reunion the previous August she had looked younger and healthier than anyone there, including the two of us with our shiny foreheads and short grey beards.

**The two of us (Gordon on left, Gary on right)
with Janice Yano at our 55th high school reunion.**

Gary's note contained a link to her obituary at legacy.com, which Gordon immediately clicked on. "Janice Yoshiko Yano Aoki," the top line of the obituary read, "In Loving Memory." We never knew Janice had a middle name. We were also reminded by the obituary that she had married Bob Aoki, another good high school friend, right after graduation from South. With stars in their eyes they moved to Anchorage, Alaska, where wages were high and work was plentiful. Their youthful marriage lasted long enough for them to have two daughters, Teresa and Cathy, before ending in divorce.

Gordon's eyes scanned quickly down the page. Born: December 10, 1943 Hunt, Idaho. Passed Away: January 10, 2018. Wait a minute. Go back. *Hunt, Idaho*? Where the hell is *that*? Gordon looked that up too. Here's what he found on Wikipedia:

> Hunt is an unincorporated rural area north of Eden in Jerome County, Idaho, United States. The area was named after Frank W. Hunt, a former Governor of Idaho. It was the home to a Japanese American Internment Camp now marked by the Minidoka National Historic Site.

> *Minidoka National Historic Site—a Japanese American Internment Camp.*

Janice was born exactly three weeks before the two of us first sputtered for breath at Salt Lake City's old Holy Cross Hospital. On the day of our birth, December 31, 1943, our father was in New Guinea as a Field Director for the American Red Cross with American troops, who were mercifully being granted some R & R during the Pacific War with Japan after Pearl Harbor. And on the day of our birth, Janice Yoshiko Yano was a tiny prisoner in the Minidoka War Relocation Center in Hunt, Idaho, along with her parents, Mitsuru Yano and Mikiko Sugino Yano and her two older sisters, Irene and Lillian.

As adults we learned about the internment camps that were quickly instituted by executive order in early 1942, following the Japanese attack on the U.S. naval base at Pearl Harbor. There were nearly a dozen of these camps, whose inmate populations ranged between 7,000 and 19,000, and they were spread out in remote spots on the map in California, Arizona, Utah, Colorado, Wyoming, Idaho, and even Arkansas. A total of 110,000 to 120,000 Japanese American citizens were incarcerated in these camps for the duration of the war. We knew all this but never thought to make the connection between our country's ruthless security policies during wartime and what that must have meant for the Japanese kids we grew up with and attended school with in 1950s Salt Lake City. We don't know where Janice's parents were born or when they became U. S. citizens—whether they were naturalized or American born—but they definitely were citizens prior to Pearl harbor. *Non*-U.S. Citizens of Japanese heritage—proud parents of three beautiful daughters—would never have named them *Irene, Lillian, and Janice*.

We remember Lillian from when we were kids growing up in the early 1950s in Salt lake City. She and her sisters lived then in an old, Victorian, two-storied dwelling on Fifth East right across the street from Liberty Park. Lillian was truly beautiful, with straight, shining black hair, gently bobbed at her shoulders. At Liberty Elementary, our older brother Don had a schoolboy crush on her. We remember going with Don to the Yano's house on more than one occasion, with various excuses for him to get a glimpse of Lillian. As a senior at South High, Lillian was vice president of the Pep Club, a member of the House of Delegates, the Social Arts Club, the French Club, the Swimming Club, and the Tennis Club. She sang in the A'Cappella Choir and Girls Glee, was awarded Honors at Entrance at the University of Utah, was a graduation speaker at South High's 1960 commencement ceremony, and ironically performed in "The Mikado"—South High's musical extravaganza for the 1959-60 school year.

**The Mikado, performed in 1960 by the South High Acapella Choir
and drama class.**

We don't recall much about Janis' oldest sister, Irene until, as sophomores
at South, we watched transfixed as she and two other South High alumni
girls soulfully sang, in achingly beautiful, three-part harmony, "Sentimental
Journey," at an alumni assembly in the fall of 1959.

"Sentimental Journey" was a hit song by Doris Day and "Les Brown's
Band of Renown" that coincided with the end of WWII and became the unofficial homecoming song for hundreds of thousands of victorious, American
soldiers, returning to their loved ones after the defeat of Imperial Japan and
Nazi Germany in 1945. That's when our dad came home too. And, 14 years
later, Irene Yano, who spent two to three years of her young life in a Japanese
American Internment camp in Hunt, Idaho, sang her heart out on the stage
of Salt Lake City's South High auditorium.

Then there was Janice—diminutive, perky, spunky, smart-as-a-whip
Janice Yano.

Janice Yano, South's sophomore class vice president, 1960.

In the fifth grade at Liberty Elementary Gordon announced that he didn't like girls. But the truth was—in secret emulation of his brother Don's childhood romance fantasies—he had a crush on Janice, which he demonstrated by finding creative ways to annoy her. She was cute and smart and a competitor, even then, with sassy retorts to all of our silliness. Meanwhile, the Yanos had moved from Fifth East to another old Victorian house on Edith Avenue, between Fourth and Third East. All the better for us! Janice's Edith Avenue house was an elbow bend down the alley from where our best friend, Lorin Larsen, lived in a duplex on the north side of 1300 South. Lorin and the two of us—in the dumb mode of prepubescent boys—routinely raced past her front porch on our bikes, showing off, and then returned to make minor insults and laugh at our own witless jokes, while Janice pretended to be exasperated by Gordon's clumsy attentions. Gordon says he could be wrong, but he thinks Janice liked him too.

Later, when we went on to South High, Janice continued to excel at school, both academically and socially. She was elected vice president of the sophomore class, was in the Pep Club, made straight A's her junior year, and, as a senior, served as the campaign manager for Dave Shiba, who ran against Gary for the office of student body president. Shiba, it turns out, was another one of our Japanese American classmates. He had been elected president of our sophomore class and, in his junior year, was elected again to office as second vice president of the entire student body.

And what about Bob, Bob Aoki, Janice's high school boyfriend and husband to be? Bob Aoki didn't attend Liberty Elementary with us and Janice, but we got acquainted with him at Lincoln Junior High, and he became what we considered to be a good and loyal friend. Bob and Gordon occasionally met to play tennis on the public courts at Salt Lake City's Liberty Park. Gordon remembers one occasion when a twenty-something year old blowhard tried to order him and Bob off the court so he could take it for himself. Bob refused to budge and dismissed the guy's bluster as being nothing more than a tired string of "clichés." "Clichés?" Gordon had to go home to look up the word in a dictionary. He thought clichés referred to some kind of fencing or wrestling tactics.

In Gary's sophomore yearbook, Bob wrote: "I've always perked up and listened when I heard the name Shepherd. . . I think a lot of you and your brother, and don't take it light. A friend is like a candle flame; blow it out, and a smoking wick is all that remains." *Your bud, "The Mikado," Bob Aoki.* As seniors, when Gary ran for student body president at South, Bob supported him instead of Dave Shiba, and volunteered to draw and cut a stencil poster of a square-rigged Galleon ship—"Put South in Shep Shape," it was captioned—that became the single most effective propaganda poster of Gary's winning campaign.

Bob Aoki's poster for Gary's student body election campaign.

Bob's stockier brothers, Dick, and Larry, both started as linemen for South High football teams in the fall of 1959 and 1962, respectively. The oldest Aoki brother—charismatically handsome, Jim Aoki—was elected South's student body president for the school year 1957-58, only a dozen years after the nuclear bombings of Hiroshima and Nagasaki.

As kids growing up in Salt Lake during the 1950s, we thought nothing of all this: The Aokis, the Yanos, and Dave Shiba—not to mention Eddie Aoyogi, Matzi and Terry Mayeda, Katheleen Sako, Sue Tohinaka, and Bruce Tokeno, to name a few—were all good kids, our friends, and obviously active supporters of the democratic principles we imbibed and boasted of at South High. All of them, directly or indirectly, were exposed as children to concentration camp life in wartime democratic America in the 1940s.

After she and Bob divorced, Janis returned to Salt Lake and worked as a single mom to mother her children and rise through the ranks at Mountain

Bell. Her job took her to Denver, Colorado, where she eventually retired as a telecommunication manager. In between, she graduated *Cum Laude* with a Bachelor of Science degree from Salt Lake City's Westminster College.

Did we mention Janice also was an athlete and played sports? Not in high school, regrettably. Her teenage years were past before Title IX became the law of the land. But as an adult woman she took up tennis, golf, and skiing and excelled at all three. She competed fiercely and won a lot of tournament trophies right up to the time of her stunningly unexpected death. We're confident that her diminutive stature and soft, demure smile lulled many an overconfident opponent into relaxing when they should have been concentrating, and they quickly found themselves down 40-love before they knew what hit them.

At our last high school reunion we suggested to Janice that we'd have to get together some time and play a little tennis. She smiled demurely and asked, "When do you want to play?"

Janis Yoshiko Yano Aoki, of Hunt Idaho, Anchorage Alaska, Denver Colorado, and Salt Lake City Utah. Nationality American.

Japanese Americans as we knew them growing up in Salt Lake City after WWII.

Irene and Lillian Yano.

Bob Aoki and his brothers Jim, Dick, and Larry.

Other Japanese American classmates at South High.

Dave Shiba, and Matzi and Terry Mayeda.

Eddie Aoyogi, Katheleen Sako, Sue Tohinaka, and Bruce Tokeno.

19.

COPS AND EGGS

"Can you see them? Are they still coming after us?" Ari Ferro's voice cracked a little with mounting tension.

"No, I don't see them anymore!" Gordon called out from the back-seat, peering anxiously through the back window as Ari's speeding 1940 DeSoto squealed slightly around a tight bend in the dark on City Creek Canyon Road, for an instant blocking the view from behind. A second and a half of relieved silence, then: "Oh, Oh! I see them now, they're gaining on us!" Gordon announced, as the Desoto finished rounding the bend, and the rapidly rotating, beaming red light behind us reappeared again in the back window.

"Better slow down," Gary, sitting up front with Ari, urged. A siren and high beam headlights now accompanied the flashing red light. "Maybe we better stop."

How the hell did this happen? How did we get into another dumb fix with angry Salt Lake City police and a splattered cop car windshield?! And to make matters even worse, Kathleen McLean and Donna Schipaanboord, the innocent daughters of our Liberty Park Ward bishop and his second counselor respectively, were sitting paralyzed with Gordon in the back seat.

Ari Ferro's house—which as kids we considered to be a mansion fronting Fifth East and Liberty Park—occupied a half-acre of land that backed up to Denver Street, right across from our new home on a dead-end circle at 1166. The Ferros had a sailboat they stored in a ramshackle, wooden, open-sided shelter in their spacious back yard. Ari raised pigeons as a hobby and kept them in another old wooden structure adjacent to the boat storage. One early summer evening in 1960, in-between our sophomore and junior years at South High, we were chatting with Ari about his pigeons while he showed us a new one he had just acquired. He also showed us a number of small, blue-tinged eggs he had accumulated from his older birds. "What do you do with the eggs after you take them from the nest?," Gary asked.

"Just toss them," Ari answered. "They aren't fertilized, so they can't hatch."

"Oh," the two of us said. Biology wasn't our forte, and we didn't know that birds could lay eggs without male fertilization.

We don't recall whose idea it was to employ those eggs as missiles to toss at hypothetical targets (as long as they were "just going to be tossed out anyway"). We had heard from older friends about "egging" expeditions and it sounded like harmless fun. We had eggs, Ari had a car, *ergo*: we had opportunity! While discussing our options, we spotted Kathleen McLean and Donna Schippaanboord—next door neighbors and long-time school mates—strolling around the Denver Street Circle. We called their names, and they both came over to Ari's backyard to see what we were doing. Donna was outgoing and funny, Kathleen was reserved and observant. They were both very good Mormon girls, not known to engage in any sort of delinquent behavior. We showed them Ari's pigeon coop but didn't mention anything about egg tossing.

Left to Right: Ari Ferro, Donna Schippaanboord, Kathleen McLean, 1960.

As 16 year-olds, we had all recently obtained drivers' licenses through Salt Lake City's high school driver education program. However, neither we nor Donna or Kathleen had a car (or even access to our dads' cars). But, as already indicated, Ari did. His parents had helped him acquire an old, 1940 Desoto with a stick shift transmission that he had previously let the two of us try driving on quiet neighborhood streets. Would Donna and Kathleen like to go for a spin with us? We were almost surprised when, after a moment's hesitation, they both agreed. By this time it was getting dark. Gary sat up front in the passenger seat next to Ari, Gordon placed himself in the backseat behind Ari, and Donna and Kathleen settled themselves next to Gordon. Between his shoes, Gordon provided a safe harbor for a paper lunch sack containing a half dozen of Ari's pigeon eggs.

1940 DeSoto.

Where to? Well, our boyhood friend Lorin Larsen had recently moved from our Liberty School neighborhood with his family to Salt Lake City's "Avenues" in the northern foothills overlooking Salt Lake. We could drive up there and show the girls the Larsen's new home. But no lights were on as we passed by, so we continued slowly driving around the steep pitched, regularly laid out streets of the Avenues—all of them lined with a diverse array of charming older homes bordered by trees and carefully kept flower gardens. A silhouetted figure stood with a hose, hand watering his little slope of grass on a corner lot. Gary said, "Pass me up an egg." The front passenger side window was rolled down; Gary stuck his arm out and with an upward motion, lobbed the egg over the car roof in the direction of the man with his hose. Did the egg land on its target? We didn't wait to find out as we took a fast turn around the corner and disappeared into the darkness. Donna and Kathleen just looked at each other with wide-eyes in the backseat, both of them stunned by what Gary had done.

Where else should we go? Feeling a trifle guilty about egging an innocent citizen, we turned up Canyon Road into Memory Grove Park, just below the grounds of the Utah State Capitol building. It was common knowledge that on summer nights young couples could be found making-out on the sloping lawns of the park. We puttered slowly along and, sure enough, we spotted the outlines of several unsuspecting, supine figures on the sidehill grass. Somehow these seemed like more worthy targets than a conscientious property owner watering his lawn, and several more eggs were lofted from our car windows. This time we definitely heard outraged yells before speeding off again into the protecting invisibility of the night.

In those days, one could drive straight north through Memory Grove up to the entrance of City Creek Canyon, then turn onto the narrow winding road that heads south back to the Capitol building. That's what we did. Two eggs remained in the bag at Gordon's feet in the back of the car. Head lights loomed in front of us coming around a bend from the other direction (City Creek Canyon Road then allowed for two-way traffic). On an impulse, Gordon reached into the bag, extracted the eggs, cradled them in the palm of his left hand, and then, relaxing his fingers, allowed the rushing air to sweep them away as the approaching car neared his window. Nothing, not a sound. Then, oh, oh, a little red light appeared in Ari's rearview mirror, and it started getting bigger behind us as Ari pushed his foot down on the accelerator.

Ari brought his DeSoto to a stop just above the Capitol Building, at a point where one can view the entire Salt Lake Valley below, resplendent with glittering lights all the way out to the Point of the Mountain, 20 miles south. The police car, red light still flashing, pulled up just a bit in front of us and stopped. A grim looking officer exited from the passenger side of his squad car and approached the DeSoto while his partner remained in their vehicle. "Okay, whichever one of you threw those eggs, get out and come with me. The rest of you stay in your car and follow us." Without a word, Gordon opened his side door and accompanied the officer back to the squad car, where he sat silently in the back seat. Neither one of the cops said a word to him as they drove back into town. Gary thinks maybe Donna and Kathleen might have been quietly whimpering a little bit, but he can't declare that half-memory as a fact. What was a fact is that we were all pretty shook up and thought our lives were probably ruined.

Ari trailed the squad car down the steep descent from the capitol building on North State Street, straight to the old, hulking red brick police department that squatted at the intersection of State Street and First South. There was an underground entrance on the First South side of the building, and that's where we drove, into the bowels of the police department, which turned out to be a large, cement-floored garage for police vehicles and maintenance equipment. Both officers emerged from their car with Gordon in tow and gestured for the rest of us to get out to join them in the middle of the cavernous space. We exited from the DeSoto and bunched together in mounting trepidation. Night duty cops were beginning to move toward us from different crannies of the garage to see what was going on. Were we going to be cuffed, read our rights, taken to a holding cell?

Old Salt Lake City Police Department, circa 1960.

"Okay, you kids. Grab these and get to work!" commanded one of the officers, extending to us a couple of buckets filled with sudsy water, some sponges and scrub brushes, and a water hose. "You better make this car spotless!"

What? Was this going to be it? Just clean up the egg splatter on the windshield and hood? As it turned out, yes, but not quite. We scrubbed the windshield and hood as scrupulously as we could, but that was not enough. "Scrub down the whole car!," the arresting cops exclaimed. And not just outside, but inside too.

Their buddies, who had been standing around making wisecracks, were called upon to make an inspection after we had stepped away from our scrubbing efforts. "Not good enough! Do it over again! Get it right this time!" was the quick and raucous verdict.

Okay, we could now relax a little, join in the spirit of laughing at ourselves as the butt of police jokes rather than being marched off to some juvenile center. Just as four years previously, when Gordon had dirt-clodded a cop car at the intersection of Herbert Avenue and Third East, they were going to let us go scot-free: No citations for juvenile delinquency; no taking of names, home phone numbers, and address; not even warning phone calls home to predictably angry parents.

We stopped smiling and laughing after we drove out of the underground garage. Donna and Kathleen kept guiltily looking back and forth at each other but said nothing as Ari steered his DeSoto back to the safe confines of our Liberty Park Ward neighborhood. We pulled into the narrow backyard driveway to the Ferro's home on Denver Street circle. Were we going to say anything about this little escapade to our parents? The two of us and Ari were most certainly not. Donna and Kathleen didn't really say. A few days later, we learned that, in fact, they had felt-duty bound to confess their unwitting complicity in our delinquency. Fair enough, but the puzzling thing to us was that neither Donna's nor Kathleen's parents, so far as we knew, ever complained to Ari's parents or ours about how we had jeopardized their daughters' safety and spotless reputations.

One idiotic lesson that we might have gathered from this and previous unpunished misdemeanors was that we were somehow invulnerable, that we could disregard rules and push the limits of adult tolerance while remaining personally unscathed. Although often heedless and willing to take occasional risks, we fortunately were not truly stupid. The lesson that actually dawned on us, following the egg-throwing episode, was that we had been undeservedly lucky in that and other minor moments of mischief that could have spiraled out of control to the harm of others and to our own lasting detriment. This does not mean, of course, that overnight we became angelic choirboys, impervious to worldly temptations. But we did begin gauging more prudently the expanding options and choices before us as young people growing up in post-World War II America. At the same time, we were largely oblivious of the taken-for-granted perks of white privilege then (and now) in our society that helped to cushion our several brushes with the police. At the time it never occurred to us that had our skins been black or brown, we surely would have been in serious trouble, and our parents most certainly would have been notified by police authorities, not to mention being subjected to the accusatory gossip of neighbors; they, as well as we, would have paid a much stiffer price for our juvenile indiscretions. In retrospect, our Caucasian DNA was arguably the true and unmerited lucky charm that most distinguished the benign consequences of many of our youthful misadventures in the city of the Saints.

20.

ALL THE SMART GIRLS
BECOMING WOMEN

When we were kids growing up and just beginning to notice that girls were different than boys, we concluded that girls were smart. They didn't seem to get into trouble, they got good grades on tests, their handwriting was neat, and they were good spellers. The idea that girls are smart has never left us. That was our experience growing up and it remains so today.

Granted, at Liberty Elementary in Salt Lake City where we first became cognizant of girls, Phillip Starr was unanimously recognized as the smartest kid in the school. But we mainly concluded that to be true because Phil seemed to be a child prodigy on the piano. All of the teachers at our school loved and praised him, and we thought he must be a genius. Actually, maybe he was. The only grade he got lower than an A his entire life as a student in Salt Lake City's public schools was a B in gym, his sophomore year of high school. After that, Phil signed up for R.O.T.C. and never had to take any more gym classes. He was a National Merit Finalist his senior year and accepted a full-ride scholarship to Stanford University

Okay, so Phillip Starr was the boy exception who proved the rule: the smartest kids when we were growing up were girls.

At Liberty Elementary, for example, our next-door neighbors Kathleen Mclean, Donna Schipaanboord, and Kathy McClure always did their homework and got top grades; Lynne Madron and Annette Bowman always got A's too; so did Linda Brown, Raelynn Symes, Helen Moody, and Carolyn Olson; and let's not forget Carol Jean Christensen and Janice Yano—especially those two. We say especially those two because the two of us developed schoolboy crushes on Carol Jean and Janice, both of whom were A students. As Gary was to say later in life (and it applied to both of us): "I was always attracted to smart girls—I tuned into their intelligence like signals from a radio tower."

When we went to Lincoln Junior and then South High, girls didn't become any less smart, there were just more of them and, wow, were they ever smart and talented. For seniors at South, the biggest academic recognition was to be awarded Honors at Entrance. To qualify for this recognition, the minimum grade-point required our senior year was 3.909 (this was prior to the grade-inflating practice of giving college-prep students extra-credit points, sending award-winning GPAs today over 4.000).

Of the 15 South High seniors who qualified for Honors at Entrance in 1962, *eleven* were girls: Linda Bailey, Linda Booth, Annette Bowman, Marilyn Downs, Kathy Carling, Nancy Foster, Susan Hemmingsen, Sylvia Jackson, Judy Owen, Christine Schmidt, and Kathy Woolf.

South High students of the class of 1962 who achieved Honors at Entrance.

And yes, as already acknowledged, Phillip Starr was one of the four boys awarded Honors with a perfect 4.000 GPA, because only grades in *academic* classes were calculated for the award. Of the 11 girls on the list, Gary—at one time or another—dated three of them: Linda Booth, Kathy Carling, and Nancy Foster. Karen Demke missed by less than a tenth of a grade point from making the list, and Gary dated her too. For what it's worth, Gordon went to a school dance with Marilyn Downs our senior year (she was our class valedictorian, edging out Phil Starr by a tie-breaking perfect attendance record stretching back to the ninth grade).

Since Gordon was generally doing poorly in school at the time, he rarely had classes with the smartest kids. But he once took a geometry class with Kathy Carling. Virtually every time Mr. Jarrett needed a student to go to the board to demonstrate the proof for an especially tricky problem, it would be Kathy. Gordon sat slack-jawed and dumbfounded as he watched Kathy casually breeze through the incontrovertible proofs of ancient Greek theorems and their corollaries. But back to our statistical thesis about smart girls. Of the forty-five students from South's entire student body of 2,000 who achieved straight A's during the 1961 fall semester, thirty-four were girls. That's 76 percent. We rest our case.

"Yes, well, very nice" Gordon's wife Faye says about all of this. "Girls should be respected more for their brains. But what about *political* equality at your democratically touted high school? Did girls ever get to run for student body president or for class president, when you attended South?"

"Well, you see," Gordon obfuscated, "in those days at South, smart girls would be *campaign managers* for student body elections, and very frequently, they *subsequently* were elected to be student body officers and class officers. So, for example, our senior year, Linda Booth was elected student body Secretary, Mercy Johnson was school Historian, and Susan Fenn was elected Secretary of the senior class!"

South High Scribe

Vol. XXXI; No. 1   South High School, Salt Lake City, Utah   Tuesday, September 5, 1961

ELECTIONS TOMORROW
Campaign Managers Speak

Mr. Shiba   Mr. Shepherd   Mr. Richeda   Mr. Starr

Cub Calendar

Sept. 6—Campaign Assembly in the morning. Primary election after the assembly.

Sept. 7—Final election for President and Vice-president. Short announcement assembly.

Sept. 8—Nomination for other Student Association officers. Football game—South at Ogden.

Sept. 12—Primary election for Student Association officers.

Sept. 13—Final election for Student Association officers.

Sept. 14—Nominations of class officers in special class meetings.

Sept. 16—Primary election for class officers.

Sept. 19—Final election for class officers.

Sept. 22—Football Game—Bear River at South, 8:00 p.m.

Sept. 22—Football Game—South at Granger.

Introduction Of New Teachers

In 1961, only boys ran for student body president; girls were always campaign managers.

"Did they ever run for *president*. Was a girl ever elected *president*? Faye persisted in asking.

"Well, no, actually . . . no," Gordon was forced to admit.

"Why not?" she persisted.

And the answer was, "I don't really know," but the truth is he did know. The truth is that girls were not candidates for student body president, or class president, at South High or any other high school in Salt Lake City in 1962 because it was contrary to the traditional rules and restrictions of the society in which we lived at the time.

Sheepishly, Gordon had to make the following admission: "After high school, temporarily unmotivated boy-dopes like me were allowed time to get themselves sorted out and encouraged to think they had greater potential, began pursuing occupational careers that required more education or training, which often landed them in advantaged positions of authority over smart women."

Case in point: Even though Carol Jean Christensen's family moved away from our Liberty Elementary School neighborhood prior to sixth grade, she still remained in our thinking as the epitome of a smart girl. But here's the thing: Carol Jean was one of the few girls we grew up with who allowed her brains to dictate a future career for herself—as a medical doctor—rather than simply accepting the prevailing cultural dictum that relegated young women to domestic roles as housewives and mothers, regardless of their intellectual aptitudes and other talents. In contrast, many of the smart girls we grew up with—despite their top grades, scholarships, and other acclaimed achievements that today would likely have propelled them into professional careers—did not prioritize discovering and exploiting their potential in the larger world of serious affairs. They were not encouraged to do so, and many of them probably were actively discouraged from entertaining such thoughts. Most were definitely encouraged, however, to latch on to a likely young man, get married, and have a family. This is not to disparage wanting and having children. Not at all. But being a mother does not preclude also aspiring to have a meaningful outside-of-the-home-career, as we have learned over the last sixty- plus years while the world has gradually inched forward in the direction of greater gender equality. Like everything else, personal priorities are enmeshed in historical time-sequences. Nevertheless, Doctor Carol Jean (Christensen) Cordy married and had children and a grandchild, too, despite the ingrained patriarchal impediments of her growing up years.

But times have changed. A great many of the social restrictions saddled on women and girls have melted, if not altogether evaporated over the passage of the past sixty years. In the present century, the educational, occupational, and political advancement of women is an emerging reality. The world has finally started recognizing the equivalent talents and skills of women and to permit and encourage equal female participation in many previously male-dominated sectors of society. In addition to being conscientious moms, women are now presidents of universities, CEOs of large corporations, police and fire chiefs, truck drivers, military officers, editors of newspapers, town and city mayors, judges, state governors, elected members of Congress and supreme court justices, as well as school teachers and nurses. But bias persists in other arenas. Male sexual misconduct and exploitation of women continue to disgrace us. Significant and persistent male-female pay discrepancies for the same jobs continue to plague many workplaces. And what about the ultimate bastion of leadership in our country? Why has the United States of America—the world's erstwhile citadel of democracy, a country that produced public schools like Salt Lake City's South High in the 20th century whose dedicated teachers and administrators preached and attempted to model democratic values of justice and equality for young people—never put a woman president in the White House?

All the smart girls of our youth are now women. Will they (and a sufficient number of smart, younger women and the men who admire them) come together powerfully enough to make political history? It's about time. Let's welcome smart girls and smart women with high hopes for what they will be able do for the future of our struggling country.

21.

WE THOUGHT THE WORLD
WOULD BE BETTER

Wayne Miller and Mike Ellis were among the five African American kids in our 1961-62 senior class at South High, a central Salt Lake City school that had a total student population of approximately 2,000 the year we graduated. Of the entire student body, twenty-four (1.2 percent) were African Americans. On the basis of these numbers, South was atrociously labeled by some of the kids attending wealthier, lily-white schools in the region as a "nigger" school. Gordon especially heard that foul epitaph as sports editor for the *South High Scribe* when our teams were playing on the fields and gyms of other schools.

Both Wayne and Mike were athletes who played for South. Neither is still living. Wayne died of "natural causes" in 2007. We're less sure about Mike's exact date of death, but it wasn't from natural causes, as he was only 25 years-old. So, let's begin with his story first.

We met Mike Ellis in the eighth grade at Lincoln Junior High. Located on the corner of 1300 South and State Street, the block that once housed a neighborhood educational institution named for our greatest president has today become another thicket of small shops, eateries, business office spaces for lease, and the Salt Lake County Probation Services building. Our vague recollection is that Mike lived with either his grandma or aunt in an older apartment building with stairs, somewhere in the central city area between State Street and 500 East, and 300 South and 900 South. These street coordinates also unofficially defined Salt Lake's "ghetto" neighborhoods, where a majority of our African American classmates lived.

Mike was always a big kid, husky and quick on his feet, with athletic reflexes. He was good at basketball and could throw baseballs a long way too, as well as knock people down in our junior high games of flag football. Gordon learned this when they shared a gym class. But he was also an easy-going, friendly kid with a big grin and a ready laugh.

His good-natured tendencies notwithstanding, Mike had a few after-school fights—not meanly provoked by him, we would wager. We remember one fight—in "Durmer's Alley," across from Lincoln on 1300 South. A blondish tough kid had challenged Mike in gym class to meet after school. He was there waiting in the alley with his friends when Mike showed up, alone. Mike wasn't grinning. The adolescent fighting norms of the day were fisticuffs and no kicking. But if Mike was going to fight a white kid surrounded by his friends, he wasn't going to just talk tough and play macho games; he was going to whale the hell out of him and get it over with quickly, and that's exactly what he did.

At South, Mike threw the shotput in the spring and, in the fall, played left tackle on the football team. He was Big Number 75. On his white, South High Cubs helmet he hand-painted the name of his football hero—"Big Daddy" (Lipscomb), all-pro tackle for the fabled Baltimore Colts—in blue script, South High's primary color.

Mike Ellis with his "Big Daddy" football helmet.

The South High Cubs had a losing season that year, and there weren't many opportunities to cheer. One game stands out in our memory, though. It was against the Granite High Farmers (coached by future BYU Hall of Fame coach, Lavell Edwards) and was played on their home turf in Salt Lake County at 3300 South and 500 East. The Farmers ran an old fashioned single-wing offense and proceeded to ram the ball down South's throat for a score of 21-0 at half time. As sports editor, Gordon trudged into the locker room with the team to hear the players lambasted by South's head coach, Dale Simons. "I thought you were *real* football players," Simons snarled. "You seniors! You're letting this *junior* carry you on his shoulders!" Simons pointed at junior Mike Gold, Mike Ellis' broad shouldered, strawberry blonde line-mate at right tackle. Ellis sat with his head down, he was sick, he had a temperature, and he had to excuse himself to go throw up.

South High Football Coach, Dale Simons.

The second half was a different game. South scored twice and shut down Granite's single-wing attack. In the closing seconds South was moving the ball again into Granite territory, but the gun went off and the game was over. Another loss. At least the team could hold up their heads; Coach Simons would have to grudgingly admit that they had finished the game like real football players—especially Mike Ellis, drenched in sweat with steam rising off his shoulder pads, as he wearily boarded the team bus for the short ride home.

At the end of the football season, Mike Ellis, Big Number 75, was awarded all-state honors by both the *Salt Lake Tribune* and the *Deseret News*, the only one of his teammates to be thusly acknowledged and acclaimed.

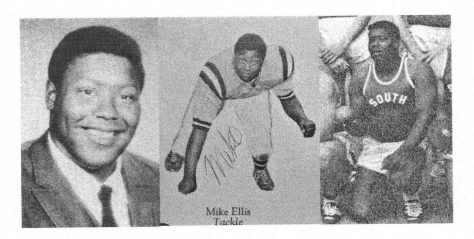

Mike Ellis
Tackle

Big Mike Ellis, awarded all-state in football for South High in 1961.

One weekend night later that year, Mike, in the company of another friend, showed up at our Denver Street Circle home after downing a few beers. They were not roaring drunk, but Ellis was tipsy and had to catch himself from stumbling when they came into the living room. Big Mike was mortified. He straightened to his full height, in his blue and white letter jacket, and remorsefully blurted an apology to Gary: "I'm real sorry, Shep. I don't mean to disrespect you and your home and your parents showing up here like this."

We have another particularly vivid high school recollection of Mike Ellis. Gordon became buddies with another Mike—Mike Mitchell, a white kid and football teammate, who was co-captain of the South eleven and Gordon's best friend at South.

Mike Mitchell, co-captain of the 1961 South High Cubs.

"Mitch," as everybody called him, was the proud owner of a 1956, two-tone red and cream-colored Chevy Impala hardtop with a wrap-around wind-shield, which he kept in impeccable condition. Ellis always road shotgun when we cruised Main Street. One Saturday night while cruising, we pulled into Snelgrove's on 2100 South. Painted pink and built in Art Deco style, Snelgrove's was Salt Lake's snazziest ice-cream parlor. Inside it looked like a restaurant, with linen table clothes and napkins. And you ordered from a fancy menu, with dozens of imaginative ice-cream dishes from which to choose.

We slid into a plush booth and waited for a waitress to take our order. Other customers were being waited on too, many of whom had been seated after us. We waited some more. Then, Mitch beckoned a passing waitress. She glanced at Mitch, then at Mike Ellis, winced, and kept on walking. Our ears and cheeks started burning. We looked at Ellis, he shrugged his shoulders and said, "Let's leave." It wasn't just a hateful waitress that night. We later found out it was Snelgrove's policy not to serve "colored customers." Salt Lake City, circa 1962.

As with many of our other high school classmates and friends, we lost touch with Mike Ellis after graduation. For us there followed a year of freshman studies at the University of Utah, six months of military basic training in California and Oklahoma for the Utah National Guard, and two years as Mormon missionaries in Mexico. When we got back from Mexico in the summer of 1966, we resumed our studies at the University of Utah and also reconnected with our good friend, Mitch. The following year, Mitch's wife, Karen, had complications while giving birth to her second child. Mike Ellis willingly donated needed blood for her. But then, in1968, Gordon learned from Mitch who—while stoically blinking back his tears—informed Gordon that Mike Ellis had put a shotgun in his mouth and pulled the trigger. We can't pretend to know what drove Big Mike to such a desperate end. According to Mitch, he had lost the cheerful grin that was his trademark in high school and seemed depressed and even angry much of the time. Mitch was asked by Mike's family members to be one of the pallbearers at his funeral.

Damn. Damn. Damn. This wasn't the future that any of us had foreseen. The democratic ideals we uncritically embraced at South High in 1962 didn't comport with the realities of American society a mere six years later in 1968. Yes, 1968—the year that the Reverend Martin Luther King Jr. was gunned down in Memphis after supporting a rally for Black sanitation workers; the year that Senator Robert Kennedy was shot to death in Los Angeles campaigning for president on a platform that strongly supported civil rights for both black and brown Americans; the year that virulent racism boiled over at home, and a controversial war was being fought by our generation in Vietnam.

And Wayne Miller? Well, without pretending to comprehend the various struggles with which *he* contended while growing up as a minority kid in Salt Lake City, or later as an adult living and working in the city of his birth, it's apparent that Wayne's life took a different track than Mike Ellis'. Like Big Mike, we met Wayne Miller at Lincoln Junior High in gym class intramural sports. Unlike Big Mike, Wayne was lithe and sinewy, with not an ounce of fat on his soon-to-be six-foot frame. And, in contrast to Mike's gregarious boisterousness, Wayne was quiet, diffident if not downright shy, and a good student. In high school, Wayne played piano in the dance band, was one of eight classmates selected to represent South at Boys' State in 1961, and subsequently was elected to the South High Board of Delegates his senior year. He was never challenged to an afterschool fight that we know of and, had he been, he would probably have coolly walked away. Even without sports, Wayne Miller was one of the most well-liked and respected kids in the school.

But, of course, it was in sports that he acquired his chief renown among his classmates. By the time he started high school, Wayne was the fastest kid in the sophomore class. He went out for football and seemed destined to become an all-star running back. But he developed a mild case of Rheumatic Fever and was diagnosed with a heart murmur. His doctors forbade him from playing football his junior and senior years but allowed that he could run track and play basketball.

On the track team, Wayne ran the 100 and 220-yard dashes and anchored the 4 x 220-yard relay team. We remember South's first track-meet of the 1962 season at Olympus High School, at the feet of Mount Olympus in eastern Salt Lake County. It was a chilly, overcast day in late March. Snow still thickly covered the mountains behind the track, and the thinly clad runners were shivering. Since Gordon was the school's sports editor, he was granted permission to stand on the track at the finish line to witness the first race of the day, the 100-yard dash. He stood there in frozen awe as he watched Wayne Miller—a vision of surging power and grace—storming directly at him, ten yards in front of his nearest competitor. Standing next to

Gordon at the tape was his counterpart sports editor from Olympus High, who exclaimed, "*Jesus!* that Black kid from South runs like *Man O' War*" (the fabled racehorse from the Roaring Twenties).

South's 1961-62 basketball team was short, even for a high school team of that era. The tallest senior on the squad was a measly six-two (and he wasn't even a starter). Wayne was an even six feet. Wayne didn't play guard, however, and he didn't play forward, either. He was the center. He was the center because he could jump. He had a short, muscular torso, long legs, long arms and big hands. Did we mention already that he could jump? He was quick; he was fast, and, oh yes, he could jump. Taller centers on opposing teams were too slow to block his short-range jump-shot. And they also discovered that he could spring high enough in the air to swat down their dinky layups inside the paint. Wayne soared for rebounds and, like the big guys, he could dunk.

Gordon remembers a game at Granite High again, watching the Granite Farmers in their warmup drill before the game, their big guys lumbering up to the basket and showing off with two-handed dunks. Then he turned to watch Wayne and the Cubs warming up at the other end of the court—Wayne Miller with the ball, loping toward the basket, and then launching upward as though shot from a catapult to hurl a smashing dunk through the net with one hand. Gordon stood in adolescent awe and hoarsely whispered out-loud: "Wayne, you thrill me!" Yep, that's what he said—it was a spontaneous, heartfelt expression from a kid who idealized sports heroes, but who was not generally known for public displays of expressive feeling.

Wayne Miller, number 22 (and Tim Christensen, number 34) vs. Granite High, 1962.

South went to state that year in both basketball and track, playing well enough to win some games against bigger opponents at the state basketball tournament and placing third or fourth at the state track meet. At the end of the school year the South High coaching staff unanimously named Wayne Miller as the school's outstanding athlete. This is what Gordon had to say about Wayne in a short summary of his achievements on the sports page of the *South High Scribe:*

> The best senior athlete and the all-around best senior at South
> High is Wayne Miller. Wayne is a showcase of self-improve-
> ment, coachability, desire, and plain hard work. To begin with,
> Wayne is not a natural athlete. Instead of natural ability he was

given a body capable of high achievement. Wayne has taken it from there, practicing, working and molding himself into an outstanding performer. Illness prevented Miller from playing football, a sport that easily could have become his best. Instead, Wayne poured his concentration into basketball and ended up as second high scorer on this year's team with a 14 point per game average. More important to the team was Wayne's tremendous rebounding and intangible something that seemed to add fire to the Cub attack. Track comes easiest to Wayne, who is one of the top sprinters in the state. He runs like a smooth moving thoroughbred, picking up speed as he goes. Wayne's long, sleek legs, dangling arms and hands, broad shoulders, and short, v-shaped torso make him look taller than his actual six feet. Draped around his bones are 175 pounds of slabbed muscle. These physical features, coupled with his willing attitude, have been responsible for making Wayne Miller senior athlete of the year.

Two years after graduation from South High School, when we were preparing to leave for Mexico on Mormon missions, we sent Wayne a formal invitation in the mail to attend our missionary farewell. He wasn't a Mormon, but we hoped he would come. He didn't. But after all, there were other friends from school who were invited who didn't come either. Had he showed up, though, Wayne Miller's face would have been the only black one in a sea of white. As the Reverend Martin Luther King used to say, the most segregated places on Sunday morning in America are the Christian churches—regrettably, still true today.

Years later, Gary, who had been the student body president our senior year, made the following glass half full-half empty remarks about Wayne to an audience at the 10-year reunion for the South High Class of '62:

We listened with faith to Dr. Backman's lectures on democracy, and we applauded Wayne Miller with our hands and hearts when he spoke to us at the Award Dinner at the tail-end of the 1962 school year. But, I remember too that Wayne was quietly taken aside during the drawing of dates to attend that celebration and was assigned to escort a black girl who, but for the felt need to arrange for Wayne an "acceptable" partner, would not otherwise have been in attendance.

As with Mike Ellis, we didn't see Wayne after high school nor after our church missions to Mexico. Through the grapevine we learned that he became a supervisor over youth sports for Parks and Recreation at the Central City Recreation Center on 600 South and 300 East—right in the middle of the old neighborhood where he grew up as a kid.

It came as a shock to learn, in 2007, that Wayne had passed away prematurely at the age of 63. From his obituary we learned that Wayne obtained a Masters' Degree at the University of Utah and, after retiring from City Parks and Recreation, went to work as a counselor at Valley Mental Health Clinic in Salt Lake. In his spare time, and for fun, he played piano for appreciative audiences at area dining spots and other venues, both public and private. Among other things said in his memory, Wayne Miller's obituary stated simply, "He was always quiet, dignified, and respectful of others."

Amen, brother. Your respectfulness of others was reciprocated by everyone we ever knew who also knew you. Rest in peace, Wayne, and you too, Mike. We fear now that the country we live in today has failed to progress very far in the direction of acknowledging in actions—and not just words—our shared humanity and sense of mutual respectfulness. We hate that. We nonetheless continue to prize our youthful association in a time and place when we thought the world would be better for us than it was for our parents, and even better for our own children than it was for us. And in too many ways, it isn't.

**Wayne Miller scholar, musician, and South High's 1961-62
outstanding athlete.**

22.

TEEN SPIRIT

Youthful Idealism and The Spirit of Democracy

Gordon: "BOOM! All of my senses were instantly charged. The hair on the back of my neck raised up, and, as though forcibly drawn by an irresistible power, I too found himself rising to my feet. 'What the *hell*?!' I thought out loud, my heart racing. I was surrounded by nearly two thousand adolescent youths, most of whom I didn't know, all standing and yelling their lungs out. It was a perfect, deafening din, yet somehow disciplined and focused; the reverberating sound-waves had nothing else to penetrate but my brain and the brains of all the other fervently standing kids in the densely packed auditorium."

It was September 8, 1959, our first sophomore day of school at South High. We had never attended a South High pep rally before—we didn't even realize that there was going to *be* a pep rally that day. All we knew was that we were supposed to attend a schoolwide assembly right after meeting with teachers and our homeroom classes. The assembly wasn't in the gym. It was in the auditorium, a classy, 1930s, vaudevillian-looking theater in the middle of the school, with mezzanine and balcony levels that were designed to seat an audience of 1,200, but somehow was supposed to squeeze in a student body of 2,000.

The school band was in the orchestra pit, and, on stage, senior and junior students were putting on a skit. Suddenly, BOOM! In startling unison the drummers hit their big base drums as hard as they could; the band launched into the first bars of the school's fight song; the student actors on stage instantly shed their costumes and revealed their true identities as that year's South High cheerleaders. Then holy bedlam enveloped the auditorium.

Holy Bedlam in the South High auditorium.

In the early 1990s, "Smells Like Teen Spirit" was dubbed an anthem for the apathetic kids of Generation X and became Nirvana's biggest hit. (Okay, so what if Kurt Cobain's Teen Spirit actually referred to a popular deodorant.) Recently, at a restaurant get-together with some of Gordon's university colleagues, an English professor said, "I hate that shit," by which he meant adolescent school spirit. Well, of course, he does. It's juvenile. He may even have hated it when he was a juvenile student in 1960s Louisville, Kentucky. But if he had been a student at Salt Lake City's South High in 1959, we wager he'd have been standing hoarsely on his feet like the rest of us.

Gordon: "Disgracefully, for the next three years I was an indolent, disengaged student (mercifully allowed to graduate with a 1.7 GPA). I nonetheless embraced unreservedly the religion of South High School. I say religion because it *felt* like religion is supposed to feel."

The auditorium was our sanctuary where the true believers of South High's idealized democracy gathered for communion. On occasion our communion might be solemn and celebrated in hushed tones. But more often it was electrically charged, collectively exuberant, and even joyously transcendent. It wasn't high church, it was charismatic and pentecostal. In those moments we were one: one voice, one heart, one spirit. We felt like we belonged to something bigger than ourselves.

South High front steps, foyer, and auditorium doors.

Sure, there were doctrines too, which the spirit of our gatherings reinforced and validated. They were the elementary doctrines of American democracy—liberty, equality, and justice.

We believed we practiced these doctrines in our student body elections. Dr. Ralph V. Backman (with an undergraduate degree in sociology, master's degree in philosophy, and Ed. D. in educational administration) was our adult guru principal and South High's apostle of the essential connection between democracy and public education. Unlike the other city or county high schools, Dr. Backman insisted that our student elections be held at the beginning of each school year in the *fall*. Nominations for office would be democratically made by all students the previous spring in their homeroom classes. But subsequently Dr. Backman wanted incoming sophomores—as novitiates to South's democratic traditions—to participate in the election of their student body officers.

During the summer, the four junior students (always boys), who received the largest number of supporting votes in the spring as nominees for student body president in their senior year, selected campaign managers (always girls) to help organize and run their campaigns for office. Notwithstanding the obvious gender discrepancies at play, the biggest summer events in anticipation of the coming school year were August "campaign parties," which each candidate was expected to put on at somebody's house who had a backyard big enough to accommodate hundreds of kids dropping by to check things out before school started.

Nominally, these parties were for the purpose of making campaign posters to hang on the long walls of South High during the week before the election. Everyone was invited to find some magic markers, a poster board, and get to work. But what really happened, of course, was that the best artists in school were heavily recruited by the different campaign managers to produce appealing propaganda posters in conformity with catchy slogans that had already been decided upon—slogans like: *I Want to be Led by Fred; People Can't Get Enough of Starr; All Footsteps Lead to Shiba; Put South in Shep Shape* and *Leadership with Our Leader Shep.*

THE CAMPAIGN

Election posters in the halls of South High for the school year 1961-62.

While the artists applied their art, everyone else milled around listening to pop records playing in the background, munching on potato chips and homemade cookies, and, acting nonchalant while scoping out members of the opposite sex to see if there were any new faces, or if one could make eye contact with the shy boy/girl that sat across the aisle in algebra class last year. AND, the various presidential candidates and their campaign managers all made it a point of personal respect and compliance with South's unity norms to attend one another's parties and compliment one's rivals. Real life electioneering, making bilious promises and casting aspersions on one's opponents, was considered bad form. The school was looking for a symbol, someone whose character and demeanor would personify our idealized devotion to equality and fair play, not an unctuous bully or blowhard. The spirit of South High would reveal to us the anointed one in due time, we innocently believed.

When school commenced the first Monday after Labor Day, the Halls were festooned with banners and plastered with campaign posters. The aforementioned pep rally assembly got things started with a BOOM, and, in heartfelt unison, we unitedly sang "On South High, we'll stand behind you forever!" Forever, as it turns out, is a long time. Pledges of eternal devotion are the stuff of religion. A mere week later a campaign assembly would be conducted at which the four candidates spoke, expressing their hopes for the school in the year ahead. This was when the anointing spirit of democracy was expected to fall on the chosen one. The chosen one would not be boastful or bombastic. He would speak from the heart with sincerity and humility. A majority of students would know this, we believed, and be given the gift of discernment to choose correctly.

South High election day, Fall 1961: Gary giving his candidate speech on the stage of South High's Auditorium. Classmates, Alma Mansell, Nancy Foster, and Paul Eddington can also be seen performing various parts in the election drama.

Votes were cast in everyone's homeroom class, taken by the homeroom's elected House of Delegates representative to Dr. Backman's office, counted in the presence of the office staff, the candidates' campaign managers, and the student editors of the yearbook and student newspaper. The final results were then announced at yet another school assembly to thunderous applause. Win or lose, everyone was expected to close ranks and bear witness to the presumptive wisdom of the democratic process. From that point forward, our weekly, communal assemblies in the auditorium were not begun by Dr. Backman or any other adult administrator or teacher but by our democratically elected student body president. Without fanfare or announcement, our president would step quietly onto the stage, and cheering students would unitedly rise to their feet, in respect for the office and in collective confirmation of their loyalty to the school and its democratic ideals.

Sure, we were naïve in our idealism, immature in our pride and narrow loyalties, and blatantly ethnocentric in our uncontested belief of the innate superiority of our school and its traditions. What American high school worth its salt wouldn't produce students with similar attitudes and convictions?

But let's be honest too. Decades after departing from our sacralized sanctuary to struggle individually for a place in the coldly indifferent world of adult occupations and professions, we retrospectively rhapsodize about our youth—selectively perceiving our youthful communal virtues and glossing over our shared problems and shortcomings. We professed equality and fairness, but our school was a place where some exclusionary social cliques also formed. On occasion, self-righteousness outweighed tolerance and humility. Girls' accomplishments took a backseat to the athletic exploits of boys on school teams. Boys, not girls, were expected to symbolize the school's democratic values by running for student body president. Members of the state's dominant religion could be witlessly insensitive to the religious preferences of others. Ethnic minorities were sometimes made to feel like mere symbolic tokens that belied both personal and institutional undercurrents of latent racism. And scores of lonely kids might not have worn the right clothes, or cared about the right kind of music, or joined clubs, or participated in extra-curricular activities, or even give a flying-flip about our precious democratic traditions.

Playing devil's advocate, we might inquire: How different were the group mechanisms for stimulating and reinforcing quasi-religious feelings of loyalty and transcendent commitment in high school from those perfected by, say, the Nazis at Nuremberg? Or more recently implemented by White Nationalists and neo-Confederates at Charlottesville and other public venues? Or on garish display at various political pep-rallies that serve to name and impugn the ugly enemies of the homogenized people cheering in the bleachers? Or from the rituals of any other manner of inward-looking and outward-despising tribalism that defies the righteous realization of our shared, global humanity?

Hmmm, well, let's take a *deep breath* and not get too carried away by retrospective cynicism. Let's not be guilty of throwing out the innocent baby with the polluted bath water. Fervent feelings of devotion to a cause are not really the problem—let there be *more* devotion, not less. Imperfection and discrepancies between our ideals and our personal pettiness and hypocrisy are not the real problem either—let there be *more* idealism, not less. The real problem lies in the actual cause to which people are devoted. *What is the cause?* A review of history's many conflicts—in every country of the world, including our own—reveals a shameful number of avaricious and xenophobic "causes" that render unholy the group mechanisms for promoting unyielding devotion and commitment. Yes, unholy.

But school spirit, teen spirit, *youthful idealism* as the means for inculcating democratic values of liberty, equality, and justice are not unholy. The few grains of altruism our species may possess at birth must be nurtured, encouraged, and channeled as young people grow up, searching for themselves, and wanting to belong to something of meaning and value beyond their own egos. Shouldn't that something be in our schools as much as in our churches—and not in exclusive private schools, but public schools—where the children of all races and religions can learn it together? *E Pluribus Unum.* Dr. Backman was right. A healthy democracy requires healthy public schools, and vice versa. Even if imperfectly taught, imperfectly learned, and imperfectly applied, let our children be infused with the spirit of democracy at an early age. Why belittle or demean this today in our occasionally disillusioned years of old age? As Gordon's wife said to a recent student intern at the county juvenile court where she was chief of staff: "Convince me you can change the world, and I'll give you the chance to do it."

Yes, let there be school spirit, teen spirt, youthful idealism, and the elementary doctrines of democracy. Rising to our feet, we stand behind you forever.

23.

SMALL MOMENTS OF GLORY
When Baseball Was Our passion, Season III

As sophomores at South High in 1959-60, we looked forward with high hopes to trying out for the Cubs' baseball team. South's coach was hard-ass Dale Simons, who in his own youth had been a baseball player of some renown. Simons ordered us new kids who were trying out to get in line to show what we could do with a bat against live pitching. Simons himself was on the mound throwing the pitches.

South High baseball coach, Dale Simons.

When it was Gordon's turn, he let the first pitch go—it was a little low and outside. He froze on the second pitch, which was a trifle high and inside.

"Get out'a there!" barked Simons, waving Gordon out of the batter's box. "We haven't got all damn day for you to be choosey!" That was it. That was Gordon's only shot to make the team, and he blew it. Gary, noting Gordon's failure, took a couple of swings when it was his turn (at pitches that were off the plate, which he probably wouldn't have swung at in a real game), but he failed to connect solidly. Neither one of us made the team. Were we crushed by our failure after so many aspirational years to play the game? Maybe not crushed but humiliated for sure. Neither one of us, however, vowed to relentlessly work on improving our game and try out again as juniors the following year. Instead, we both decided to become sports writers and cartoonists for the school's newspaper, *The South High Scribe*.

Sample cartoons by Gordon (top) and Gary (bottom) for the South Scribe.

Meanwhile, that summer we played slow-pitch, church softball for the Liberty Park Ward and also tried our skills at fast-pitch softball as members of a Salt Lake County Parks and Recreation team that recruited players from all over Salt Lake. Technically, of course, softball is not quite the same thing as baseball, but we loved playing both. Besides guys like us, who went to South High, our county rec team also had players from East (including our second cousin, Earl Coombs, who was the state 100-yard dash champ his senior year) and West High. Our coach was Larry Maxwell, who a decade earlier had starred in basketball for South and from 1963-1994 was head basketball coach at Highland High, where his teams won five state basketball championships.

We played all of our games at White's softball park (since torn down) across the street from the Utah State Fairgrounds on North Temple. We did surprisingly well, winning all of our regular league games. Maybe the biggest factor in our success was a result of Gary inviting an unlikely pitcher to join our team by the name of Dennis Steiner, whom he had met in his sophomore gym class. Steiner didn't play on any sports teams at South, looked nothing like an athlete, combed his hair in a "Fonzie" style pompadour, and hung out with kids who were more interested in auto mechanics and hotrod culture than sports. But somehow, somewhere, he had developed genuine fast pitch softball skills, whipping his arm around his head and snapping it across his hip to propel the ball with high velocity and pinpoint accuracy.

We played the Elks Boys Club for the league championship, and they were loaded with star athletes from West high school. Their coach was John Caputo, a famed athlete in his youth and, at the time, sports director of the Elks Club. He coldly assessed our team (in a private conversation with Coach Maxwell that we overheard) as not belonging on the same field as the Elks Club team. Their pitcher was a Japanese American kid who, like Dennis Steiner, didn't look like an athlete, but he could really smoke his pitches. We couldn't hit him and were lucky to get runners on base from occasional walks or infield dribblers. Dennis pitched well for us but was nicked for a handful of runs. Gordon closed out our last inning with an inglorious called strike three, after both Gary and Bill Gehrke had preceded him with their own hapless whiffs at the ball. Coach Caputo had been right. But Larry Maxwell was a classy coach—probably the best we ever played for—who understood and cared about adolescent boys striving to grow up. Instead of bemoaning our loss and mediocre play in the final game, he congratulated us on our season and told us we had far outperformed his initial expectations.

Coach Maxwell also informed us that we, along with the Elks Boys Club team, were to be feted at an award celebration dinner the following week. We were both surprised and pleased that our runner-up finish would receive some token of acknowledgment. The award dinner was held at the old Columbus Elementary School on 500 East and about 2500 South. What we didn't know in advance was that dinner would be prepared and served to us by neighborhood girls of our approximate age who had been rounded up for duty as their reward for enrollment in other Salt Lake County summer programs. Each of us boys received a four-inch-high plastic trophy for our runner-up status, which, embarrassingly, was presented to us individually by the girls in attendance. The blatant sexism of this arrangement didn't penetrate our thoughts very deeply at the time—we probably felt more abashed than the girls did by all of this. What did penetrate was a good feeling that comes from bonding with a team of diverse and committed peers, jointly doing our collective best, and being recognized for our efforts even though falling short of our shared goal. As Dennis Steiner later wrote in Gary's yearbook: "It was fun playing ball, and we'll beat them Elks Club boys next time!"

Dennis Steiner, 1961.

The following summer we went back to playing baseball—this time in the "Automotive League," which was sponsored by local car dealerships in Salt Lake City for 16-17 year-old boys. Once again we competed at Municipal Ball Park (today, Herman Franks Park), where our Little League and Cop's league teams had played most of their games. For the first time in our ball playing days, however, the two of us were not chosen to be on the same team. Gary's team—Carlson Chevrolet—was decidedly mediocre, with only so-so hitters, like Gary and Bill Gehrke, and poor pitchers who gave up a lot of runs. But Gordon's team—Ken Garff Oldsmobile—was very good, solid at every position. Kenny Caputo was back on second base, and Gordon once again played shortstop, sucking up almost everything that came his way in the infield and getting timely hits at bat. Undoubtedly, though, the player who made the single largest contribution to the team's success was their regular pitcher, Johnny Flores, a compact, good natured, Mexican American kid who threw a nice breaking curveball and a sneaky fastball with outstanding control. Johnny rarely walked a batter and didn't get rattled in tight situations.

Garff Oldsmobile went undefeated to win the league championship and then faced an "all-star" team composed of selected players from the league's other teams to end the season.

The special allure of the 1961 all-star game was that it was played at Derks Field (now Smith's Ballpark)—the home of the city's triple-A team, the Salt Lake City Bees! (Coincidentally, the two of us were employed that spring and summer to sweep the grandstands at Derks Field after games and other scheduled events). Derks boasted a big league quality baseball field with an infield as smooth as a pool table, velvety, manicured grass, and outfield fences set at 330 feet down the left and right foul lines from home plate and a distance of over 400 feet to dead center. We were in awe. On the first play of the game, however, Gordon committed a glaring fielding error by letting a routine groundball go through his legs at shortstop (he was expecting a bounce but the ball zipped slickly across the manicured infield without so much as a hop). Chagrinned, Gordon atoned by going two for four at bat and knocked in two of his team's four runs, and Garff Oldsmobile eventually triumphed over the all-stars, 4-2.

Salt Lake City's Derks Field in the 1960s.

That was the summer of 1961. After graduating from high school in 1962, we worked at our dad's laundromat and self-service dry cleaner off of California

Avenue in the Glendale neighborhood, a mile west of Derks field. (This investment venture folded after six months due to a paucity of customers interested in the new-fangled way to do their dry cleaning.) There was no organized league baseball for us that summer. At eighteen we were too old for Automotive League, and American Legion ball was an extension of high school team baseball, which we had whiffed out on as sophomores. That's when we returned to playing soft ball for the Liberty Park Ward.

Gordon was scuffing the dirt around third base with his cleats, waiting for the next McKinley Ward batter to step up to the plate. It was the first round of the 1963, LDS Church "All Church" softball tournament. The Liberty Park Ward's softball team had earned the right to play in the tournament by defeating Harvard Ward for the Liberty Stake championship a week earlier by one run in the last inning. Gordon, who had singled and then gone to third on another hit from Gary, scored the winning run by going for home when the next batter hit a groundball to the Harvard Ward shortstop. The shortstop threw high to the Harvard catcher, who leaped, caught the ball, and came down hard with his cleats on Gordon's backside as he slid across the plate: SAFE! Liberty Park was going to All Church!

Advancing to the All-Church tournament, Gary and Gordon had cautioned their teammates about who they would be up against: McKinley Ward, a team stocked with outstanding players who had attended South High with us: Alen Owens, Richard Ablehouzen, and Mike Mitchell among others—especially Mike Mitchell, who routinely smacked high, arching homeruns into parking lots when he was up to bat.

Jessie Wunderlich—three years older than us—was Liberty Park's pitcher and star player. After two innings, the score was tied 0-0, but McKinley had runners on first and second with two out. Wunderlich delivered the next pitch and, *Crack!* The McKinley batter smashed a rising line drive past Gordon at third base. Two runners were in a position to score. Gary was playing rover (free to roam between infielders and outfielders) and sprinted to his right, stretched out in a horizontal leap, and . . . Yes! Snagged the liner with a backhand catch, before tumbling into a somersault on the ground. Inning over! Game still tied, 0-0.

Sad to say, that was the high-water mark of the game for us. McKinley Ward sluggers in subsequent innings continued to hit the ball hard (especially Mike Mitchell, with a pair of homers), and we went down by a score of 6-3. McKinley went on to win the All-Church tournament, and Mike was named Tournament MVP. That approaching fall, the two of us, along with Mike, Ron Swenson, and several other South High friends, would commence three months of combat basic training for the Utah National Guard at Fort Ord, California, followed by three more months of advanced training at Fort Sill, Oklahoma. The following spring the two of us would report for LDS missionary training in Provo, Utah, to learn Spanish in preparation for serving LDS missions in Mexico. It looked like our baseball days were over.

Though our youthful passion for baseball has long since cooled, we still occasionally reminisce about our playing days, fondly recalling our small moments of glory on the diamond while ruefully reviewing some of our muffs and disappointments. Fair enough, but perhaps the obvious point to be gently made to us after so many years is that our mother was perfectly right when she reminded us that it's only a game. So why, as grown men, do we continue reminiscing about ancient baseball feats and failures? Of course Mom was right, and yet . . . And yet something of who we are today was formed by dreaming about and playing the game when we were young. Given a chance to redo our lives, we wouldn't change that part. Perhaps in a redo we would forsake our boyhood convictions of the preordained supremacy of "natural athletes" in sports, practice our skills more diligently, and fortify the modest strength and speed which nature bestowed upon us such that there might have been more moments of glory and fewer muffs and failures for us now to reflect upon.

Fanciful redo's are, of course, self-indulgent delusions. What is not delusion was the happiness we experienced playing the game at a decent level of competence and knowledge and—may we also say—acquiring an enduring conception of heroes in so doing. Baseball established for us the idea that heroes are individuals worthy of respect and admiration who don't boast of themselves, but step up to deliver the goods for their teammates when a game is on the line, whether in baseball or any other joint endeavor. To the true heroes of every generation: Play ball!

II.

Moving On and Coming Back Home

24.

FATEFUL DECISION

Not long ago, Gordon received an interesting request from one of his granddaughters. This is what she wrote:

January 20, 2019

Hi Grandpa! This is Aftyn.

I was wondering if you could help me out. For my Honors English class, we have been asked to interview someone 60+ years of age about a "critical moment or experience in your life that has profoundly affected your worldview and/or has shaped the person you have grown to become." I thought to ask you for this assignment. With your response, I will write a short narrative essay that only my teacher will read. First, please reply explaining your event and its effect on you. After I get your reply, I will then ask you five simple questions about other aspects of your life that connect with your events. (Example: If your event happened in your childhood, I might ask 'What era or decade did most of your childhood occur in?') Some of my questions might be already answered in your event response, but I will still ask so I can get a direct response. You can take some time to think about this, I just need a reply by the 25th. Thank you so much for helping me!

Now retired from the university where he had taught for 36 years—and eagerly open to interesting assignments that give him a priority excuse for not doing his household chores—Gordon responded to his granddaughter with alacrity.

January 21, 2019

Dear Aftyn,

I've attached my response to your question concerning a critical moment or experience in my life that that has importantly shaped me and my worldview. I tried to keep it short but that's not easy for me to do 😊. I hope that won't be a problem for your project. In any event, I look forward to answering your follow-up questions.

Love,

Grandpa Shepherd

Although I didn't realize it at the time, one of the critical decision-making moments in my life occurred in the summer of 1963 when your Uncle Gary and I decided to join the Utah National Guard. Let me explain. We had graduated from high school the year before and had completed our freshman year of college at the University of Utah in Salt Lake City. I loved the social aspects of high school but had been an indolent, unmotivated student. I put a little more effort into my freshman classes at the University of Utah, but there too I proved to be a mediocre student.

During the summer of 1963, many of our old high school buddies (only some of whom went on to college) were planning to join the National Guard. Some were thinking about marriage and most were working full-time jobs. Even though the United States wasn't officially at war with anyone at the time, there was still a military draft to which young men over the age of eighteen were potentially subject. If you were drafted, you would be assigned to some branch of military service, go through military training, and then spend two years of your young life as a peace-time soldier for Uncle Sam. Two years. Wow. That could interrupt and put on hold a lot of youthful plans.

Joining the Guard was another option, It was a way to fulfill one's "military obligation" and avoid the draft. As a guardsman, you could choose your branch of service and only have to spend six training months away from home. The *downside* to this arrangement was that you would then owe five and a half more years of attendance at monthly weekend drills and two weeks of summer camp training every year to your local National Guard unit. But most of my buddies thought this was a preferable option to two years of fulltime duty, and they didn't have to argue very much to get me and Gary to join with them. Having given it very little thought, we went with our friends to the local National Guard Armory on Sunnyside Avenue and Guardsman Way and signed our names on the dotted line for a six year military commitment as weekend warriors. We were nineteen years of age and joining the Guard simply seemed like the normal thing for boys like us to do at that stage of our lives. We had no real idea about what we were getting into.

So, how did all of this become such an impactful, turning point experience or event in my life (and Gary's as well)? Frankly, much of our experience in army training and the National Guard was negative. Can negative experiences be important to one's learning, growth, and understanding of themselves and the world? Sure.

Sparing you a lot of gruesome details, we both quickly learned that we were not a good fit for the military. I learned I'm too independent and proud to function well in authoritarian organizations. Gary's the same way. Neither of us are whiners or suck-ups, and we're more than willing to do our share of work in a job with a meaningful purpose. But we don't like being bossed around. We don't like rigid rules. We don't like being arbitrarily ordered to do things for which we're not given a reason. We don't like harsh punishment and demeaning indignities imposed for minor or unintended infractions. And so on. Needless to say, we both disliked military basic training. and, even more, we disliked the succeeding years of weekend drills and summer camps with the National Guard as we got older and began assuming more adult responsibilities in our personal lives.

But truly impactful decisions or experiences should be assigned more than just a negative value. There were, in fact, several unforeseen but very positive consequences of our joint decision to join the Utah National Guard. One was the way shared military experience strengthened and solidified Gary's and my brother-relationship as we were becoming young adults. We had always been close growing up, but it was in the army where Gary's welfare in meeting the daily challenges of a monolithic training system designed to break down a person's civilian identity became my priority concern (and, reciprocally, my welfare in that same system also became his priority concern). For example, during a 20-mile march in full field gear with loaded backpacks and carrying our M-14 rifles, I developed blood blisters on my feet as plump and juicy as ripe cherry tomatoes from the ill-fitting combat boots I was wearing. During the last uphill stretch Gary positioned himself behind me and pushed into my backpack to keep me moving forward and my legs from buckling as we struggled through to the end of the march together. Subsequently, Gary wound up having a hernia operation in an Army base hospital after we were sent to Fort Sill, Oklahoma for advanced training, and he spent a week and a half recovering. I would hike six miles round trip to his hospital room every evening after duty hours to visit. In a letter home, Gary wrote that I was "a hero brave and true" for my dogged devotion. The personal bonds we fortified during that intense training period sustained our resiliency under an alien kind of pressure that has endured to the present day.

Another impactful decision we jointly made (while assigned to top and bottom bunks in the same basic training platoon and barracks) was to accept LDS missionary assignments when we returned home. Would we have done so anyway? Maybe. But the fact is, we decided this when we were in military training together. That's where, in an enclosed environment cut off from outside influence, we thought about and discussed our parents' religious hopes and expectations for us, our own religious doubts, the pros and cons of missionary service, and eventually arrived at the same decision to serve—committing ourselves to do the best we were capable of in spite of our doubts. That kind of commitment was precisely what had been lacking in my life up until then.

Gary, left and Gordon, right attired in Dress Green uniforms upon graduating from basic training at Fort Ord, California in 1963.

As Mormon missionaries both of us were sent to Mexico. Needless to say, two years of missionary service in Mexico was another impactful experience. Those two years, plus the time spent in army basic training, gave me a fertile timeout period of three years before going back to school at the University of Utah. I needed those three years away to find myself. During that time I matured. I learned self-discipline. I learned how to focus. I learned how to set goals and achieve them. I learned how to study. I learned that if I genuinely applied myself I could convert weaknesses into strengths. When I resumed going to school I became a good student; in fact, I became a very good student and eventually pursued an academic career as a college professor (and like a good twin brother, so did your Uncle Gary ☺).

There is one other important thing about our youthful and uniformed decision to join the Utah National Guard in 1963. Two years later, in 1965, the United States dramatically increased military draft quotas and began sending American troops to fight in Vietnam. National Guard units were flooded with applications by young men our age attempting to avoid the draft. Only a few could be accepted. But Gary and I were already in. We were safe from the draft, which meant we were safe from being sent to fight and possibly die in a war we didn't believe in. But one of our missionary companions—who began taking classes with us at the university when we got back from Mexico—wasn't so lucky. Unlike us, he hadn't joined the National Guard as a teenager out of high school. Consequently he received his draft notice, was inducted into the army, sent to Vietnam, and was badly wounded in action. He came home, eventually recovered from his wounds, but was never the same, sunny person again. His turning point moment wasn't in Mexico, it was in Vietnam.

Had our fortunes been reversed, had our missionary friend been the one to join the guard in earlier years instead of the two of us, would I be writing this little memoir now for my granddaughter's English assignment? Maybe, maybe not. We'll never know. I can confidently say in retrospect, however, that blundering into the Utah National Guard in 1963—no matter how much we disliked the experience that followed—was one of the most fateful and important decisions of both Gary's and my young lives.

25.

WELCOME Y'ALL TO BRAVO COMPANY!
Boys In Training for Uncle Sam

W e were wedged together with about three dozen other young men on wooden benches in the back-end of an open-air Army transport truck, tightly straddling heavy, stuffed duffel bags between our legs. We were seated in the last vehicle of a five-truck convoy pulling away from the "Reception Center" barracks at Fort Ord, California, where we had just completed "Zero Week" of our six-month Army Basic Training regimen. During Zero Week we acquired uniforms, boots, and other necessary gear; got various shots, shaved heads, dental and medical inspections; and learned basic military command structure, including a few elementary marching commands, along with a multitude of other Army regulations and procedures. Now, as we were all clumsily struggling to board our truck with jam-packed duffel bags, a passing column of jogging soldiers sang out to us, "You'll be *sooorrry!*"

They were right. Five minutes later a different song assaulted our ears—a startling chorus of loud yells and curses accompanied by heavy banging on the sides of the truck. Suddenly, the back tailgate opened and slammed downwards, revealing a crowd of angry men in army fatigues brandishing batons and screaming at us to "get the fuck off this Goddamn truck as fast as you can or we'll beat the living shit out of you!" We had been exposed to a fair amount of profanity among our peers growing up, but nothing in our previous experience had prepared us for the brutal onslaught of denigrating language now being unleashed at us without any apparent justification.

The new recruits closest to the back literally spilled out onto the street asphalt on top of their duffel bags as a result of being yanked in front by our new overseers and pushed from behind as panicky recruits tried to comply with the din of profane commands to get off the truck. The two of us both managed to avoid falling on top of the several new comrades who were splayed out on the ground, and who were instantly being wacked by batons and screamed at to get up. A man with spittle spraying from his mouth confronted us as we staggered to straighten ourselves and our gear and yelled: "Goddam it! I said run!—*run* you candy-ass pussies!" while we struggled to lug our 75-pound duffel bags—up a steeply graded street to fall-in to formation with all of the other recruits similarly jumping and falling from the five trucks now parked in a line. Numbered in this sweaty, fearful line-up of mostly nineteen-year-old boys were about a dozen friends from South High School (including Mike Mitchell, Ron Swenson, David Kelly, Marty Yeager, Harro VanLeeuwen, and Brent Rice).

"Welcome y'all to Bravo Company!"

What the devil had we gotten ourselves into? We had expected military basic training to be hard and demanding. But this? What was this? What was happening to us did not remotely comport with our idealized preconceptions of American patriotism and honorable military service to one's country.

Our shocked, dissonant feelings and confusion were not soothed later that night when, after we had been assigned to our barracks as members of the 5th Platoon of Bravo Company, we met our tough, no-nonsense platoon sergeant, Sergeant Owens, and were assigned bunk locations in alphabetical order. The two of—Shepherd, Gary and Shepherd, Gordon—stuck together, with Gordon on top bunk and Gary on bottom at the end of a row of bunks closest to the latrine area. Late that night, when we were just starting to doze off following a taxing day, we heard loud yells and cursing emanating from the latrine room near our bunk. Gordon, semi-conscious and vastly irritated, unthinkingly yelled out in a manner that had already become normative in this new environment: "Shut the hell up in there! We're trying to get some sleep!" For a stunned moment there was no sound or movement. Then a compactly muscular army sergeant strode out of the latrine where he had been cursing out an unfortunate new recruit who had tried to find a private time to relieve himself.

"Who said that!? Who told me to shut up!? I will line up this whole platoon in your skivvies and shove my baton up your asses if someone doesn't confess—right now!"

There followed a deafening silence. Then Gordon jumped down from his top bunk. "Here, Sergeant! I'm the one who yelled!"

"Stand at attention, you stinking piece of shit!" the sergeant screamed. With his face an inch from Gordon's, and with no diminishment of volume, he continued to scream: "Get dressed double-time and get your sorry ass down to the HQ in two fucking minutes!" (The HQ was the Headquarters office of Bravo Company where the company commander— First Lieutenant Carter Morey—ruled supreme during the day and where, during the night, various staff sergeants kept the watch. The sergeant screaming at Gordon was the one on duty that night.)

Gordon dressed in record time and sprinted to the HQ office at the head of the company street. When he opened the HQ door, the same night sergeant was waiting for him at the front desk. "You make me sick!" he thundered, ordering Gordon to stand at attention in the corner of the room, close to the door: "And face the wall! "I can't stand to see your ugly-ass face!" Thereafter, whenever other staff personnel came in the office, they would bang the door on Gordon as they entered. The night duty sergeant would then proclaim: "See that sorry piece of shit standing there? He told me to shut the hell up!" Upon which, Gordon would receive more growls and cuffs.

At the outset we had been willing to follow all necessary and legitimate orders, to do our best to learn new skills, to work hard, and be corrected when necessary. But we never completely got over our initial, adverse reaction to the basic training regimen at Fort Ord. We went in looking forward to growth and maturity with honor in fulfilling our military obligation to our country. But we were not looking to be bullied, dehumanized, and abused in the process. Naively, we didn't comprehend or appreciate that, what appeared to us to be a demented introduction to Army basic training, was actually then standard U.S. military procedure for making soldiers out of civilian recruits, incorporating the flawed training theory that raw recruits must first be systematically dehumanized and stripped of their civilian social identities and sense of self in order to form new, military identities in obedience to military command and authority.

We did grow, of course. We became physically stronger and mentally tougher and a lot less naïve. And, by surmounting the various tests imposed upon us during training, we developed an even keener awareness of the value of mutual support and cooperation among friends and comrades—especially between the two of us as brothers undergoing the same experience. That aspect of our social identities was only strengthened rather than torn down in military basic training at Fort Ord.

We adapted. We learned the rules. We learned what to expect, how to function, and, from our point of view, things substantially improved in the weeks ahead. Not every day in basic training was highlighted by physical and verbal abuse. Many of our actual training sergeants were battle hardened veterans of the Korean War, competent to instruct us in the various military arts, and, for the most part, they were not overly focused on humiliating and tearing us down after the first few weeks of instruction. In particular, Sergeant Owens, our African American platoon sergeant, whom we grew to respect, was tough but not vicious, and he didn't curse at us like some of the white sergeants. He emphasized that he wanted us to learn how important it was to obey orders and to develop loyalty to one's fighting unit; to learn how to stay alive in combat. Okay, we could do that.

Platoon Seargent Owens.

**Gary on right (with glasses) standing at port arms with platoon mates.
Gordon, middle (also with glasses) learning how to throw a hand grenade.**

We learned how to disassemble and clean our new M-14 semi-automatic rifles and to reassemble them and properly aim and accurately fire them at various targets. We learned how to properly attach and employ bayonets in close combat situations (an ancient military skill that by then was mostly obsolete). We learned how to wear and clean gas masks, and we were exposed directly to tear-gas without masks in a crowded, non-ventilated room—mucous streaming from our noses and mouths—so we would know first-hand what effects the masks would keep us from suffering in certain battle situations. We learned how to pull pins on live grenades and throw them within prescribed time limits (and then duck behind concrete barriers to avoid being injured by blast fragments). We were instructed in rudimentary principles of hand-to-hand combat and would fight one another in test matches. And of course, we ran. We ran up and down the foot-sucking costal sand dunes that bordered the tourist town of Carmel on the Monterey peninsula in full field gear—steel helmets, 40-pound backpacks, army boots, and slung M-14 rifles.

All of this combat training culminated in a night-time exercise of all battalion training units that had reached the final stage of their training. It was called the Infiltration Course. Our B Company numbered about 200 trainees, and there were approximately equal numbers of troops in the other dozen or so training companies in the battalion. Thus, several thousand young men were congregated on an immense field that was designed to simulate combat conditions. That night was made especially memorable by an interminable drenching rain that turned the field into a giant mud pie. At the front end of the 100yard-long field, encumbered with full-field equipment, we began crawling forward in the mud. Obstacles were strewn in front of us: barbed wire about a foot off the ground; deep and wide trenches every 25 yards or so; actual explosive devices going off at randomly selected intervals in planted mounds alongside the designated crawl-pathways; and, most disconcertingly, live 50 caliber machine gun rounds—marked by brightly colored tracers—screaming over head at a fixed height of about four feet (we were told) from the ground.

The two of us wriggled on our stomachs side by side, hugging the mud up to our faces but trying to keep it out of our eyes. We could see the tracer rounds coming right at us, and that was all the incentive we needed to stay low (not easy to do while trying to crawl under entangling barbed wire on your back with your M-14 raised slightly in the air to lift the wire). We knew the explosions going off along our sides would not harm us as long as we managed to stay aligned in our crawling lanes and not rear up for any reason. Aside from the streaking stream of bullets overhead, the worst part of the course was sliding down into the mud and water-filled trenches while staying low and keeping a tight grip on our M-14s. After surmounting the last trench situated at the end of the field, we crawled past the barbed wire-protected, mounted machine guns and then, lurching to our feet—with what seemed to be a pound of mud and water trapped in the crotch of our pants as we staggered forward—we were required to charge a stationary dummy with a padded chest screaming "kill! kill!" and plunge our rifle-mounted bayonets into the dummy. We then slogged our way to large wooden bleachers and sat shivering, drenched, and covered in mud, waiting our turn to repeat the course a second time.

The next day was Friday, November 22. Due to the just concluded late-night, muddy exertions on the Infiltration Course, we were given a half-day off from our regular training schedule to clean up equipment inside the barracks, including M-14s, boots, and brass belt buckles. Some guys had transistor radios playing music softly as we chatted and relived the previous nights' experiences while scrubbing and polishing our gear. A little after 11:00 a.m. Pacific Time, one of our platoon comrades—a soft, pasty-faced Texan by the last name of Sweeney—rushed into the barrack's bay from the latrine where he had been listening to a news program while sitting on a commode. In an excited, gleeful voice he shouted: "They've killed the son of a bitch! They shot him! He's dead!"

There was momentary confusion. What the hell was he talking about? Then, someone else who had also heard the news piped up: "It's Kennedy! He's talking about President Kennedy!" The guy nearest the joyous Sweeney—a lanky big guy—grabbed him by the throat and shoved him up against the wall. He could not articulate his anger, but the pulsating vein on his forehead, his glaring eyes and right fist raised high to strike made clear his intention. Cooler heads prevailed; Sweeney was unclutched and slunk away in shame and fear; everyone else crowded around the radio to hear the news.

The entire nation went on high alert, especially military installations around the country. For a while, no one knew for sure what was going on.

Would there be further assassination attempts on other national leaders? Were the Russians behind it? Were other enemies—foreign or domestic—involved? Was the whole country under attack? Fort Ord personnel—including thousands of trainees like us—were immediately armed with live ammo and placed on 24-hour guard duty until national security threats could be discounted. We walked night shifts on designated perimeter areas around Fort Ord in full military gear with given passwords to identify ourselves and uncover potential saboteurs or other enemies. Even though all the assassination details were not uncovered in the subsequent days (or even to everyone's satisfaction today) it was soon determined that immediate threats to our base were unlikely. The tight security measures initially taken at Fort Ord and elsewhere were called off. Instead, all Fort Ord army personnel, again including thousands of us young trainees, were mustered in full dress uniform to parade and stand at attention to witness high ranking Army officers perform military rituals of honor for the nation's fallen commander in-chief.

When we flew back to Salt Lake City (only the second airplane flight we had ever taken, the first being our initial flight to Ford Ord in mid-September) for a two-week leave of absence in December over the Christmas holidays, we had just completed and "graduated" from the combat phase of our military basic training. We arrived home visibly bigger and more mature looking in appearance generally (including unfortunate hints of thinning hairlines). Our older brother Don noted right away that we had gained weight, maybe developed a few new muscles, and he seemed a little more respectful. Our younger sister Sue was temporarily shy and abashed by us. Mom and Dad seemed proud. We were in high spirits, thrilled to be back among family and friends and familiar surroundings after being separated for the first time from such essential elements of our civilian identities. We were slated to begin the second phase of our basic training the day after New Year's Day, where we would presumably acquire the skills essential for our designated military occupational specialization (MOS) as "forward observers" in artillery school at Fort Sill, Oklahoma. But for the time being we reveled in seeing old friends and partaking of family holiday rituals we had previously taken for granted.

Gordon (left) and Gary (right) at Fort Sill, Oklahoma, for artillery training after completing basic training at Fort Ord, California.

When we did return to the Army's smothering embrace at Fort Sill, we were keenly aware of being on the downhill slope of our training, and that we would soon be free from this alien interlude in our lives. At Fort Sill we received rudimentary trigonometry instruction in order to learn how to plot azimuth coordinates for directing artillery fire; dressed in artic gear in order to practice our newly acquired skills in wind-chill temperatures of 30-degrees below zero on the high plains of Fort Sill's artillery range; watched on television as Ed Sullivan introduced The Beatles to America; and counted down the days to our release while Gary spent two weeks in a base hospital recovering from a hernia operation.

The world was changing and was about to change even more, and so were we. But not as soldiers for Uncle Sam. Our military experience had been impactful, but we had failed to identify with the Army—with its strict military procedures and unquestioning obedience to superior officers. We learned that we were not good at blind compliance or the stifling of personal imagination, however necessary that might be to the efficient functioning of military organizations in times of war. We were increasingly aware of the escalating war in Vietnam and the fact that, because of our Utah National Guard status, we would be unlikely combatants in that bloody conflict. Instead, we could concentrate on other priorities, such as resuming our education at the University of Utah. But as our first priority, we determined to submit ourselves to the organizational strictures of another authoritarian, intensely focused goal-oriented institution: The LDS Church and its exacting missionary program for young adults like us. Paradoxically (given our newly-discovered dislike of authoritarian, regimented training), we were about to change our army fatigues for the suits, white shirts, and ties required of Mormon missionary soldiers in God's army of the latter-days.

26.

FAREWELL
Salt Lake City, May 17, 1964

The following account is based on a tape recording
made of the proceedings reported below.

It had already been a long meeting. Too long, really: three preliminary speakers, two musical numbers, and the usual congregational hymns and passing of the sacramental emblems of bread and water to an overflow crowd of ward members and visitors. The Liberty/Liberty Park Ward Chapel, constructed in 1908 and situated fifteen blocks south of Temple Square in Salt Lake City, had recently been renovated but still lacked air-conditioning. Windows had been opened in hope of catching an occasional breeze, and the rhythmic motions of hand-held fans was increasing as many of the congregants attempted to circulate the still air. Increasing also was the scattered wailing of infants and the fidgeting of young children who had already passed the limits of their endurance.

The Liberty/Liberty Park Ward Chapel in Salt Lake City.

In a quavering but earnest and resolute voice, Marjorie Coombs Shepherd was now addressing the congregation. "This is certainly a thrilling sight, to look down at all the faces of our dear friends and family. And it's also a thrilling occasion for us, as you can well imagine. It's something that we've looked forward to for a long time. I guess I've looked forward to it ever since I came home from my own mission and anticipated the time that I would have children to send into the mission field. Today we deeply appreciate your presence here and your words of encouragement to us."

Marjorie was forty-eight, a mother four times over, and devout in her LDS faith. During the Great Depression she had left her home in Salt Lake City to serve an eighteen-month proselyting mission for the LDS Church in the economically devastated regions of North Carolina, Kentucky, Tennessee, and West Virginia. It was there that she met "Shep"—her husband to be, a returned Mormon missionary who was touring the area where he himself had labored for the LDS Church several years previously. At the podium this day, in the Mormon ward where she had raised here children, Marjorie expressed elation and relief. At last two of her children had decided to accept their religious duty to serve God in the mission field. There had been some doubts—her eldest son, Don, had refused the call and married out of the church—but now the family's missionary tradition would be sustained. It was these related themes of religious heritage and her family's moral duty to live up to that heritage by faithfully serving the church that dominated the remainder of her remarks.

"As we were singing the opening song," Marjorie continued, "'Shall the Youth of Zion Falter,' and the verse that says, 'true to the faith that our parents have cherished, true to the truth for which martyrs have perished,' I couldn't help but think in my mind of *our* heritage which we have. Our boys have a wonderful heritage. When I think back, on both sides of my family— my mother's and my father's, and Shep's mother's and father's families, back to great-grandparents and, in two cases, great-great-grandparents of the boys who joined the church and gave up everything they had to accept the gospel—it makes me grateful that we have that heritage. I can't remember who it was, but I recall hearing someone say that the pioneers came out here willingly because they were forced to [laughter]. And in a way that's true. They *were* forced out of their homes. They didn't have anywhere else to go. They were driven. In some cases their homes were burned. Some of them even gave their lives. And yet, they had their free agency; they didn't have to do this. But I'm thankful that our grandparents and great-grand parents had the courage and the faith that the Lord promised to those who were willing to give up everything, that they might have eternal life. I'm thankful too that I haven't been put to that kind of a test. I don't know whether I would have the faith to carry me through or not. But I'm thankful for what has been handed down to me, and I hope that my children will feel this gratitude and appreciation for what is their heritage."

Reaching the conclusion of her brief comments, Marjorie reasserted the firmness of her convictions and offered words of admonition and bless- ing to her sons: "In closing I would just like to bear my testimony to you brothers and sisters, and especially to my family and children. Even though we may look back with pride upon the heritage we have, we can't sit back and rest on the laurels of our forefathers. Each and every single one of us have missionary responsibilities that our boy now have. I know that if they are prayerful and they work hard and strive to learn the Spanish language, if they will have love in their hearts for the people with whom they come in contact, if they will overlook their differences and faults and see only the good and be willing to accept them as they are, I know that the Lord will bless them."

As Marjorie took her seat, the congregation readied itself to hear what Alvin Shepherd would have to say concerning his sons' appointments to serve the LDS Church for two years in Mexico. Alvin (Shep) was an expansive, gregarious man who enjoyed being with people and loved to reminisce with old friends. If not formally eloquent in his speech, he was nonetheless a self-confident speaker who seldom prepared or used notes. Although popular with his associates, Shep had often struggled financially, moving from one sales job to another as he attempted to overcome old business debts and support his family. But today was a day to savor, a day to share with friends and loved ones.

"Brothers and sisters, I'm so happy tonight to be here with you," Shep began. "You know, all of us at some time or other have our problems and discouragements. Sometimes we wonder about the struggles we have to make. As I have sat here tonight and as I have seen the faces of you grand people who have come to be with us, to help us rejoice in the occasion of our boys going into the mission field, I thought that all the problems that you have and I have—all seem insignificant and so far away when we have the spirit of our Heavenly Father to be with us, when we have our friends and our relatives and those who are close, whom we love, with us on an occasion of this type."

It was also a day for Shep to reflect on his experiences, to identify himself with his sons and connect their approaching experience with his own. It was a time to reaffirm kinship links and acknowledge the sustaining reciprocity of the local religious community of which he was a part. "I must mention one or two names tonight. Sitting in the back of the hall there's a man who came in just as the service was starting with his wife: Brother and Sister Kjar. Brother Joseph Kjar was my bishop when I was called over thirty years ago to go into the Southern States Mission. My mother was his ward clerk. A short few months after my father was killed, Bishop Kjar saw fit to call me into the mission field. And now it's been just a few short months since my mother passed away, and Bishop McLean has seen fit to call Gary and Gordon into the mission field.

"I was reading my missionary diary not so long ago, and every once in a while I would find a reference to feeling the closeness of my father, when I was depressed or sorrowful in my mission. And then I thought of my mother. I'm sure as our boys go into the mission field that there's no one who ever lived who wanted to see them go on a mission more than my mother— their grandmother. And I'm certain her influence will be with them, as well as their grandfather's.

"We have most of the high council and their wives here tonight, the stake clerks, former stake presidents, and the current stake presidency of the Liberty Stake. These brethren on the stand are men that I have learned to love and appreciate. They have supported me, and I hope I have supported them. And so I am grateful my brothers and sisters for the friends that are here. Others have called, unable to be here. And of course we're grateful for the relatives who are here."

Shep paused as he surveyed the congregation. There was an unusually large number of young people in attendance—schoolmates and friends of the twins. These associations now became the theme of the remainder of Shep's extemporaneous discourse. "Our lives are full. But the thing that's been great, brothers and sisters, is our children. All through their lives they've had lots of friends, and it's been such a pleasure as they've grown up to have their friends in our home, to get acquainted with them. I look around now and see many of them that Gary and Gordon have grown up with. It makes you happy and thrilled to know that these boys and girls—young men and women now—have played such a part in our son's lives, and that Gary and Gordon have played a similar part in the lives of their friends.

"I think of Philip over there, Philip Starr, who's going to Stanford University on one of the finest scholarships to be given; a brilliant, outstanding young man. Philip and Gary, of course, served together in the student body presidency at South High two years ago. Nothing would keep Philip from being here tonight, from being on the program to play a piano solo. He came down from school, made a special trip. I understand he's got to hurry back to California. He's got a tough exam back there tomorrow morning. I don't know how clear his mind is going to be for that exam.

"And then I think of David Lingwall over here. David has come in and out of our home for years; he doesn't have a lot to say at times. But I was thrilled tonight with the clarinet solo that he played. I think many of us were waiting to what he was going to play before he finally began [laughter]. But once he got started, he did an excellent job. We love you, David. I hope our boys are an inspiration to you.

"Then these other two young men sitting here have also been into our home a lot. Mike Mitchell came into the church about a year ago. Before that he wasn't a member. But didn't he give a sweet prayer to open this meeting? Mike was an outstanding athlete at South High—captain of the football team his senior year. He played softball with our boys. The team from the McKinley Ward—which he now belongs to—went to the All Church tournament, and Mike was honored as the outstanding player of the tournament, before he was even a member of the church. And the thrill that came to us when Mike came over one day and said, 'Gordon, I want to be baptized now. I want to join the church. Would you baptize me?' You know brothers and sisters, it's marvelous to live in a home and have the young people come into your home and see these things happen.

"Lorin Larsen here, he's going to give the closing prayer. He's grown a little taller than the rest of them [Lorin stood more than six feet five inches tall]. When he served in the army national guard he chose, and I think they encouraged him, to join the MPs [military police]. When he stands up, you'll see why [laughter]. Lorin has got his own mission call. He'll be going next month to the Eastern States New York Mission and will have a grand time serving at the World's Fair."

Then, after reiterating his personal convictions and gratitude, Shep concluded by invoking the blessings of God for the congregation and for his children: "May the Lord bless you all. May he bless Gary and Gordon, and may he bless Donald and their little sister Susan. Touch their hearts. Bless them with a desire of service and love and understanding."

Alvin Brighton Shepherd and Marjorie Coombs Shepherd.

Gordon was nervous. Over the years he had become almost phobic about public speaking. Ever since turning twelve years of age, he had stubbornly refused to accept any church speaking assignments, even after Bishop McLean had become quite insistent in his requests. Mormon youths are supposed to be exposed to regular opportunities for public speaking so that when the time comes for them to render missionary service (or accept other adult religious duties) they will be prepared and more effective in their performance. But this time Gordon *was* prepared. That is, he had spent a considerable amount of time thinking about and rehearsing what he should say on the occasion of his missionary farewell. There was, however, the distinct possibility that once he faced an audience he would blank out and have nothing to communicate except stammered emotions. This was precisely what Gordon feared most. Unlike his father, he had no trust in his ability for extemporaneous expression.

Alvin Shepherd squeezed Gordon's arm, whispered a word of encouragement, and suddenly Gordon found himself moving toward the pulpit as though in a trance. It was now his turn to say something. He stared at the microphone for several uncertain seconds and then began in an awkward cadence: "Our newly-remodeled chapel is certainly beautiful. But I don't know about this stand—the way it seems to serve your right up into the jaws of the audience [laughter]. I think you can tell how I calm I am [laughter]. I must have cut myself shaving a dozen times today" [more laughter as the congregation took cognizance of the tape on Gordon's Adam's apple].

Inane comments, perhaps, but the laughter was bracing. The generous receptiveness of the congregation encouraged Gordon to believe that he was going to be alright, and that he could handle this speechifying business as long as he had sufficient time to prepare his thoughts. He proceeded to express a litany of appreciation and gratitude to those who had meant the most to him while growing up, beginning with his parents. A strong sense of duty (one shared by Gary) toward fulfilling parental aspirations was clearly evident in his brief tribute: "I think I'd be very ungrateful if I didn't express a number of thank-yous. I'd like to thank my parents for everything that they've done. They're strong people. They're strong in the church. Their faith is strong. They've laid whatever foundations we possess. They've set an example, and they've set a standard. Now it's true we've not always risen to that standard. In fact, many times we've fallen way short. But my mother and father have done everything in their power to raise us as God has commanded. They will be blameless before him."

Gordon then spoke of his brother Gary, relating a single anecdote from their recent army basic training experience to which he attached religious significance. He told of how the sight on Gary's M-14 rifle had been bent the day they were supposed to qualify in marksmanship at the firing range at Fort Ord, California, affecting his ability to shoot accurately. A minimum score was required in order to graduate from basic training. Anyone scoring less than the minimum would be held back (at least that was the threat made by training officers) and would have to repeat the course while his comrades moved on to more advanced training assignments in other parts of the country. Fearful of separation and feeling completely helpless, Gordon crouched behind a convenient sand dune and prayed for diving assistance to help Gary through the test: "the first-time," Gordon admitted, "that I have prayed earnestly for help in many years." At the end of the day, Gary's score on the rifle range was the exact score needed to pass. "Most important," Gordon concluded as he reflected on the experience, "it was together in basic training that Gary and I further strengthened our brotherhood and mutually confirmed our desires to serve missions for the church.

"I've got another brother and a little sister," Gordon continued. "Don, maybe you're not aware of the admiration and respect that I have for you and your artistic talent. I know that we had many a battle royal in our younger years, but I'd like you to also know that, in between brawls [laughter], Gary and I never passed up the opportunity to drag our friends downstairs to show off your artwork. And Sue, I probably won't even recognized you when I get back after you will have grown so much. But I want you know that you've been a wonderful little sister, and I love you."

Having acknowledged indebtedness to family first Gordon went on to single out his closest boyhood friends for appreciation—particularly Lorin, Mike, Dave, Phillip, and Ron Swenson—as well as several adult neighbors and local church leaders who had played influential roles in both his and Gary's formative years. All were being recognized as part of the intimate social network that helped to shape and channel the course that had brought both Gary and Gordon, within the structure of Mormon society, to this religious turning point in their lives. "I would like to thank all those who influenced me," Gordon summarized, "who have taught me, who have set an example for me, who have stood out high in their character and accomplishments. In expressing thanks tonight I think there is just one whom I could thank, and it would be sufficient for all. And that, of course, is the Lord. Perhaps going on a mission is a good way to do this. Perhaps it's a good way to pay back a portion—a small portion—of the many things he has given to me."

For Gordon, this was the first time that he had made such public confessions. It seemed to him that the occasion demanded it, that if he was going to accept a mission call he should do so with serious intent and commit himself to work hard to overcome his fears, his pride, and other perceived weaknesses; that he should commence now to speak as a willing and dedicated representative of his church, even though he realized that his religious faith and understanding were still weak and underdeveloped. He had given careful thought to what he was going say next—it was to be a declaration of a new attituded and his determination to succeed in performing the missionary role that he and Gary were about to assume.

"It seems to me that today is a pretty important occasion. In fact, I'd like to go so far as to say that you here are witnessing a great event. Now it's not a great event because the Shepherd brothers are going on missions—it's not a great event because we're being shipped out of the country for two years [laughter]. And it's certainly not a great event on the basis of today's proceedings alone. But it is a great event because two young men have been called by God to preach his gospel. And that because of this, no matter how poor or mediocre we may prove to be as missionaries, there will be somebody who will recognize the truth and be brought into the church. And is this not a great event? Is it not a great event when the membership of God' church is increased? That because of it there will others who will be able to participate in the greatest work in the world today, that of building up the kingdom of God on the earth. Are these not all great events? Is this not cause for celebration? I think it is. And I think we've been shouldered with heavy responsibilities. I'm particularly apprehensive about the responsibility that's been given to me. I know that the only way that I will be able to carry out this responsibility is through constant prayer and by remaining close to the Lord; that if I do this I will be blessed. I will be strengthened. I will be given guidance, and I will be able to the work that is necessary."

Gary and Gordon, 1964 missionary farewell portrait.

Like Gordon, Gary was not especially fond of public speaking. Still, as student body president of his high school, he had gained valuable experience and a modest measure of self-confidence in addressing large gatherings. Striding toward the pulpit, Gary eyed the big clock positioned on a side wall of the chapel. The meeting had already run ten minutes over its scheduled time, and another ward congregation that shared the chapel was waiting outside to enter and commence their own Sunday service. As the final speaker, it was clear he would have to hurry. "Time is very short, brothers and sisters. As a matter of fact it's gone, and so I'm afraid I'm going to have to save my sermons for the Mexican people [laughter]. But there are still a few things I would like to say."

The few things Gary had to say were quite similar in both their form and content to the remarks just concluded by Gordon. There were the same kinds of acknowledgments and tributes to the same individuals, particularly to his parents and twin brother. There was the same underlying confessional tone in reference to perceived shortcomings and follies of the past supplemented with a determined resolve for atonement through committed effort and reliance on God's help. These are attitudes typical of those who submit to the demands of a call to discipline themselves in the service of what they believe is a transcendent cause.

"I would like to let you know that it's a real pleasure to be standing where I am this afternoon," Gary said next. "It's a dream of our parents come true and a hope of mine fulfilled, that both Gord and I might be found worthy and willing to serve a mission for the church. And it's a pleasure too because of you people who are here this afternoon. A good friend of mine once asked me when it was that I was the happiest in life. I thought that was a good question, but I didn't have a good answer. I think I do now. I enjoy myself most when I am in the company of my good friends and with people whom I love and respect. And so, as you can see, I'm very happy this afternoon. Thanks to Mike Mitchell, who's been almost like a brother to Gordon. Thanks too to Lorin, Ron, Dave, and Phil, because they've been our brothers too.

"I remember a General Conference when President David O. McKay said that one of the greatest blessings that could come to a father or mother would be to have a son or daughter sincerely say that they had been born of good parents. My brothers and sisters I say to you that I have been born of good parents whose greatest concern has always been for their children. For this I am very grateful, and of them I am very proud. I just hope that we can live up to the high hopes they have for us and that some of the disappointments along the way to this afternoon can be made up.

"People often ask me: Do I like being a twin? Well, I don't know what I would ever have done without my twin brother. So many times Gord and I are almost the same person in thought and feeling. We've been constant companions for each other all through our lives. Gord's a challenge to live up to, because he's a better and stronger me in so many ways. He is a strong person. He has a strong character, strong convictions, and he stands up for the things he believes are right. The things Gord stands for are good; they're going to pay off in the mission field. Who could ask for a better friend than my twin brother?

"Today I'm also grateful for my older brother Don. I'm proud of the many successes in art and at the university that he's achieved. And of course there is our little sister Susan, who so eagerly observes and wants to follow all that we do. I love her very much too."

Gary concluded, as did Gordon before him, with a declaration of his resolve to commit himself to the missionary cause of the LDS Church and a confession of his dependency on the grace of God to see him through the tests to come. "I'm happy with my call to serve in the Mexican Mission and for the opportunity I will have to strengthen my own beliefs and increase my own testimony of the truthfulness of the gospel. I know my testimony will grow stronger than it is now. This has been promised to me in my patriarchal blessing. I've also been promised that through diligence and conscientious effort I will be blessed with wisdom and understanding, and that I will have the spirit of the Lord to be with me in all things. It is my hope and prayer this afternoon that I may be worthy to receive these blessings, that Gordon and I may both serve honorable missions, and that we may return home again having done the best work of which we were capable."

The meeting had been a long and taxing one. Many of the speakers' remarks had been repetitious in both form and substance. Nonetheless, it may be presumed that most of the congregation left that day feeling that the religious expectations of Mormon society had been satisfied. The idealization of certain core LDS religious values had occurred. A suitable amount of sincerity and seriousness had been displayed by the fledgling missionaries, demonstrating the kind of character transformation expected of Mormon youths as they cross the threshold into adulthood. The values of family, kin, and community bonds had been rhetorically reiterated; and in fact, the local religious community itself—in the process of assembling for and witnessing this farewell event—had been reaffirmed in its collective commitment to the missionary cause of the LDS Church.

As for us, motivated more strongly by a sense of shared duty to fulfill our parents' hopes than by our own religious convictions, we readied ourselves to sustain our family's faith tradition by becoming self-disciplined students of Spanish and missionary disciples of the LDS Church in Mexico—a country whose language, people, and culture would dominate our consciousness and concerted efforts for the next two years of our lives.

27.

MEXICO

*D*own in Mexico/There's song they know, Chiapanecas!/It's a lively thing/ You can't help but sing . . . Come and eat a fat tamale/Come and drink some fresh atole/Eat and drink you need not hurry/Though you pay none do not worry ~ Verse fragments from songs we learned studying about Mexico at Liberty Elementary in the fifth grade.

México, creo en ti (Mexico, I believe in thee) ~ Refrain line from Ricardo López Méndez's patriotic poem, *El Credo Mexicano*.

Pobre México, tan lejos de Dios y tan cerca de los Estados Unidos (Poor Mexico, so far from God and so close to the United States) ~ Political lament popularly attributed to 19th century Mexican president, Porfirio Díaz.

"You know," the border official said in lightly accented English to the two of us sitting in front of him, "the thing we don't like about you *Norte Americanos* is that you think you can buy everything, that you can bribe us whenever you want." He shook his head in sad but righteous indignation as he refused to even look at the three 100 peso bills (at the time, the rough equivalent of $25 U. S.) that Gary had placed on his desk.

Gordon was aghast: "What the Sam Hill was Gary doing!?" Gary looked the official in the face and then calmly pulled out three more 100 peso bills and laid them on top of the first three.

The official glanced down, barely nodded his head, and, while scooping up the bills, jerked his thumb over his shoulder and said, "Alright, get out of here; go tell your parents you can cross back in."

After having spent two years as Mormon missionaries in the central interior and southernmost reaches of the Mexican Republic, we were in the northern border city of Nogales, about 70 miles south of Tucson, Arizona. We had just surrendered our visas and crossed the border to meet our parents and younger sister, Susan, who were waiting for us on the other side. Our plan was to re-enter Mexico as tourists, so we could travel back to the places we had fallen in love with and introduce our parents and sister to the many Mexicans whose lives had touched ours and ours theirs. That plan was only momentarily sidetracked when the two of us were escorted into the border official's office to be informed that, without the visas we had just surrendered, we could not reenter the country as tourists.

Gary shrugged as he and Gordon walked back with the good news for their parents and sister: "Yeah, sure, it's illegal to offer bribes," Gary said, "but after living in Mexico City for so long, I learned that that's often what you have to do in order to get things done around here. It's the norm. You guys working in the jungles and mountains of the southern mission, are *campesinos* (peasant country bumpkins) when it comes to negotiating with government officials and big city cops. The main thing right now is, for fifty bucks, we're going back to Mexico. Otherwise, we'd be heading for Tucson." And about this, Gary was unquestionably right.

When we located Dad, Mom, and Sue waiting for us in the parking lot we told them everything was settled, that we were good to go. But we didn't tell them how things had been settled. What followed after recrossing the border into Mexico was a cram-packed, ten-day journey and tour of both our mission areas that generated its own set of adventures and anecdotes worthy of being told elsewhere (see *Mormon Passage: A Missionary Chronicle*, University of Utah Press, 1998).

In March, 1964, after the two of us completed six months of regular army basic training for the Utah National Guard at Fort Ord, California, and Fort Sill, Oklahoma, we met for "worthiness interviews" with our Liberty Park Ward bishop, Gilbert McClain. Bishop McClain refrained from conducting a relentless interrogation of our youthful peccadillos, judged us sufficiently worthy to serve, and we immediately submitted applications to become LDS missionaries. We were 20 years old. A few weeks later we received our official missionary callings and assignments from church headquarters in Salt Lake: Gary was assigned to the Mexican Mission with headquarters in Mexico City; Gordon was assigned to the Southeast Mexican Mission with headquarters in Veracruz. We were both delighted. As kids we had first studied about Mexico in Mrs. McDermaid's fifth grade social studies class at Liberty Elementary. Our initial learning at the age of eleven about Mexican music, food, geography, and a warm, generous people living south of the U. S. border had left a lasting, positive impression.

Prior to actually leaving for Mexico, both of us spent three months at the Language Training Mission (LTM) in Provo, Utah, for a crash course in Spanish and intensive memorization of the lessons we would soon be using to persuade potential Mexican converts to embrace our inherited Mormon faith. Neither one of us had previously studied Spanish in school. Both of us pushed ourselves to the limits of our ability to learn the language and meet the demanding memorization objectives of the program. Especially for Gordon—who had been a lackadaisical student in high school—this was the first time he had ever disciplined himself to doggedly pursue a rigorous course of study.

In late August, 1964, the two of us boarded a plane together with other novice missionaries to Mexico City, which is where we parted company for two years when Gary deplaned with several of our companions from the LTM. Gordon continued his flight on to Veracruz, a port city on the Gulf of Mexico, with two other newly-minted missionaries from Prove. Of their parting, Gary wrote in his journal: "With a large, painful lump in my throat, and fighting off sudden, surprising chills in my heart and welling tears, I shook hands goodbye with Gordon for the first time in our lives. It's not likely we'll see each other again during this mission. And yet, though separated, I know we will go about our work as missionaries and not be hindered by our mutual loss."

Later, Gordon wrote to Gary: "Once in the air again after leaving Mexico City, I kept looking out the plane's window at the darkness and lights from cities and towns below, wondering what these places held in store for us in the months to come." The reality was, of course, we had no true way of adequately anticipating what lay ahead: the cultural tests and physical challenges of living in a vast, foreign country where differences of material abundance between rich and poor were even greater than in our own; the small triumphs and exuberant moments of prideful accomplishment in the face of a certain amount of opposition and adversity; our genuine growth and maturation as young adults; the development of lasting friendships with many of our missionary companions (alongside mutual aversion with others); the surprising solidarity and instant warmth and identification with church members in Mexico, a thousand miles from home; and, of course, the particularities of those places and people who—for an intensive period of our young lives—would become the objects of our admiration and fondest hopes, as well as numerous disappointments and frustration.

Upon arriving in Mexico, we quickly discovered that, notwithstanding our proud memorizing achievements in Provo, we could barely understand a few words of spoken Spanish, let alone carry out a simple conversation with native speakers. As Gordon put it in his first letter to Gary: "Gar, I don't know about you, but for me it's been like starting from scratch with the language (so fast, so difficult to follow) . . . It's one thing to have all the lessons memorized and quite another to communicate spontaneously with people." In turn, Gary reflected in his journal: "Received a letter from Gord today. . . He's been having the same problems as me: sick with the food, trouble with the language, a hard time really getting down to brass tacks, etc. I know he'll pull through—it's me I worry about." A good foundation for ultimate language competence in Mexico had been laid for us at the Language Training Mission, but it would take months of frustrating effort and exposure to native speakers before we gained reasonable confidence in our ability to communicate effectively.

Gordon (left) and Gary (right) writing letters and in a missionary journal, circa December, 1964, as new missionaries posted in San Martin and Mexico City.

Unlike our negative experience of enforced obedience to rigorously imposed rules in Army basic training, in Mexico we were predisposed to believe that mission rules were ultimately sanctioned by God and, of course, we were not subjected to physical or verbal force to make us conform. Rather, we were intrinsically motived to conform. We wanted to do the right thing. We believed the things we had been taught growing up by our parents and admired local church leaders would be reflected in the experiences that

God had in store for us in Mexico as we crossed the threshold of adulthood, securely following the inherited religious tradition of our Latter-day Saint ancestors.

In addition to Mexico City, Gary's mission boundaries included the cities of Guadalajara and Querétaro north of the capital, Morelia and Manzanillo to the west, and Chilpancingo and Acapulco to the south. Headquartered in Veracruz, Gordon's mission boundaries were staked out by the cities of Jalapa and Poza Rica north of Veracruz, Puebla and San Martín to the west, Minatitlán and Mérida to the east, and Tuxtla Gutiérrez, Villa Flores, and Tapachula to the south.

This 1997 map shows 16 LDS mission headquarter cities in Mexico. During the time we were in Mexico (1964-66), there were only 5 missions. In 2020, there was a total of 35 LDS missions in Mexico, with 7 separate missions in Mexico City alone. Image courtesy of the University of Illinois Press.

Both of us spent months in apprenticeship roles as "junior companions," following the lead of our more experienced, senior companions. During this period, Gary and his companions succeeded in converting dozens of Mexicans to the LDS faith, especially in the immense, urban confines of Mexico City. Meanwhile, Gordon and his companions were relatively less successful in recruiting new church members in the smaller and more traditional towns and cities of Southern Mexico. After a year of toiling in missionary ranks as a junior companion, Gordon was suddenly promoted to seniorship and sent with a new companion to "open up" a distant town to Mormon proselyting: Villa Flores in the remote mountains of Chiapas, a couple of hundred miles from the Guatemalan border. Shortly thereafter, Gary was elevated to a supervising position in Mexico City, was promoted a few months later to become an assistant to the mission president, and subsequently was sent, with Keith Flake (cousin of future senator Jeff Flake from Arizona as his companion), to open up the Pacific coast city of Manzanillo to Mormon proselyting. At about the same time, Gordon returned to Veracruz to become his mission president's assistant, where he spent the last five months of his mission in Mexico.

Needless to say, over this period of time we experienced a tremendous amount of growth and maturation—not only with regard to language and missionary skills, but also as young adults, capable and willing to take on adult responsibilities. We began to realize that, even though we were relatively inexperienced youths, our missionary status conferred upon us an adult religious authority which our investigators and converts took seriously. We, along with our missionary companions, were thrust into religiously important pastoral roles that required us to bless children and the sick or dying; conduct religious services, including funerals; arrange marriage ceremonies; act as confidants and family counselors to Mexican adults overwhelmed with personal problems; as well as teach and convert religious seekers and perform baptisms.

Changes in missionary status over time were accompanied by a corresponding change in our perceptions of missionary work and companion relations. As senior companions we became directly responsible for what we did or did not accomplish. We were no longer able to second-guess the judgment of our previous senior companions or knowingly shrug our shoulders when the work seemed not to be progressing well. Problematic *junior* companions soon became a persistent theme in our letters and journal accounts. Although we made occasional cynical comments during this phase of our missionary careers, our rhetoric (recorded in journal entries, letters, and mission publications) became more pious and platitudinal as we assumed positions of authority and increasingly identified with the formal structure of the mission organization. Our disdainful, impertinent comments about the religious beliefs and practices of those whom we were trying to convert also increased, as we had to assume the lead role in prodding investigators and battling with both Catholic and Protestant detractors.

We, like other ambitious missionaries, regarded official mission work norms (the number of hours worked per week, the number of doors knocked on, lessons given, baptisms performed, etc.) as representing a minimum standard of acceptable performance and routinely pushed ourselves to exceed them. From similarly motivated companions we learned that it was dedicated consistency that paid off in the long run, and we were willing to make the necessary investments of ourselves in order to be successful, thereby cultivating and sustaining the high regard of our fellow missionaries and mission leaders. Such an orientation closely approximates the ascetic religious attitude celebrated by Max Weber as the "Protestant Ethic," namely: the psychological reciprocity of believing oneself to be chosen of God and the relentless compulsion to devote one's resources in a sober, calculated effort toward the accomplishment of a sacred cause in the company of other devotees.

Not to disparage the religious experience of others, but it was this kind of devotion that we often identified as spirituality. When in our journal accounts or correspondence we spoke of being guided by the Lord—of having God's spirit—it was the rhetoric of high morale, exhilaration and happiness in the cause despite (or occasionally because of) some degree of deprivation and adversity. We experienced spirituality when achieving unity of action with comrades, and, perhaps most important, as a growing self-confidence in our ability to do missionary work—especially in our ability to speak and act from both experience and spontaneity in coping with problematic situations in a foreign land.

It was when we were both assistants to the president in our respective missions that we began formulating plans through the mail and by phone to reunite with our parents at the U.S. border in order to return with them to the places in Mexico where we had served for two years. A small but significant part of our planning included a surreptitious meeting in San Martín—the town where Gordon had first been assigned as a novice missionary upon arrival in 1964—which was adjacent to the boundary of Gary's mission area, 90 miles east of Mexico City. We say surreptitious because we had made plans to meet without consulting or getting permission from our respective mission presidents—Jasper McClellan, President of the Mexican Mission and Seville Hatch, President of the Southeast Mexican Mission. (Both of these men were Anglo Mormon "colonists" who had grown up in the LDS community of Colónia Juarez in the northern Mexican state of Chihuahua.)

Excerpt from Gordon's missionary journal, dated June 23, 1966: "Back in Veracruz. No admonitions from President Hatch about the fiascos of our trip to Tapachula [including Gordon's arrest and a night spent in the Tapachula jail for failure to have his visa in his possession when unexpectedly confronted by Mexican immigration officials who boarded a bus he was traveling on]. He simply told me and Porter [Gordon's companion as assistant to the president] that he was glad we were home safe and sound, and that we should start making preparations for district conference in Puebla day after tomorrow. This is a conference I've been looking forward to for weeks. Gary and I have made plans to meet in San Martín Saturday afternoon."

Excerpt from Gary's letter to Gordon, received June 23, 1966: "Hearing your voice again on the phone after almost two years was unbelievable. Now the twenty-fifth of June is almost upon us, but I feel more like its December, it's Christmas Eve, and I'm eight years-old. See you shortly. Your brother, Gar."

Excerpt from Gordon's missionary journal, dated June 26, 1966. "Conference in Puebla Saturday was excellent . . . [but] I found my thoughts wandering to contemplate the prospects of meeting Gary later in the day at San Martín. After conference ended, London [the mission secretary], Porter, and I piled into our Volkswagen and headed out to the dusty little *pueblo* where I began my mission. How should I act? How should I feel? Unrestrained excitement? Tears and shouts of joy? Well, it just wasn't that kind of reunion. Both Gary and I characteristically restrain our feelings in public. But beyond this, our personal bond is so secure and mutually understood that it seems to transcend the need for such displays.

"We met on the outskirts of San Martín and introduced our respective companions. Gary was with Elder Garza, the other assistant to President McClellan in Mexico City. I joked, with little room to talk, about Gary's receding hairline; he commented on my emaciated appearance (exaggerated I'm sure, by Elder London's larger-than-my-size navy blue suit—which occasionally I borrow for conference apparel ever since losing my only suit to a thief in Veracruz). Past and present were quickly bridged as we drove into town . . . [where we] discussed our release plans and the possibility of the folks coming down in August to pick us up. After an hour or so of pleasant conversation, it was time to go. We all shook hands, exchanged *abrazos* [hugs], and pronounced our *hasta luegos* [see you laters]. Gary and Elder Garza got in their car, and we watched as they turned east to Mexico City. We then headed in the opposite direction, toward Puebla and Veracruz."

Gordon (left) and Gary (right) with our respective missionary companions Bill Porter, Steve London, and Santiago Garza in San Martín, Mexico, June 25, 1966.

Two months later, Gary was granted permission by President McClellan to cross mission boundaries on a bus from Mexico City to Veracruz in order to attend Gordon's *relevo* (farewell release) from the Southeast Mexican Mission. The two of us—with President Hatch's blessing this time—then boarded another bus back to Mexico City. On the way we read each other's missionary journals and, in so doing, conceivably germinated the idea for writing a collaborative book someday about our missionary adventures in Mexico. Gordon spent several days in Mexico City with Gary, meeting some of his convert families and co-teaching several missionary lessons that Gary had scheduled with other persons who had indicated an interest in investigating the LDS Church and its teachings. As Gary had done in his behalf in Veracruz, Gordon attended Gary's *relevo* in Mexico City as the final speaker at his farewell event. The following day, the two of us flew to Nogales to meet our parents and sister Sue, who were waiting for us at the U.S./Mexican border.

When we returned home to Salt Lake City in August 1966, the discrepancy between the relatively enclosed world we left behind in Mexico and the mass dissent and social upheaval taking place then in the United States could scarcely have been more dramatic. Like many other youths of our generation, we had passively supported what seemed to be the obviously justifiable moral and political goals of the civil rights movement for Black Americans. After our missions we became increasingly disturbed by the LDS Church's apparently intransigent racial policy, which at that time was to withhold lay priesthood and temple privileges from people of African ancestry. We also came to oppose American prosecution of the war in Vietnam and, as with civil rights, passively sympathized with the anti-war movement then gaining locomotive momentum on college campuses around the country. These movements massively called into question the rightness of taken-for-granted authoritarian systems, and they had an impact on our thinking as we readjusted to secular life.

Perhaps most important, our re-immersion as students at the University of Utah provided a new and stimulating outlet for our awakening intellectual interests, which had remained largely dormant during our missionary hiatus. However unconsciously and gradually, our missionary experience had contributed greatly to our intellectual maturation, as for the first time in our lives we disciplined ourselves to study and learned to concentrate systematically on a particular set of teachings for making sense of the world. The overall plausibility of those ideas had never in our experience been effectively challenged before. But now, at the university, removed from the intensive plausibility structure of the mission organization, and with much the same motivation to succeed as students as we had sustained while functioning as missionaries in Mexico, secular systems of thought and critical analysis gradually began to have more appeal for us than the theological doctrines of the Mormon faith.

Despite our missionary experience in Mexico, neither of us followed the Mormon norm of an active career of religious callings and organizational assignments in the lay structure of the LDS Church. We became interested in the study of sociology and pursued graduate degrees. Gary obtained his Ph.D. from Michigan State University, and Gordon received his from the

State University of New York (SUNY) at Stony Brook. We have subsequently collaborated on research and writing projects of mutual interest.

Although we have become detached over the years from the religious commitments of our youth to the LDS Church, we have cultivated an active scholarly interest in the study of religion in general and Mormonism in particular. Many relatives and friends, both in the church and out, may see this as perverse, but we do not. In pursuing our own paths, we have never wished to injure the religious sensibilities of other people. We continue to value our Mormon heritage and look back without regret on our missionary days in Mexico as a time of challenge and growth in our lives. Our missions afforded us a singular opportunity to be exposed to a distinct culture, its language and especially its people, whom we learned to love and appreciate in ways that provided us greater insight into the strengths and weaknesses of our own culture. In turn, these insights sparked our interest in attempting to understand the variations of human life in different times and places that we later pursued as students of sociology.

28.

HELLO SOCIOLOGY

It was the fall of 1966. Gordon and I had just completed two-year missions in Mexico for the LDS Church, and prior to that we had spent six months in Army basic training in California and Oklahoma. Now I was sitting in my first sociology class on the first day of school at the University of Utah in Salt Lake City. The instructor was young, a new assistant professor by the name of Charles Anderson. He was speaking with passion and urgency about the failure of so many Americans to engage morally, intellectually, and directly with the world in which they lived—content, instead, to "merely sit back and bask in the dark glow of their idiot boxes."

This was a phrase that captivated my imagination: "So many Americans . . . merely sit back and bask in the dark glow of their idiot boxes." I wrote it down. It was literate. It was pithy. It spoke to and reflected a fundamental truth. (I avoided owning a TV for the next twenty years, partially as a result of that statement.) I had always been interested in history and literature—I had done a lot of reading in both. I had no idea what sociology was. I was just filling up my schedule with required courses after a three-year absence from school. But now here was a young man standing before me, not a whole lot older than myself, speaking with the eloquence of a writer, the moral clarity of a philosopher, and with the critical analysis of a historian, but one who pierced the complexities of our own time rather than those of a bygone era.

I was hooked. It was the Sixties. Vietnam was raging. The Civil Rights Movement was surging, tugging along in its wake the emergent feminist movement and a dozen other liberation movements. The youth counter culture was blossoming. Urban riots were exploding, and political assassinations had moved from the realm of fiction to horrifying reality. Taken-for-granted assumptions of authority and tradition that upheld structures of inequality were being massively challenged on all sides. I remember waking up many mornings with a slight adrenalin rush in anticipation of what new outrageous development that day might bring. The study of sociology seemed a perfect fit for the times. I wanted to understand these times, to participate in them more fully, and maybe—with the increased insight I thought sociology might give me—to help change, for the better, the little part of the world that I lived in.

My brother Gordon had also enrolled in an introductory sociology course that semester. He also was intrigued and exhilarated by what he encountered. In a concurrent social psychology class, we were both reading *Escape from Freedom* by the psychoanalytic philosopher, Eric Fromm, as well as some of the writings of Theodor Adorno on the authoritarian personality and its relationship to the rise and sustenance of fascism and the anti-Semitic horrors of Nazi Germany. We pondered the shocking, interlocking significance of Stanly Milgram's experiments on obedience to authority. Later during that fateful year, we read Fyodor Dostoyevsky's celebrated chapter from *The Brothers Karamazov*, "The Grand Inquisitor"—a meditation on the massive difficulties that impede human potential for freedom and choice. In sociology we were reading C. Wright Mill's declaration on the means and purposes of sociology, what he called *The Sociological Imagination*.

While driving an Army truck to Eastern Wyoming and South Dakota as part of a National Guard training exercise, Gordon and I explored for hours in conversation the implications of our readings and were elated to discover that we had indeed begun to acquire Mill's "sociological imagination"—a perspective that allowed us to apply the analytical concepts we had learned at school to achieve a richer comprehension of events daily erupting in the world around us and that we were experiencing in our own lives.

Our growing conviction that the study of sociology could take us somewhere we wanted to go—and that we might be good at it—was strengthened by other encounters. I took a class in small group dynamics. Again, the instructor—Don Hastings— was young, new, and intense. He assigned a flurry of what seemed, to un-versed freshmen and sophomores, impossibly difficult, sophisticated writing by the likes of Bales, Parsons, Shills, Emerson, and Homans. He told us to write critical synopses of what we had read and understood. I struggled mightily to comprehend what I read and then to write a coherent synthesis that employed a conceptual vocabulary I was just barely learning. I felt like I must have failed. I was stunned to get back my essay with a note from Professor Hastings congratulating me and asking permission to make a copy of it for his files. My self-confidence began to edge up a bit. Not only could I talk competently to my brother about what we were jointly learning, I could also, apparently, write something more formally in a way that impressed my professor.

Gordon and I both took a course in the sociology of religion—something we didn't know you could do. (We gradually discovered that one of the great appeals of sociology is that it can apply to anything that involves social interaction between human beings—that there can be a sociology of any human activity one may be interested in and has adequate knowledge about.) In any event, the instructor was Lowell Bennion, who was Assistant Dean of Students, a theologian of some renown, an early American student of the sociology of Max Weber, and an adjunct professor in the sociology department. He was also a very humble man. One day, at the beginning of a class period, he gave a sincere apology for having been, in his estimation, inadequately prepared in his presentation of material during the previous class. He said he could do better and, with our permission, would like to try to go over that material again. We were stunned. We hadn't noticed anything amiss before. But it hadn't been up to his own standards. I was moved by such a display of professional commitment and public openness to his students.

Lowell Bennion introduced Gordon and me to Max Weber's analysis of authority—a concept we had explored in other courses but not from a specifically sociological perspective. We were particularly interested in Weber's treatment of charisma as a type of social authority that eventually must become routinized, or transformed, into forms of institutional control after it has accomplished its revolutionary mission. We have followed this interest up to the present time in the research and writing we have done on the role of revelation in the development of new religious movements.

There were a number of other influential courses and teachers during my undergraduate years, but one particularly worth mentioning was the first applied statistics course Gordon and I took, which was just being instituted as a department requirement for majors. We were not well-grounded in mathematics, and we were not thrilled at the prospect of taking this course. We did initially struggle. But the instructor, Ray Canning, approached his task with care and sensitivity, recognizing the quantitative deficits and attendant anxieties that many of his students had. He admitted that he himself had come somewhat late to statistical analysis as a student, and yet here he was now teaching us and perhaps knowing better than some others how best to anticipate and address the more perplexing aspects of statistics that he knew awaited us. By the term's end, both Gordon and I had gained a hard-won appreciation for the essential role of statistical analysis in producing verifiable empirical work.

Several years later, as an almost finished Ph.D. candidate in sociology, with several additional advanced statistics courses under my belt, I found myself in a nearly identical situation when I agreed to teach a newly required statistics course for the School of Social Work at Michigan State University. I found myself making the same little speech of reassurance to that anxious group of social work students, admitting my own earlier inadequacies, but pointing out I had overcome these to the degree necessary to now be their teacher. I told them that if they would make an honest effort, I would work with them until everyone would be able to grasp basic statistical procedures and, more importantly, understand how and why these procedures could be applied to help answer research questions that could not otherwise be resolved.

Gordon's and my decision to go on to graduate school in sociology seemed easy, even inevitable. We wanted to do sociology, to be sociologists. That meant getting a Ph.D. That meant many more years in school. It meant forestalling a decent income for an unforeseen amount of time in pursuit of an ephemeral career that might never, in fact, materialize. Nevertheless, with encouragement from faculty at the University of Utah, and with a like-minded commitment from Gordon, we sent out our applications for graduate school in the winter of 1969.

My application, acceptance, and eventual journey to graduate school were inextricably tied to development of a relationship with Lauren Snow, my future wife. Lauren and I were first introduced on a blind date arranged by mutual friends. Lauren was a 19-year-old math and chemistry major working as a student in a campus virus research lab chopping up chick embryos, preparing cell cultures, and sterilizing glassware in an autoclave. She had decided she wanted to join the Peace Corps and go to Afghanistan when she graduated. I had always been attracted to smart girls—I tuned into their intelligence like signals from a radio tower. Here was a very smart girl. Independent minded, with a social conscience to boot. And cute, too. We hit it off.

Meanwhile, one of my two graduate school applications elicited a positive response—it was from Michigan State University. What to do? East Lansing was a long way from Salt Lake City, even further from Afghanistan, should Lauren actually wind up in the Peace Corps. I happened to be taking a marriage and family course at the time. The research cited in our text clearly showed a strong positive correlation between length of courtship and marital success. Age of partners was also a strong success factor. It caused me to reflect that I had known Lauren for all of three months, and that she was still three months shy of her 20th birthday.

**Lauren graduating with a B.A. in math and chemistry from
the University of Utah, August, 1969.**

What to do indeed? I ignored the findings from my courtship and marriage
text and asked her to marry me. I mentioned the Michigan State contingency.
She weighed her options for a day or two and then said, yes, she would marry
me and forgo Afghanistan, if I would contact Michigan State to see if they
would hold over my program acceptance for the following year, so she could
complete her own undergraduate degree at the University of Utah. This was
an equitable and reasonable counter-proposal. And that's what happened.
Michigan State deferred my arrival for a year, and, five months later, Lauren
and I married in mid-September of 1969. We had previously contracted to
rent a tiny basement apartment at 1620 Browning Avenue in Salt Lake City
for $75 a month on the night American astronauts landed on the moon—a
fitting metaphor for our own unimagined and seemingly implausible future
together. Lauren took added coursework during the succeeding school year,
which enabled her to graduate in a total of just three years. Meanwhile,

during that same year, I wrote a master's thesis on the relationships between political and religious ideologies and individual cognitive style.

In late summer of 1970, we loaded everything we could of personal value and necessity into a little red American Motors Rebel—permanently damaging that unfortunate vehicle's springs—and then, with exactly $100 cash between us, took off on Interstate 80 going east to Michigan. Gordon accompanied us in his own over-loaded little Dodge Dart; he had been accepted for graduate work in sociology at SUNY Stony Brook. He had meanwhile also married and had a baby daughter, who with his then-wife Beckie remained behind in Utah until Gordon could secure living quarters and an extra-income-job on Long Island.

Gary and Lauren with their heavily loaded Rambler Rebel just prior to driving to Michigan to start graduate school.

On the morning of our departure, both Gordon and I, in our separate Salt Lake City apartments, arose early to complete final packing, and then each of us threw up—an old occurrence resulting from tension and what we called an early morning "paper route stomach." En route east through the Rocky Mountains and great plains, we dined on cold chicken noodle soup directly from cans and slept on the ground in sleeping bags at rest stops or behind rural town gas stations. We parted company near Toledo, Ohio—Lauren and I heading straight north to East Lansing, while Gordon continued motoring east to New York City. One concrete fragment of that trip that reflects the tenor of our thinking then resides in a small poem that Gordon pieced together in his mind while driving and subsequently sent to us in a letter after reaching his destination. It's called "Shiloh," and is prefaced by a brief note that went like this:

Dear Gary and Lauren,

Just a note to let you know that I was captured and held as a political hostage by the Black Panthers. (Ha! Ha!) Following my "escape," I made the Big City about 2:00 in the afternoon and my destination two hours later. The physical plant at Stony Brook is in shambles. Most of the buildings are new but already scruffy, and the grounds are incredibly unkempt. Oh well, these are things of the flesh. I will withhold judgment until partaking of the spirit.

While driving in Pennsylvania after our parting, I pulled off the freeway to gas-up at a local grocery and filling station. On the way back to the highway, I noticed a small sign pointing to a narrow road that disappeared into the hills. The sign read: *5 miles to Shiloh.* Before gassing up, I'd been reflecting on the shootings of anti-war student protestors at Kent State this past May, so, to pass the time I composed a short poem (I guess you'd call it that) in my head and wrote it down when I stopped for the night, even though this Shiloh was not the actual Civil War Shiloh of my so-called poem.

SHILOH *

Concrete highways now cross the palm of this land,

where once its sacred sod

was darkened

by the righteous blood of young Americans,

who killed each other

in the name of God.

Would that the silent hills around this field of agony

unseal their awful witness,

the trees burst burgundy and scarlet,

a drenching rain

to stain the rocks with rust

that penetrates forever.

To be a flush of shame

at the savagery,

at the reckless spilling of precious life,

at our incapacity to restrain

our insanity.

Lauren and I conjured up our own images and reflections as we cruised through—what to us parched-desert-Westerners seemed to be—a lush, surreal green Michigan countryside between Detroit and East Lansing. Unlike Gordon, though, we wrote no commemorative poetry to capture our thoughts. But we certainly did encounter a brave new world of beginnings as graduate students at Michigan State. Those, however, are tales of further influences, learning experiences, and growth for another recounting.

For now, I will just note that I admired Lauren's trust and even courage in joining me on this initial adventure, far from the comforting security of family and home, into an unknown future teeming with "strangers in a strange land." At least that's how we thought of it and talked about it. We knew we were literally poised at a cross-roads and that whichever turn we chose would change our lives forever. We had faith—perhaps it was naïve faith—that this unknown future would be a good one, and that together we would find ways to surmount whatever obstacles might be thrown up before us along our chosen path.

Is there a moral to all this autobiographical rambling? Perhaps one can be found for a putative audience of young people who are contemplating the prospects for their own career paths. I would say to such an audience that all of you are either edging closer to a turning point crossroads in your own life or are even standing squarely on it right now. What happens next will be significantly shaped by forces beyond your personal control. The story of all success is typically sprinkled with good fortune—being in the right place at the right time or knowing the right people who can help.

But prior to being in that right place and time, there has been a preparation process, an accumulation of knowledge, skills, insights, attitudes, and values that you have picked up along the way. When opportunities do come to you—whether calculated and worked for in advance or purely by chance—you need to be able to recognize them, seize them, and then magnify them by applying those skills and qualities of character you have spent your life developing. Openness to change and a willingness to embrace change will help. So will a basic trust in yourself and in what you have learned. A little naïve faith might help too.

As an adjective, the Hebrew word Shiloh may be translated to mean tranquil or peaceful. As a place name it refers to a place of rest. As a proper noun, it may also be translated to signify the bringer of peace.

29.

MORMON PASSAGE

As a graduate student at SUNY Stony Brook in the 1970s, Gordon's Ph.D. advisor was a junior faculty member by the name of Erich Goode. Erich's primary area of specialization was the sociology of deviance, as understood from a social constructionist perspective. Subsequently, he also developed an interest in Memoir writing. As a sociologist, Erich is interested in the ways memoirs are constructed. He is especially interested in how memoirists are influenced by their relationships with other people and their subsequent reactions to memoirists' recollections and interpretations of their mutual past.

Gordon hadn't communicated with Erich for several years when he unexpectedly received an email asking him to participate as a respondent to a survey Erich was undertaking. "Hi Gordie," he wrote (Erich is the only person who calls him "Gordie," but Gordon doesn't mind):

> It's been years since we communicated. How are you doing?
> I have retired from teaching—from Stony Brook in 2000 and
> from the University of Maryland in 2007. One of the things
> I've gotten interested in recently is the writing of memoirs. I'm
> doing a piece on memoir writers—from beginners to authors
> of full-length books. In making up a list of authors who have
> published full-length memoirs, I thought of you as a possible
> respondent because of you and your brother's book *Mormon*

Passage (University of Illinois Press, 1998). If you're willing to respond to a brief questionnaire, I'd very much like to send it to you. I'd like to ask you a few questions about your writing experience. Thanks very much, Gordie. I look forward to your response.

Best and warmest wishes, Erich.

Naturally, Gordon agreed to participate in Erich's survey, and forthwith Erich sent him an interview schedule consisting of nineteen open-ended questions—not so brief after all! In his introduction to the questionnaire, Erich explained, "I'm mainly interested in you discussing your relationship to writing memoir—why you wrote your memoir, how you began doing it, how you did it, the social life you have around it, who influences it, what inspired and influenced it, both in terms of past biographical influences and in terms of your life today, the social circles in which you interact and with whom you're engaged that read and shape your work, provide feedback, suggestions, and so on, that caused you to write certain things in a certain way. I do have a schedule or list of topics, but I want you to talk as much as you want and feel free to say anything you feel inspired to talk about."

After reading over the subsequent nineteen questions, Gordon decided he would take to heart Erich's invitation to be "inspired" and compose an essay structured around his leading questions rather than write categorical answers to each one separately. Here's a summary of what he had to say about his and Gary's collaboration in writing *Mormon Passage*.

Upon our return from Mexico as youthful LDS missionaries in 1966, both Gary and I were drawn to the sociology of religion as undergraduate students at the University of Utah. Our main influence was an LDS scholareducator by the name of Lowell Bennion. In 1933, Bennion earned a Ph.D. in sociology at the University of Strasbourg under the tutelage of Eric Voegelin and

Maurice Halbwachs and wrote his dissertation on the methodology of Max Weber. When we attended the University of Utah, Bennion was Assistant Dean of Students, but he also taught occasional classes in sociology. The text he used in his sociology of religion course was Thomas O'Dea's cogent little Prentice Hall volume, *The Sociology of Religion* (1966). O'Dea's book plus Bennion's classroom teaching hooked both of us. Through Bennion's class we also were introduced to O'Dea's landmark study in the sociology of Mormonism entitled *The Mormons* (University of Chicago Press, 1957). O'Dea's two books had a major impact on our emerging interest in the sociology of religion in general and the possibilities of applying a sociological perspective to Mormon studies in particular. Gary and I both wrote term papers for Bennion's sociology of religion course on Mormon topics. Gary's paper was a comparison of the leadership styles of Joseph Smith and Brigham Young, and mine was on secularization and Mormon accommodation to the normative demands of contemporary American society.

Gary and I parted ways when we went to graduate school (Gary attended Michigan State). Since neither of our Ph.D. programs offered courses in the sociology of religion, we put our undergraduate interest in Mormon studies on the backburner and concentrated on the required graduate curriculum at our respective schools. Gary ended up finding a faculty member at Michigan State willing to direct a dissertation on LDS versus Catholic modes of moral socialization for children. I, on the other hand, fell under Erich's influence at SUNY Stony Brook whose social constructionist approach to the study of deviance intrigued me, and I ended up writing a dissertation on the relationship between science and the mass media in general and the public debate over marijuana use in particular.

After graduate school, Gary and I both focused on getting some publications out of our dissertations. But I also had in the back of my mind a project that would get us back together again on a Mormon topic, namely a content analysis of LDS conference reports as a way to study the salience and change of thematic religious concerns over time. As a result of my dissertation work, I had developed confidence in my ability to employ content analysis methods to extract quantifiable data from published documents. This, in conjunction with Gary's superior familiarity with Mormon history sources, seemed like a good combination. We wanted to move beyond our dissertation topics and already knew we were effective together as a team, a realization regularly reinforced since early childhood. What resulted from our first scholarly collaboration was *A Kingdom Transformed: Themes in the Development of Mormonism* (University of Utah Press, 1984).

What to do next? At that point we were contemplating the possibility of two more books on Mormon culture. Having researched and written about the historical adjustments of LDS teachings and institutions in contemporary society, we decided we were well positioned to continue writing on 1) Mormon growth through missionary recruitment; and 2) problems of member retention and types of defection from the faith. *Mormon Passage* was the end result of project number one and, for better or worse, project number two never got past the talking stage. Our original plan for a book on the Mormon missionary system was quite different from the memoir approach we eventually pursued. What we first had in mind was a conventional scholarly treatment that would be anchored in historical and statistical data obtained from the LDS Church, direct observation of missionary training on the BYU campus, and interviews with missionaries, mission presidents, and missionary training staff. I was awarded a sabbatical leave in 1986 to pursue this project, and spent four months in the Salt Lake City/ Provo, Utah, area to acquire the data we wanted. It was discouraging. Church authorities whom I contacted were not overly enthusiastic about our project. They had their own institutional research division and were not interested in independent scholars investigating their programs. I learned to practice conniving methods in order to obtain a few random interviews, and surreptitiously gained access to the Provo Missionary Training Center (MTC) a couple of times for observational purposes, but I repeatedly ran into bureaucratic stonewalls and found it difficult to get any statistical data from official church sources. LDS ecclesiastical officials were (and are) highly sensitive to the church's public image and are loath to lose control over institutional information. I slowly came to the conclusion that we probably weren't going to get enough of the kind of data we had envisioned for our proposed book. I began to think nostalgically of my earlier research based on content analysis of public documents that didn't require official permission or impose institutional obstacles and limitations on accessing needed information.

One of the former instructors at the MTC whom I tracked down in Salt Lake City had files of correspondence with various missionaries from the field over the years of his tenure at the MTC. He generously said we could copy and use his documents if we wanted, but I began thinking to myself, "hmmm, our own missionary journals and correspondence are as good as this stuff, and we're not beholden to anyone else but ourselves if we want to think of them as primary source materials." Providentially, as it were, Gary had already been word processing our handwritten correspondence and his missionary journal entries as a self-indulgent hobby project. Eureka! Why not dump our frustrated plans for a conventional scholarly analysis of the Mormon missionary system in favor of a case study narrative based on our own mission field documents?

Both of us had read Oscar Lewis' *Children of Sanchez*, and were impressed by the reiterative, multiple narrative he constructed in his informants' own words as a way of drawing readers inside the lifeworld of Mexican urban poverty. We had also read *The Autobiography of Bertrand Russell* and liked his correspondence with various 19th and 20th century notables attached at the end of each chapter as much or more than his preceding chapter narratives. These two books shaped our thinking about how to structure a case study of Mormon missionary life using personal documents in a narrative format to convey to readers the missionary experience from an insider perspective. The original draft manuscript of *Mormon Passage* was a massive 800 pages plus, and it wasn't called "Passage;" it was initially entitled, "Brothers in Mexico." The length was a problem for prospective publishers and so was the title—too confusing as to the actual subject matter of the book. We sent queries to several big name academic publishers, who showed little interest, and also to the University of Utah Press, which had published *Kingdom Transformed.* But under new management, they turned us down because they didn't want to be typecast as an outlet for Mormon studies. We even offered the manuscript to Signature Books, a Salt Lake City publisher that specializes in Mormonrelated academic books, but were flat-out rejected. That hurt.

We thought our material was intrinsically interesting but realized we needed an objective, experienced editor to give us some advice. We consulted with Lavina Fielding Anderson in Salt Lake City, who had years of experience writing for and editing scholarly journals in Mormon studies. She simultaneously provided encouragement and gave us good critical advice. She liked the writing very much in the personal documents but admonished us to beef up the scholarly context for our narrative accounts by writing a solid introductory chapter as an overview of the LDS missionary enterprise. "Be a *resource* to your readers," she admonished to our chagrin. "Give them updated information in sparkling prose about missionary training and practices that they don't already know about."

So—in sparkling prose or not—we wrote an introduction replete with references and footnotes on the contemporary LDS missionary enterprise (my sabbatical leave efforts came in handy here). We then began to focus on The University of Illinois Press as an outlet for our manuscript. In part because the University of Utah Press had put a moratorium on publishing Mormon related topics and in part for reasons of their own, by 1990 Illinois had become the major academic outlet for scholarship in Mormon studies. Illinois was good to us. They had a sympathetic editor, Liz Dulaney, who saw promise in our work, outsourced the manuscript to competent reviewers, and provided good feedback. The main problem with the manuscript was its length. We had to put it on a crash diet to lose approximately 300 pages. This required radical editing.

We were committed to a multiple narrative account and resisted the idea of eliminating length by simply focusing on one of our stories while leaving the other out. That led to the idea of switching from one of our journal narratives to the other without backtracking in time, while using our correspondence to keep the reader updated on what was happening simultaneously to the other brother in his mission area. This allowed us to eliminate roughly half of our journal entries while integrating both of our narratives. At this point we began thinking of our manuscript as an overly long film for which we had to pare down all the footage we had accumulated to a standard commercial length by identifying what we thought were the best scenes and cutting out the rest. We even used film splicing techniques to bolster our correspondence when occasionally it was thin or left out too much essential information by grafting otherwise deleted journal segments into some of our letters so they appeared to be part of our correspondence. I would estimate that about 20 percent of our published letters were supplemented in this way. Misleading? Yeah, technically, but they were still our own words describing our own experiences, and this practice made it possible for us to shorten the "film" about our missionary days while simultaneously fleshing out the narrative and preserving what we thought were some of our more significant vignettes.

As for the title, Gary came up with "Mormon Passage" after reflecting on the dual meaning of our missionary experience: First, as a rite of passage which we had shared with other LDS youth, and second, with reference to our eventual personal passage out of the faith once we resumed our educational careers. We thought this title worked well for both us and readers of the book. We were disappointed that the editorial staff at the University of Illinois Press wouldn't budget in any photographs we had snapped as missionaries in Mexico to illustrate some of our journal vignettes, but were very pleased with the final cover and overall appearance of the book when it was published.

Front cover of Mormon Passage showing Gordon performing a baptism in Villa Flores, Mexico, 1965. Image courtesy of the University of Illinois Press.

We thought Illinois did an adequate job publicizing the book, but we were admittedly disappointed with sales, especially in Utah. Copies were available in major Salt Lake City bookstores after publication, as well as at the BYU bookstore in Provo, Utah, but the book was not prominently featured anywhere. There was no run on available supplies to purchase as gifts for Christmas or to inspire newly-called missionaries, and the great majority of sales were to academic libraries. Actually, we never anticipated that the book would sell especially well among faithful Latter-day Saints in the pews (who primarily are interested in unadulterated faith promoting stories, and certainly not in accounts that mix religious certitude with doubts or replace triumphal endings with reflexive ambiguity and loss of faith). But we were hoping for brisker sales than we got from the Mormon intelligentsia, which is largely situated in the Salt Lake City area. We participated in an "authors meet critics" session at the annual Sunstone Symposium in Salt Lake City attended by 40–50 people, and another one at the Society for the Scientific Study of Region's annual meeting the following year, but we never got on the lecture circuit, nor were we asked to speak at any Mormon gatherings. In general, reaction to our missionary memoir in both the Mormon and academic communities seemed ho-hum.

LDS Church officials, who are obligated to reinforce members' idealized conceptions of their religious duties—including lay missionary service—might be a little put off by some of the descriptions of minor deviance or normal imperfections in our missionary accounts. But we have never been contacted or reprimanded by anybody in LDS ecclesiastical ranks. Most of the people who talk to us about the book and who actually have served LDS missions say, "Yeah, that sounds about right," including my daughters Lynne and Natalie (who served LDS missions in Costa Rica and Guatemala, respectively) and my son Robert who went to Mexico City. (I also supported, by the way, my daughter Pamela's decision *not* to interrupt her education by accepting a missionary assignment.) I, in fact, always supported my kids in their religious decisions and various church-related activities even though I had abandoned my faith (as did Gary) before they grew up. It was important to their mother, who remained very staunch in her LDS commitments, and I saw no good reason to make a divisive issue of my agnosticism. In addition, my time in Mexico proved to be a very positive learning experience, which I have never regretted, and I thought it would be good for my kids too. At any rate, they all seemed to think the book was a more or less authentic reflection of their own missionary experiences a generation later in time.

The most negative reactions to the book came from a few of Gary's and my former missionary companions whom we had self-righteously singled out in letters and journal entries for criticism and moral condemnation. None of the latter had been in contact with us since our missions, and their communications with us after the publication of *Passage* were from out of the blue. One of my former missionary companions emailed me to say that he had discovered a reference to *Passage* and was anxious to order a copy. I emailed him right back to apologize for some of the unkind things he was going to read about himself; he never responded back. Another former companion contacted me with great gusto to say he had heard about the book and was going to check a copy out of his local library. I wrote right back to him, too, in order to prepare him for the critical reflections on his character recorded in *Passage*. After reading the book, he responded with a long, indignant email, saying that what I had written was dishonest, that it was a betrayal of him and the "Lord's work," but that he would pray for me and hoped that he could yet be a blessing in my life.

Gary also got several responses from former missionary companions— one in particular whom he had thoroughly trashed in his journal entries and letters to me, which we subsequently printed verbatim in *Passage* (verbatim that is, except for a pseudonym, which we used liberally throughout the text for all those companions whom, in retrospect, we had maligned in any way). Unlike my angry excompanion, this guy didn't repudiate Gary's youthful assessment of him, but wanted to "dialogue" further about the missionary experience and perhaps get Gary to appreciate that he wasn't as bad as he had been made out to be.

There have been a few other old missionary companions—not many— who have written or spoken with us about the book and, if they were por- trayed positively by us, seemed fine with our accounts of missionary life, though few if any have been effusive in their praise. The academic, analytical chapters in the book are virtually never mentioned to us by former mission- aries. Perhaps the strongest reaction to Mormon Passage, however, came from an old friend whose occasional letters from home we periodically inserted into our journal narratives. We had been out of contact with him for a number of years. Gary finally tracked him down in California and sent him a copy of the book.

Shortly afterward, Gary was in that area of the country visiting rel- atives and looked him up. Our friend was not cordial. He threw the book on the floor and said it made him sick, that in it he had been deployed and exploited as a negative foil to our good-guy personas. Incidentally, several other readers told us that he was their favorite character in the book, but this did not console him. Like my excompanion he felt terribly betrayed, especially over the revelation in one of his letters that he "flunked" his missionary interview with a puritanically rigid ecclesiastical official because of his alleged "self-abuse" problem. He had always been highly sensitive about his sexual identity and was humiliated. Rather than prove his worthiness by subjecting himself to a six-week probationary period, he withdrew his missionary application and determined he could "exercise the little bit of love that's in my heart without [ecclesiastical] approval or an outmoded moral code."

These kinds of reactions have caused me to have some regrets, and I think the same is true for Gary. We naively failed to anticipate adequately how hurtful or damaging our characterization and judgments would actually be for some individuals whom we portrayed, even though we identified them with pseudonyms. We intended for our published account to be a realistic representation of missionary life—blemishes and all— not just a whitewash job. That meant if we were including a chapter that featured a companion assignment with a slacker missionary, it was going to stay in the book from our perspectives as young missionaries. So too was the reporting of particular events that we retrospectively believed were symptomatic or typical or insightful in some way, even if they cast specific missionaries (including ourselves occasionally) in a bad light. And, regardless of our friend's feelings, we could not leave out his letters. They were too good, too articulate; they illustrated too clearly the anguish that LDS missionary expectations can generate for certain Mormon youth. But I do regret leaving in gratuitous comments that could easily have been deleted when we were trying to reduce the overall length of the manuscript. As kids, both Gary and I had a tendency (we probably still do) to make smartass comments about people for sheer entertainment, and sometimes our self-indulgent delight in making fun naturally overrides fairness. There was a fair amount of this in our missionary writings.

We could and should have been more sensitive and judicious about these self-indulgences when editing the manuscript. If a smartass, denigrating comment was made in a letter or journal entry about a missionary who played a very minor role in our narratives, why leave it in the book for that person to encounter as an adult with grown children and an idealized memory of his missionary service? What good purpose does that serve? There are a dozen or so of these little gratuitous remarks that could have been culled and taken out without changing the overall themes or tenor of the book. If we had it to do over again, we would search them out and clip them from the manuscript.

Although Gary and I have always liked to read biographies, autobiographies, and memoirs, we never aspired to be memoirists. *Mormon Passage* was hatched only after our conventional book project on the Mormon missionary enterprise failed to gestate satisfactorily and was aborted. We didn't want to see a couple of years of effort go down the drain without producing something on the subject. It so happened that Gary and I had preserved a sizeable number of documentary materials from our missionary days, especially journals and letters—not only letters to one another, but also letters to and from our parents and numerous friends with whom we corresponded. Since high school, we had fancied ourselves as good letter writers, and when we started our missions we were given journals as gifts from our parents to write in. (This is supposed to be normative for Mormon missionaries and, indeed, both of our parents had kept missionary journals, which we had seen growing up.) So we perceived writing in one's missionary journal as a kind of religious duty. Unlike us, however, few of our missionary companions were faithful journalists. It became something of a point of pride for us to maintain regular journals while most other missionaries did not. What we soon learned was that you didn't have to write a lot, just a little bit every day. But if you were consistent at it the pages grew and eventually you had accumulated a good deal of documentary material about your missionary experiences.

While we were dutiful journalists as missionaries (neither one of us has kept a journal since), when we started organizing our materials for *Passage* we became editors more so than memoirists. Reading through all of our documents ignited a good deal of memory, including keen recollections of particular events and specific conversations. But we did not begin writing a memoir as one presumably writes a historical novel—as an organized, articulated stream of consciousness about the past from the point of view of an omnipotent narrator in the present. Rather, we assembled already written journal and letter vignettes and tried to figure out how best to organize and splice them together to produce a more or less smoothly flowing narrative. As editors, we were far more focused on straightening out syntax and correcting grammatical errors in the original documents than we were in recreating or rewriting history from our contemporary points of view.

In general, both Gary and I appreciate memoir writers who are insightful and generous in their assessment of other people's strengths and weaknesses, including their competitors or enemies as well as their friends. I assume that memoirists are biased in their own favor, but I like to see a capacity for ironic detachment and modest humor. I don't like whining, preaching, or incessant chest beating. I tend to be a very private person. In casual conversations both Gary and I are good at listening and getting other people to talk about themselves. In contrast, I tend to shift conversations away from myself. I'm parsimonious about selfrevelations and monitor my words in preference to blurting my personal feelings or opinions. If I were to ever publish another memoir, there are lots of things I would leave out. I would not criticize family members or people who are close to me, even though they all have various shortcomings. I would not talk about the details of my sex life. I would certainly not talk about the details of my bowel movements (a la Allen Ginsberg in *Death and Fame* or Norman Mailer ruminations in *On God*). As I mentioned earlier, Gary and I have regrets about publishing what we retrospectively consider to be occasional insulting comments in *Mormon Passage* that were largely gratuitous and would edit them out if we had it to do over again.

So, yes, if I were to author another memoir of some kind I undoubtedly would inhibit, or at least soften, potentially damaging observations in certain instances. I would not be brutally honest or totally transparent in writing of others or myself in a personal memoir. This doesn't mean that I think memoirists should not strive for this sort of openness or truthfulness. Maybe that's what proper memoir writing requires. Maybe total honesty, introspectively expressed with careful and compelling analysis, is what makes great memoir writing. But that's not me. I can reveal some things about myself, my feelings, and my opinions of others, but not everything. I have too many inhibitions, too much compunction, too much self-pride in my Boy Scout values of modesty and loyalty for those who mean something to me to write a naked memoir.

My compunction and self-pride are linked to the issue of veracity in memoir writing. In part, memoir veracity depends on accurate memory. Both Gary and I have always had good memories for detail. I like to narrate detailed events as stories. I see mundane exchanges as potentially interesting if they involve some degree of human quirkiness, irony, humor, or contention. When I experience something or somebody I think is interesting, I make mental notes; I focus attention on those aspects of the "story" that make it interesting to me. Storytelling unites us. Gary and I make a practice of selectively interpreting the facts and events of daily life that can be constructed into narratives for sharing in conversations with other people. Doesn't everybody do this? It turns out that not everybody does, or at least not quite to the same extent that Gary and I and routinely do.

I guess my point about memory and the veracity of recall is that memory has to be practiced; it becomes a skill. And the skill of memory cannot be separated from particular interests, selective perception, and interpretations that are articulated through storytelling. I've practiced my memory skills like this since I was a kid. Gary and I used to wake up together every morning and ask, "What did you dream about?" and then we would listen to narrations of one another's dreams. After school we would mutually rehearse the events of the day, or, on family trips, engage in marathon recollection sessions in the back seat of the family car in order to make the time pass by more quickly. You can't report every single thing that is said or that happens. Even if you had perfect recall, it would be boring to report all of it. You have to be selective. For the purposes of memory you have to focus on those bits and pieces of experience that are potentially interesting or compelling elements of a story. The recall I have of the details of events that occurred years ago, including those in Mexico as a Mormon missionary, is in part a consequence of regular story sharing over the years. If people don't formulate and share stories about their experiences, I don't think they end up remembering very much. To put it another way, the fewer the stories you share about yourself, the less you remember about yourself. As I say, Gary and I have shared stories about ourselves since childhood and still do. The nature and circumstances of our twin brother relationship has always been conducive to shared recollection.

I think Gary and I have become decent editors of raw materials and manuscript drafts. I also think Gary and I are decent writers, and I think we're both pretty good at perceiving and interpreting life events with a certain kind of curiosity and detached amusement. In so far as these qualities might be important to good memoir writing, I would call them strengths. But as I confessed earlier, I privatize my personal life and am reluctant to reveal too much about my inner self to the world at large. And I would leave out or fudge information about people I love or care about if I thought it would hurt or offend them. If these are serious shortcomings in memoir writing, I plead guilty.

30.

OF WIGS AND ROLLER COASTERS:
Wherein the Phantom Demonstrates his gentle side

O ur older brother Don had a tender, caring side. But, growing up, we didn't see much of it. We didn't look for it much, either, much less try to encourage it. But as adults, the two of us did warily make efforts to build a better relationship with Don. We say warily in large part due to an overriding development that eventually affected everything and everyone close to Don: his drinking. Within ten years of his graduation from high school Don had become an alcoholic and burned through two marriages. Within another five years he lost his art faculty position at the University of Utah and a third wife as consequences of even heavier drinking.

Among the multiple sad and bitter recollections of those years, several warm and redeeming memories also emerge. One in particular involves Don's devotion to a young Black woman suffering the throes of multiple sclerosis, whom he had encountered in the late 1970s. Her name was Darlene Jennings (but Don always called her Doll). Darlene was one of ten children, a graduate of South High School, and a psychology major at the University of Utah until her MS affliction became too severe to allow completion of her studies. She lived with and was cared for by her parents in a Victorian era home on 700 South near 500 East where the old yellow brick LDS Second

Ward chapel still proudly stands. By the time she became acquainted with Don, Darlene was confined to a wheelchair, her speech was impaired, and she was unable to fully control the movements of her head and hands. Don arranged for Darlene to be dropped off at his small Avenues apartment on E Street, where he would read to her, talk with her, push her wheelchair on neighborhood walks, and take her on modest little outings when he could secure transportation.

The two of us routinely visited Salt Lake City in the summer months from our then respective homes in Michigan and Massachusetts and consequently became acquainted with Darlene as a result. We remember how attentive and tender Don was with Darlene, demonstrating interpersonal traits that we had rarely seen him exhibit toward others in our years of growing up with him. This occurred, for example, whenever Don helped her eat. He patiently waited for her head to be momentarily still from sudden jerks, then carefully raised a spoon or fork to her mouth with a bite full of food, meticulously wiping away with a napkin any crumbs or spills that might be left on Darlene's lips or cheek.

We took Don and Darlene on picnics to Memory Grove above the Utah State Capital and on longer scenic drives in the mountains between Park City and Heber City. Most memorably we took them on an expedition to Northern Utah's favorite amusement park, Davis County's *Lagoon*, in company with both of our own young families. Darlene had never been on a roller coaster ride and wanted to try it. Don didn't think he was strong enough to lift Darlene from her wheelchair, so Gary did and then carried her on to the platform and into the coaster seat. Don sat next to Gary and Darlene, and Gordon settled in the seat behind with Lynne, his oldest daughter.

The Lagoon "White Roller Coaster," built in 1921 and still in operation.

Darlene clutched tightly with both arms around Gary's neck and emitted a shriek as the coaster crested and then shot down the steep hill of the track. We hadn't previously realized that Darlene wore a wig, but she did, and the sudden, accelerating speed of the roller coaster down the first big plunge of track stripped that wig off Darlene's head in an eye blink and whipped it right past Lynne's startled face. "What kind of furry animal has just flown off Darlene's head and why is she bald?!" were the instantaneous thoughts racing through Lynne's twelve year-old mind with approximately the same speed as the displaced wig.

Darlene never stopped producing a combination of high pitched screams and laughs throughout the ride and showed no concern whatever over her lost hair. But Gordon and Lynne had spotted what looked to be a patch of fur resting on the ground adjacent to the coaster machinery while rounding a lower rung of track. When the coaster stopped, Gordon jumped off the platform, scrambled over a white picket protective fence at the foot of the roller coaster, and snagged up the fugitive hair piece. Darlene barely noticed Gordon and Lynne positioning the wig back onto her head. She couldn't stop laughing and pleaded for another ride. Both of us always admired Darlene's quiet determination and sunny disposition in the face of adversity and her utter lack of malice and her openness to all people.

And we also agree that the times Don spent caring for Darlene were probably the truest indicators of his best self; the person he rarely was with us and our parents, but the person we glimpsed when he and Doll were together—the caring, gentle, and too often unacknowledged side of the Phantom of our youth.

Don, circa 1970, while teaching as an art instructor at the University of Utah.

31.

THE CAPTAIN GOES DOWN
WITH THE SHIP

Taking a break from the professional conference we were attending as academic sociologists in downtown Salt Lake in 1989, the two of us drove our little rental car up the Avenues to LDS Hospital. With us was Gordon's daughter Lynne, who was a first-year student at Ephraim's Snow College. The day before we had learned from some of our old high school friends that Dr. Ralph Backman had been hospitalized and was seriously ill.

Dr. Ralph V. Backman: revered educator and principal at South High School—a school that had provided an educational home for Salt Lake's central city kids since the deep depression years of 1931-32. Sadly, South's doors had been shuttered the year before our 1989 conference, sacrificed at a time of inner-city population decline to preserve the city's two older high schools—East and West—who were favored by wealthier constituents and larger student populations. Sadly too, Dr. Backman, South's erstwhile captain and apostle of democracy to three generations of Salt Lake's blue-collar youth and ethnic minorities, was rumoured to be lying at death's door on the third floor of LDS Hospital. A good captain always goes down with his ship.

South High upon completion in 1931.

The three of us stood hesitantly outside his room in the hallway. We were surprise visitors, unannounced and unanticipated. As we stood there, we most of all didn't want to transgress Dr. Backman's imperilled dignity as we furtively watched the nurse take away the emesis basin in which he has just lost his lunch. So, we waited. We waited long enough for Dr. Backman to recover, to modestly compose himself and return his head to the pillows of his bed before we made our impromptu entrance.

Gary had mentally prepared a little speech: "Dr. Backman," he began, "you probably don't remember us, but . . ." Dr. Backman interrupted, his ashen face suddenly animated, and, in an emphatic voice he countered: "Nonsense! You're the Shepherd boys." The two of us had graduated from South in 1962, twenty-seven years earlier.

Dr. Backman became South High's principal in 1948. Prior to that he had been a charter member of South's first faculty when the school opened its doors in 1931. We know this because when we browsed our mother's old, first edition copy of the 1932 *Southerner* we discovered to our surprise the young face of Mr. Ralph Backman, with a full head of hair, soberly gazing from the faculty page. He was listed as a social science teacher.

Dr. Ralph V. Backman, 1931.

Beginning in 1932, Ralph Backman quickly moved up the administrative ladder to become Dean of Boys at South, while continuing to teach debate, psychology, sociology, and

U. S. government. Later, as principal of the school, Dr. Backman was unquestionably in charge, but never in a rigid, Captain Queeg sort of way. Instead, he led by both lofty precept and personal example. The educational programs he advocated were based on a pragmatic, democratic philosophy of ultimate trust in individuals to subordinate self-centered interests to the good of their shared community. To illustrate his approach, we excerpt portions of a public statement written by Dr. Backman that he titled "Our Philosophy."

> South High aims to reflect the best that America has to offer
> its youth . . . consistent with the principles of democracy in
> both theory and practice . . . The strength of our nation will
> be determined by the degree to which our youth have respect
> for the laws of our country and the welfare of the many. The
> education we provide is aimed at developing self-respecting,
> self-reliant citizens . . . At South the environment contributes to
> the growth of democratic attitudes and practices and respect for
> all persons . . . All students are provided with the opportunity

to help shape and carry out the functions of South High School, of which they are an integral part.

Dr. Backman valued collegiality with his staff; he implemented democratic structures of student governance and encouraged active student involvement in South's many extra-curricular programs; he set high standards for academic performance and conduct while holding the reverent respect of the school's students as well as its teachers.

Wait a minute: Did every student at South share our respect for Dr. Backman? No, undoubtedly not—that sort of perfection is only found in Utopia and 1950s Disney movies. But it's no exaggeration to claim that the great majority of South's students unequivocally respected him and, like us, they youthfully conflated his persona with the school as an institution that advocated the fundamental values of American democracy. Even if you were a delinquent twit,

Dr. Backman never spoke down to any student; he spoke to us as though we were educated adults, as though we were willing and capable of assuming democratic trust and responsibilities and, amazingly, many were stirred to live up to these idealized expectations.

Already holding a MA degree in Philosophy from Stanford University in 1935, Dr. Backman achieved an Ed.D. degree in Educational Administration from the University of Utah in 1960.

Dr. Ralph V. Backman, 1961.

"What have you fellows been doing with your lives?" Dr. Backman inquired of us as we stood at the foot of his sickbed. We briefly summarized ourselves, and then Gordon introduced his daughter. Dr. Backman's nausea temporarily forgotten, he focused his revived attention on Lynne, as though she were the only person in the room: How did she like college? What was her major? What were her future plans? And so on. As we prepared to leave, he told us, "When I'm well enough to get out of here and go home, feel welcome to come see me again. I'd like that."

Well, rumors of the Captain's pending death were slightly exaggerated. He prophetically recovered sufficiently from his illness after our visit at LDS Hospital to return to his Salt Lake City home. Dr. Ralph V. Backman lived two more years before dying at the age of 88. A good captain goes down with his ship, but his legacy survives through the resilience of a grateful crew that carries on, applying the seamanship lessons they learned under their captain's steady command and tutelage. God bless our dedicated public-school educators—true captains of our country's future, providing essential instruction and civic guidance to our children in an increasingly diverse and multicultural society, whose democratic institutions are dependably challenged in stormy seas by waves of intolerance, fear and ignorance. Rest in peace Dr. Backman, wherever you are—the ship of public education remains in good hands. The democratic ideals which you championed of union and equality in a diverse society—though sorely tested today—are still alive.

32.

HERE COMES THE SUN
Talking with Student Survivors at Kent State

Confidentiality concerns have led us to employ pseudonyms
for several of the individuals described in this essay with whom
we have conducted personal interviews.

In the spring of 2002, Gordon was in Michigan taking advantage of that marvelous academic institution known as a sabbatical leave. He was teaching a course in social psychology as a visiting professor for the Oakland Sociology Department and collaborating with Gary in an ethnographic study of an intriguing religious communal group called the Children of God. But that was not what preoccupied our interest during the first week of May that spring. That week we drove to Kent, Ohio, to renew some acquaintances and participate in the annual May 4 commemorative events at Kent State University. On the Kent State campus thirty-two years earlier, four students had been shot to death and nine wounded by Ohio National Guard troops in a protest demonstration against the Vietnam War. Gary's personal interest in learning more about the tragic events that transpired at Kent in the spring of 1970 had been stimulated by our shared academic interest in the study of social movements—especially the civil rights and antiwar movements of the turbulent 1960s.

In 1989 Gary learned that a reunion and conference were being planned by former members of Students for a Democratic Society (SDS) in conjunction with the 20th anniversary of their being banned from campus, one year before the Kent shootings. Hatched at the University of Michigan in 1961, SDS quickly caught on among student idealists looking for an organized way to put into action their egalitarian social and political values. For a meteoric few years in the mid to late 1960s, SDS became the largest and most influential student organization of the New Left before imploding into increasingly militant and squabbling factions, including the notorious Weather Underground. The 1989 SDS reunion at Kent State, at which Gary satin, featured retrospective talks on 1960s student radicalism for social change by such former SDS national officers as Carl Oglesby (who, coincidentally, was a Kent State alumnus), Mark Rudd (who led the student occupation of administration offices at Columbia University in 1968), and Bernadine Dohrn (one of the principal organizers and leaders of the Weather Underground). While retrospective views at the conference ranged from some regret ("Our democratic values and goals of equal justice in America were correct, but our turn to violent confrontation was the march over the cliff") to continued defiance ("We did what we had to do—including violent confrontation—in order to vigorously challenge a corrupt militaryindustrial complex that exploited and oppressed minority groups, because nobody else was willing to do it"). At the same time, all of the speakers reflected with sadness on the high cost of protest paid by the slain and wounded students at Kent State; many expressed hope in the future prospects of a new generation of student activists who would be more concerned about pursuing careers of social justice than corporate profits.

While at the conference Gary began introducing himself to Kent State alumni and others in attendance, explaining his social science interests in both past and contemporary social movements and began cultivating a snowball network of contacts who agreed to be interviewed at a later date. Over the years, in fact, Gary conducted a number of open-ended interviews and brought Gordon into the project as well. For us, the principal question was: Who were these erstwhile radicals? What were their stories, their personal histories, and what were they doing with their lives decades after the electrifying, defining events of their youth?

So we drove to Kent again in 2002 for the annual candlelight vigil in commemoration of the slain students to ponder the legacy of their violent deaths, and also to attend a memorial service for one of the more beloved Kent students of 1970 who recently had died of natural causes, far away from the quiet college town which, once upon a time, had been engulfed in a moment of chaos and killing.

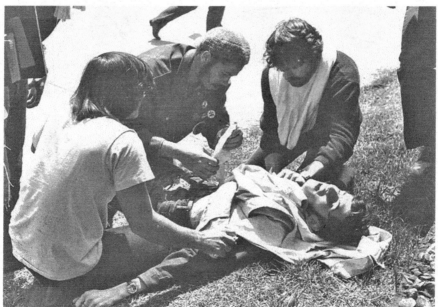

Ohio National Guard troops moving out to push anti-war demonstrators from Blanket Hill in front of Taylor Hall; students fleeing into an adjacent campus parking lot after the guard opened fire; fellow Kent students applying first aid to wounded John Cleary. All images courtesy of May 4 Collection. Kent State University Libraries. Special Collections & Archives.

Gordon: I've rescued an old letter I wrote my wife Faye that contains a summary description of Gary's and my experience at the memorial and my impression of some of those who gathered to pay their respects. Since my once supernatural memory has become increasingly degenerate in old age, I now resort to that letter for a snapshot view of a few hours of observation from our 2002 visit to Kent, Ohio.

May 5, 2002

Dear Faye,

In our brief phone conversation last night I never got around to telling you about the memorial service Gary and I attended for a former student radical at Kent State. His name was Mike Brock, and apparently he was a big, burly, generous, fun-loving guy with a soft spot in his heart for animals of all kinds, especially dogs, and an unquenchable taste for beer. Some years after the Kent shootings he moved to Fairbanks, Alaska, and became the owner and proprietor of a popular beer joint called the Howling Dog Saloon. They showed some video segments at the memorial service of him at his bar in Fairbanks, and in middle age he looked and talked a lot like a country version of Norm, from "Cheers." Before becoming transformed by student idealism at Kent State in the late 1960s, Big Mike was originally from Buffalo, New York, and was a nonobservant Jew. In innocent irony the memorial service ended up being held at the campus Catholic Newman Center, whose officials were decent enough to welcome an aging band of former student radicals.

The memorial was organized by one of the surviving students—Tom Grace—who was shot down by the Ohio National Guard on the back side of Blanket Hill on May 4, 1970. Grace is now a professor of history at SUNY Erie Community College in Buffalo, New York. On the day of the shootings, Big Mike was also on Blanket Hill protesting against the U.S military "incursion" into Cambodia and defying the Ohio Guard, which had been ordered into Kent to suppress student protest demonstrations over the weekend. When the shooting ceased, and the guardsmen had retreated back to their perimeter line, Big Mike found Tom Grace, bloody and lying in agony. He picked him up and carried him in his arms to Prentice Hall, a nearby student dormitory, where Grace received emergency medical attention.

Gary and I got to the Newman Center early. The only person there when we arrived was Guy Phermetti, who was tuning up his guitar in preparation for his part in the memorial service (in a soft voice he sang, "Here Comes the Sun," by George Harrison). Guy was a Vietnam vet from Texas who somehow ended up as a student at Kent State. His first day on campus was May 4, 1970, and he has lived in Kent ever since. Tom Grace came in while we were chatting with Guy, carrying a large vase filled with wildflowers, which he placed on a piano bench next to an enlarged, poster-size photo of Mike Brock as a young man, sporting a walrus mustache and black shaggy hair and sitting on the front stoop of an old house with his pet dog, a big golden retriever. Tom introduced himself to me and said hi to Gary, whom he already knew from Gary's previous visits to Kent. Nice guy. Short, slender, thoughtful, soft-spoken and loyal. I think he was the only one at the service who wore a tie. He still walks with a pronounced limp from a National Guard bullet that shattered his ankle on May 4, 1970.

Tom Grace, Kent State student survivor who went on to become a history professor at SUNY Erie Community College in Buffalo, New York.

Others began filtering in, a small gathering of about 35–40 mourners in all. Did you ever see the movie, "The Big Chill?" It reminded me of that. Gary and I were deliberately there early so we could see people come in and try to figure out who was who. The service was not actually conducted in the Newman Chapel but in the adjacent social hall (which Protestants like you usually refer to as the fellowship hall). Gary and I helped Tom set up folding chairs facing an old piano and speaker's lectern. The eulogy was given by Joe Whojamacallit (I used to be so good at remembering names). From the neck up Joe looks like an Old Testament prophet, with sharp facial features, piercing eyes, full head of hair, gray beard and great bushy eyebrows. From the neck down he looks more like a middle-aged mortal. Joe also was on Blanket Hill May 4 and, like Big Mike, faced the guard's guns and went to the aid of another wounded student, Alan Canfora, whose story as a student agitator at Kent State was told in the last chapter of *Fire in the Streets*, by Milton Viorst.

Canfora arrived a little late for the service and wound up sitting behind me and Gary on the last row of folding chairs. He chatted briefly with us but failed to introduce his girlfriend, who looked to be in her late 20s. The rumor in Kent is that she won't let him party much with his buddies anymore, and that Alan has become domesticated. Sitting in front of us was Gail Roberts, the defiant young woman in James Michener's book, *Kent State: What Happened and Why*, who threw a bottle at a police cruiser on May 1, Friday night on Water Street in downtown Kent where students were jamming the bars. That helped to fuel a riot, causing the Kent Chief of Police (whose daughter is now the manager of the Inn of Kent, where Gary and I typically stay in our periodic visits) to urge Mayor LeRoy Satrom to call for the National Guard. Gary suspects that Gail might have had something to do with the burning down of the ROTC building on campus the following night, or at least knows who did.

We interviewed Gail several years ago, and she has kept in touch with Gary through email. When Gary asked her why she was wearing an old blue and white stripped knit hat to the memorial service, she whipped it off and showed us her shaved head. We declined to ask why her hair was cut so short, but she smiled broadly anyway and volunteered to say that at least she had more hair than we did, which was an irrefutable fact. Gail is a lawyer in Akron now, but I'm not sure who her clients are. I think she does a lot of *pro bono* work for lower income people, who otherwise get railroaded by the legal system.

Gail Roberts as a young, radical Kent State student addressing anti-war protestors the weekend before the May 4 shootings. Images courtesy of May 4 Collection. Kent State University Libraries. Special Collections & Archives.

We saw Howie Emmer and Bill Andrews come in and sit down on the other side of the room. Bill was another student who confronted the guard on May 4 and was guilty, as a police report at the time said, of "throwing a tree" at the guard (it was a tree branch). Bill was one of twenty five students who were indicted for riot and other related offenses by the Portage County Grand Jury. He fled the state and hid out with friends in Pennsylvania for a few weeks, but decided to turn himself in. He eventually was acquitted but did time waiting for trial in the county jail. According to Gail, his nickname while in jail became "Free Me Bill." Today, Bill teaches high school in an inner city, Cleveland ghetto. In the 1980s he went to Vietnam for a year so he could personally apologize to the Vietnamese people for the Vietnam War. Five or six years ago Gary and I went with Bill to a bar on lake Erie, and he almost got us into a fight defending a black kid, who he thought was being picked on by some blue collar red necks.

Howie Emmer was not in Kent on the day of the shootings. He had been kicked out of school and banned by court order from stepping foot on the campus for his part in organizing and carrying out a number of highly disruptive actions at Kent in protest of the war the previous year. Howie led the local Kent SDS chapter and was instrumental in recruiting Joan Carter into taking an active role in the Kent State SDS. Joan, as you may remember, was the speaker I got Rick Scott to invite to UCA a couple of years ago to give an Honors College lecture on students and social change.

Like Howie Emmer, Joan was off campus the day of the shootings. Her angry father had ordered her home the year before because of her political activism and neglect of her studies. After disobeying her parents again by hooking up for a short sojourn in a revolutionary Weatherman commune in Columbus, Ohio, Joan began distancing herself from active involvement in radical politics, went to graduate school for a Ph.D. in English literature, married a symphony composer, and now teaches at Case Western Reserve University in a Cleveland suburb.

After leaving Kent in 1969, Howie also joined the same revolutionary commune in Columbus. Unlike Joan, however, he eventually went underground with the Weatherman faction of SDS. Today he teaches third grade to Hispanic kids in a Chicago ghetto. Several years ago Gary tried to contact Emmer through Joan about granting us an interview, but he declined on the grounds that we might, however naively and innocently, be used as dupes for the FBI's ongoing investigation and surveillance of old student radicals. As soon as Big Mike's memorial service ended, we split up and Gary made a beeline over to talk with Howie (who ended up cautiously agreeing to interview with us at some unspecified time in the future). In the meantime, I found Bill Andrews talking to Jerry Lewis, the retired sociology professor who first proposed the annual Kent State candlelight vigil and associated commemorative events in 1971, the year after the shootings.

In middle age, Bill is a big, baldheaded man and is a very funny, entertaining guy. He started to get into an argument, however, with the one black person attending the memorial, a gray haired male wearing a wiry beard and an African dashiki by the name of Scotty. I had never heard of Scotty before, but apparently he also had been a student at Kent some time before the shootings. Scotty is a Vietnam vet, and he and Bill were arguing about whether war protestors blamed U.S. soldiers for the war. Bill said no, only Johnson, Nixon, McNamara, and other politicians were blamed—but not the soldiers. Scotty said, "Bull *shit*! I was there man, don't tell me what it was like to come back home from Nam!" I was starting to get a little nervous when Gail Roberts sauntered over and changed the conversation. She said she needed a smoke and wanted to go outside. I went with her, and Scotty came along to bum cigarettes. We sat on a bench in the freezing wind while Scotty and Gail chain-smoked and complained about how biased the news media were. I don't know what specific, recent news story provoked that harangue, but it wasn't too hard to agree with Gail's scathing critique. My teeth were chattering, but, by taking us outside, Gail had deftly defused Bill and Scotty's recriminating argument about the Vietnam War, which had scarred them both in different ways.

Mark Pacifico was also at the service, but he didn't stay after to visit. Instead, he hurried off to help Kassy Hogan (who is now his wife) make final preparations for the commemorative May 4 events scheduled to begin at noon on the campus commons adjacent to Blanket Hill and the Victory Bell, which was to be solemnly rung at 12:24 p.m., the moment in time when the Ohio National Guard fired their fatal fusillade thirty-two years ago. The Victory Bell, by the way, was the fateful site where Kent Students gathered to hold their rally in protest of the Nixon Administration's expansion of the war in Cambodia. General Robert Canterbury, commanding General of the Guard, determined that the rally was an illegal gathering and ordered his men, with tear gas, fixed bayonets, and loaded M-1 rifles to clear the field of dissident students, pushing them over Blanket Hill to the day's deadly denouement on the other side of Taylor Hall. Mark arrived as a freshman student at Kent State a year after the shootings and immediately became involved in ongoing radical student politics at Kent. Although he was an east coast, city boy from New York, Mark stayed on in Kent, continuing to take occasional classes in school and holding a variety of different jobs in the area. Mark remained a committed political activist throughout the reactionary Reagan years, but he probably stayed put in Kent because he fell in love with Kassy, who is ten years his junior.

The Kent State Victory Bell where, on May 4th, 1970, students assembled to protest the war in Vietnam.

Kassy, born and raised in Virginia, first came to Kent in 1980 as part of a college touring production of a play about the Kent State shootings. Kassy played the part of Allison Krause, one of the four students who was killed by the guard, and she so strongly identified with the role that it changed her life. Right away she met Alan Canfora and fell in love. She thought they were going to get married, but Alan eventually backed out of the relationship.

Subsequently, like Mark, Kassy stayed in Kent to become actively involved in the struggle to build a monument to the slain students on Blanket Hill and secure university support for May 4 memorial events. Until quite recently the KSU administration has had antagonistic relations with the May 4 Committee, a student organization which Kassy and Mark both unofficially advise and continue to actively participate in.

After years of carrying a flame for Alan Canfora, Kassy's heart finally succumbed to Mark's attentions and they married five years ago. Kassy works in a costume store in Kent, and Mark, who ended up with a master's degree in biology and extensive computer experience, is currently working as a telephone pollster in a job that he hates. But it pays for his cigarettes, pizza, and coffee, all of which he refuses to give up, even though he had a heart attack six months ago.

Well, it's an intriguing group of people. There were many others at the memorial service whom Gary and I didn't know or didn't get a chance to visit with. Life goes on, but for these and many other Kent State alumni of 1970, their subsequent histories and personal identities were fundamentally transformed by the events that occurred in a little Ohio town over three decades ago. Did their fateful choices and actions—during a profoundly divisive period of crisis in America—make any difference in anybody else's life besides their own? In spite of their youthful years, were they bold actors participating in the construction of history, producing searing moral lessons for the benefit of future generations of Americans? Or were they simply naïve and idealistic victims of their time and place, pulled into a maelstrom of larger societal contradictions and conflicts beyond their ken to adequately comprehend or change, with little meaningful legacy to offer us now in the 21st century? Reality is always complex, and the passage of time softens our memory of the deadly passions of bygone eras. But if forced to choose, both Gary and I hold to the mythic truth of the first interpretation.

You'll have to come with us to Kent some time. I'd like that.

33.

VIETNAM FROM A SOLDIER'S POINT OF VIEW

The name, "David Phillips," attributed to the person written about in this essay is a pseudonym.

Gary's 1994 talk entitled, "Prophets, Bomb Shelters, and the End of Time," had been well received. On Gordon's recommendation, Norb Schedler, director of the University of Central Arkansas' Honors College, had invited him as a guest speaker for the college's colloquium series. Following a Q&A session with Honors students and other guests at the lecture, Gordon introduced Gary to one of his former students who had been in attendance—a forty-four year-old, non-traditional student by the name of David Phillips. Gary quickly tuned into the fact that David was a commanding personality who nevertheless had established a tenacious bond with his unassuming sociology professor. David had been a history major at UCA who ended up minoring in sociology after he took an introductory sociology class from Gordon. He was also a Vietnam Vet. Gordon had first learned that fact several years earlier when David was unaccountably absent for a week from his Self and Society class.

David offered to meet with Gordon in his office to explain his absence. He had been going through a difficult time. His wife had divorced him ("because I did not communicate with her"), and he was working nights at a liquor store in North Little Rock to help meet his child support payments while attending school. He was depressed and had attempted suicide. "Don't do that!" Gordon interrupted. "If you have any more suicidal ideas, I want you to call me, I don't care what time of day or night," and wrote down his phone number. The next day David came back to Gordon's office and presented to him a twelve-inch Bowie knife with a clipped point that he had carried with him in Vietnam. He asked Gordon to keep it for him—out of his reach so he wouldn't be tempted to use it on himself. That's when he told Gordon about his service in Vietnam.

David had never talked about his combat experiences, he said, but they had dominated both his consciousness and subconsciousness for twenty years. His memories were an admixture of horrific moments of desperate killing and pride in the bravery of the men whom he had trained and who followed him into battle. As Gordon listened to the pent-up release of David's suppressed battlefield remembrances, he had a sudden, crazy idea: Would David be willing to appear as a guest speaker and talk about his experience in Vietnam to his Social Movements and Social Change class, which included a section on the student anti-war movement of the 1960s? David was taken aback; doing something like this would never have occurred to him in a million years. But he also was surprisingly intrigued by the idea: How would this proposal work?

Gordon explained that Rick Scott—a member of the sociology faculty, a good friend, and also Norb Schedler's assistant at the Honors College—was already scheduled to speak to the class about his experience as an anti-war activist during the Vietnam war. Rick was a few years younger than David but part of the same cohort of young men who faced induction into the army through the military draft of the 1960s. Rick's older cousin had been killed in Vietnam, and Rick became vehemently opposed to the war. He avoided the draft by volunteering for the navy, completed naval basic training, and then applied for conscientious objector status. Amazingly, this is exactly the way things worked out for Rick. When he was released from the navy as a conscientious objector, he immediately joined an anti-war group and became a full-time activist in protest of the war.

Gordon's idea was to have David speak on Monday to his class about soldiering in Vietnam, have Rick speak on Wednesday about his anti-war activity, and, as a culmination to their talks, have both come to class on Friday to take turns answering students' questions about their very different outlooks and experiences during that turbulent period of American history. Students would then be required to submit reaction essays in response to both speakers' presentations. It was a potentially dicey proposal—potentially *very* dicey, depending on the unknown chemistry that David and Rick might generate in the classroom when they met. Maybe it was not such a good idea after all. But David said *yes*, he would do it. He said he felt intimidated by Rick's articulate eloquence, but he was willing to try it anyway (maybe as a way to confront some of his own demons).

The week Gordon scheduled for David and Rick to speak to his class turned out to be the best thing he ever did as a college instructor. It subsequently became a prominent feature of his class. Students were mesmerized by the juxtaposition of their two talks and the contrasting perspectives David and Rick offered on the life altering events imposed on them by the war in Vietnam. On one occasion, an older woman student in the class asked David a question in the

Q&A exchange with Rick. Her brother had been drafted to fight in Vietnam, she said, and was subsequently killed in combat. Halfway through her question she broke down in quiet tears and couldn't continue. David's heartfelt response was to go to her desk at the front of the room and give her a gentle kiss on the forehead, saying, "It's alright sister, I love your brother."

Gordon (as well as Gary) had opposed U. S. military involvement in Vietnam, but he also had developed a personal connection with David Phillips and greatly admired his devotion and courage in leading the men who served under his command in combat. Whatever the politics of the war or the morality of its prosecution may have been, if he had been a young man conscripted by his country and actually engaged in combat, David Phillips was the kind of officer—serious and focused, cool-headed under fire, dutiful and self-sacrificing, but also realistic and unafraid of the responsibilities of command—under whom Gordon would want to entrust his own life.

For six years the David-Rick talks were the highlight of Gordon's course on Social Movements and Social Change. Then, in 1998, David appeared in Gordon's office and said he couldn't continue. Following his last appearance to speak to the class, he had attended a memorial service for one of his Vietnam War comrades. He told Gordon he couldn't keep on meeting with Rick and talk pro and con about the Vietnam War in retrospect as though it was merely an abstract debating question. For him it was far more than that, and it was taking a soul-sapping toll on his emotional health. The following day, Gordon wrote David a letter.

October 22, 1998

Dear David,

I much appreciate your candidness. Your presentations to my class have been so successful—which is to say that students routinely consider them to be the most meaningful and memorable moments of the course—that I have failed to adequately appreciate the personal toll they have exacted from you. The only thing I really need to say is, thank you. For six years you have revealed a part of your soul to young strangers with little or no reward and at considerable psychic cost. That is enough. You have my enduring gratitude and, I am confident, the gratitude of the students who were lucky enough to attend those classes as well.

I hope you don't mind if I quote from one of the student's reaction essays last spring which I liked and kept. The student was

"James" Thien, a Vietnamese foreign exchange student with a major in history. James wrote:

Mr. Phillips' decision to join the war was representative of one who is loyal to his country and willing to sacrifice his life for it. This is not strange or ridiculously absurd. His family has a proud tradition of military service, one which symbolizes a great American patriot. As a soldier, Phillips is not a romantic fool who would keep the American flag upright while under enemy bombardment. He is a cunning warrior who understands how important it is to stay alive. He took into great consideration and caution the warnings of imminent danger. He seems to have worried about the deteriorating morale of American soldiers. Prior to his arrival he was confronted by a drunken sergeant who told him, "Remember Charles [the Viet Cong] is bad." We see a sharp distinction between demoralized comrades, destined to die upon their first tour of duty, and an efficient enemy who is stalking like a predator. Phillips was obviously aware of this and greatly appalled by it. He learned to be cautious and ruthless. He learned to be deadly serious about war. America should be proud to have someone like Phillips, one who would keep his armor shined and his shield solid when his country is trying to win a war. However, it is a reminder to all American politicians that they should never have used and exploited a good soldier like Phillips. As the result of a lost war he suffered insults and resentment upon his return, which stayed in his mind, as shown through his gripping speech, ready to explode when his bitter memories are recalled too emotionally, clearly a psychological torment. It is a pity America is sacrificing a good soldier for a lost cause. He understood well what it means to be a soldier. He is a hero.

David, I know you don't like the word hero to be loosely applied, especially to yourself, but this was Mr. Thien's conclusion, and it's not too far from my own.

I look forward to seeing again you soon,

Gordon

At first, Gordon stayed in regular contact with David who had remarried. He and his wife successfully operated their own specialty products advertising business, and David became actively involved in North Little Rock community affairs and developed a reputation as an inspiring after dinner speaker at civic clubs and local business associations. In 2000, his son graduated from high school and was determined—in spite of David's protestations—to join the Marine Corps. In October of that year, David showed up at Gordon's office to introduce him to his son, who was on leave from boot camp and attired in his Marine Corps dress uniform. David was beaming with pride, but he also confidentially expressed some concerns to Gordon about what his son might be getting into. When David had enlisted in the United States Army in 1967, his grandfather took him aside and said, "Son, you need to understand, soldiers are for war and wars are for killing." Almost exactly a year after Gordon met him in his office, David Phillip's son was on his way to Kandahar, Afghanistan with the advance Marine Expeditionary Unit following the 9/11 attacks on the Twin Towers in Manhattan and the Pentagon in Washington, D. C. (While in Afghanistan, David's son saw action but returned safely home a year later.)

Visits dwindled gradually after that. David would occasionally drop by Gordon's office to say hello when he was passing through town. On one occasion he presented Gordon with an RMO ("round metal object") coined for U. S. military officers to share and keep as a tangible symbol of their loyalty to one another. The tradition requires that you keep your coin with you at all times. In the event that a fellow officer requests or "challenges" you to produce your RMO, and you fail to do so, you must buy him and any other officers who are present a round of drinks. David had obtained his and Gordon's RMOs at the officers' club of the Little Rock Airforce Base in Jacksonville, Arkansas where he had cultivated close ties to the air force as a civilian liaison official.

On another occasion, Gordon met David at night at the modest Vietnam memorial on the grounds of the Arkansas State Capitol, which honors Arkansans who lost their lives in the Vietnam War. On the wall of the memorial was the name of a soldier whom David had known as a young man. At the memorial, under the name of his friend, David left in tribute all of his Vietnam combat medals. The next day when Gordon returned to see if he could retrieve the metals, they were gone. Consequently, Gordon had his daughter Pam, who lived and worked in Washington, D.C., go to the massive and magnificent Vietnam Veterans Memorial Wall and make some etchings of three other soldiers' names whom David had known in Vietnam: John P. Davis, William B. Eslinger, and James E. Steadman. Gordon framed the name-etchings and mailed them to David as a Veterans' Day remembrance. David wrote an appreciative response.

Dear Gordon,

A week and a few days have passed since your gift arrived. I haven't written to thank you until now because I needed to consider what I wanted to say. Sweet, wonderful memories, that I had put too far away from my mind's eye, came into clear focus when the names of those dear men registered with me. In an instant I could see them in good detail. Each one strong, young, and alive. Johnnie, Bill, and Jim. Such common names for such good people. Still, there are no better names for them, just as there are no better synonyms for the words brave, honest, and true. Thank you for giving me a gift that lets me remember these fellows lived joyfully and honorably. In their memory, I must do the same.

Your friend, David

Vietnam Veterans Memorial Wall, Washington, D.C.

The last time Gordon saw him, David expressed a new concern: he thought he was losing his memory; he couldn't remember names or certain words and sometimes would forget things, he said. It was beginning to embarrass him a little bit when he delivered a talk to the local Rotary club or the Sales and Marketing Association. Gordon jokingly reassured him by saying, "welcome to old age!" David smiled and said, "yeah, I guess that's right," but he was concerned about it and was going to see a doctor.

When Gordon retired in 2106, Gary asked him, "What ever happened to David Phillips, the Vietnam vet you introduced me to after my talk at the Honors College colloquium in 1994?" Gordon guiltily admitted he hadn't seen David for several years. He had made a number of efforts to contact him through email and Christmas cards, but these communication attempts had not been responded to. Finally, going through some old papers, Gordon came across a card David had given him with his home phone number written on the back. Gordon dialled the number. The firm voice answering the phone was David's. Gordon recognized it immediately. But, shockingly, David didn't know who Gordon was. He forthrightly explained that he was confident Gordon was someone whom he should know but that, regrettably, he was in the throes of dementia (probably Alzheimer's disease.) The relentless progress of this insidious brain disorder had advanced to the point where he could no longer remember much about his own life, let alone other people. Gordon was stunned. On the phone David seemed cognizant and capable of conversing, but he had no recollection of their friendship or of his student days at the University of Central Arkansas.

To this Gordon replied, "Okay, maybe we can just talk a little and get reacquainted on the phone." David was fine with that but cautioned he probably wouldn't be able to remember their conversation. "You see," he said, "I have to keep things as simple as I can. I have to write down and follow written instructions. I need to keep to a simple routine." He said that he walked three miles to and from his house every day to the post office on J. F. K. Boulevard in North Little Rock to check for mail and keep up his physical health. He had lost weight. "You probably wouldn't recognize me now," he said. (In his prime, David Phillips was deep-chested and broad-shouldered. He was meticulous about his dress and appearance and looked great in a suit and tie. Before Vietnam, as a freshman at the University of Wyoming, he had wrestled and played football for the Cowboys.) David apologized for not remembering Gordon but said he had come to terms with his illness and was committed to simply making the most of what remained of his life from one day to the next. They chatted for a few more minutes. David thanked Gordon for his call but reiterated he wouldn't be able to remember it for long. Gordon told David that he admired his stoical resilience, that he had been proud to know him as a friend, wished him all the best, and hung up.

Gary ruefully shook his head as Gordon finished describing his last conversation with David Phillips. Their own father, Alvin Shepherd, had died of complications related to early on-set of Alzheimer's in 1982 at the age of seventy. And now, at that point in their lives, the two brothers were seventy-two. They were lucky, they agreed. "Let's stay close and keep close to our families and friends and enjoy them while we can," Gary said, "life is way too short." Gordon fervently concurred and said he would send Gary a copy of an interview his daughter Pam had conducted with David in 1993. Meanwhile, Gordon still carries with him the two-sided RMO which David had given him as a token of enduring friendship and mutual respect.

The RMO Gordon received from his friend, David Phillips.

A summary of David Phillips' war experience in Vietnam referenced in this essay is provided below by excerpts from Pamela Shepherd's interview with David for a paper she was writing in a history class at the University of Utah on the Vietnam War. Pam's paper was entitled, "Vietnam from a Soldier's Point of View." Readers are advised that, in his responses to Pam's questions, David does not offer a romantic or heroic account either of his service or of the war and its military or political goals. His language is blunt and forthright about the brutal, grim realities of combat and its enduring impact on the soldiers who enlist to fight their country's wars.

Interview Date: November 8, 1993

Pam: What areas of the service were you in, what was your rank, and why did you enlist?

David: I was attached to the 173rd Airborne Brigade, 2nd Battalion, Alpha Company, 1st platoon. I entered the service in 1967 as an E-1 private and came out [four years later] as a first lieutenant. [David was first promoted to sergeant in Vietnam and then given a battlefield commission and command of a platoon.] I knew I would have to go, so I enlisted. My family was made up of soldiers. My dad was a colonel in the air force. All of the men in my family had served with honor. I could do no less.

Pam: In what ways did, or did not, military basic training prepare you for war?

David: Basic training gave me a feel for the army but not for war. Basic training has never been able to give a soldier a glimpse of what fighting is really like . . . Drill sergeants put pressure on you in training to ready you for the pressures of combat, but combat is too intense to simulate. Ain't no teacher as good as Victor Charley [Viet Cong or VC—the principal enemy for U. S. troops in Vietnam].

Pam: How long were you in Vietnam?

David: I served two and a half tours of duty in Vietnam, 1967-69, 1970-71, and 1972. My last tour of duty was cut short by wounds.

Pam: Where were you stationed?

David: My unit moved all over the place. Phu Bei, Pleiku, An Loc, Doly To, and somewhere in Cambodia.

Pam: When did most of the fighting take place? How did the waiting, or anticipation of combat, affect your morale?

David: A good deal of the fighting was at night . . . I used to get tense when we had to stop and dig in. I liked to stay on the move and make contact with the enemy before he found us. This may sound strange, but I believe I had a gift for combat. I could pick up on conditions and situations that were indicative of an ambush. I could read sounds and smells, light and texture. I knew when things were out of order. I took extra time to move my men so as not to blunder into anything. My men probably experienced more anxiety than I did while awaiting combat because I stayed busy preparing, watching, and reacting to changing situations.

Pam: What was your first reaction when you got to Vietnam?

David: This place is full of snakes, bugs, and people who want to kill me. It sure is hot.

Pam: Your first reaction to participating in combat?

David: War is killing. Killing will help you survive.

Pam: Your reaction to seeing VC dead?

David: I was glad they were dead.

Pam: How difficult was it for you to fight an enemy you couldn't see?

David: I kept my men out of villages as much as possible in order to cut down on having to determine who was or was not VC. VC blended in well with the locals. They had networks and contacts with ALL the villages. Anytime I went into a village, I knew there would be VC, VC families, or people who knew VC. If villagers were unarmed, I left them alone. The VC were very good at setting ambushes, then vanishing. Their actions could be frustrating. To counter the frustration, I took a "wait 'til next time, MF" attitude.

Pam: How were VC treated when captured and how did this make you feel?

David: My unit captured only three VC. The others we came in combat with were all killed in battle. The three captured were badly wounded. We patched them up and sent them to the rear. I hoped they would die. I viewed them as killers, just as they viewed me, and I had no pity for them. You see, Pam, to survive combat it helped to have the killer in me. Respect for and hatred of my enemy kept my mind on the situation at hand, which was the destruction of the enemy and the preservation of the lives of my men.

Pam: How did you go about dehumanizing the enemy?

David: You have to dehumanize the enemy in order to kill him. "Dinks," "slopes," "gooks," "slants," and "Chuck," were some of the names we used. Dehumanizing the enemy has occurred in every war. The second the enemy becomes Mr. and Mrs. Thieu's little boy he will be in a better position to kill you.

Pam: Were the people you were fighting really the enemy or was it the idea of communism you were fighting against?

David: People who carried AK-47s were the enemy. I didn't think much of ideology. Once you're in it up to your rear end, you fight for yourself and the men beside you. There's not much "Mom and apple pie" spirit left.

Pam: How and where did you receive your wounds?

David: I received three wounds. The first was a bullet wound in my left arm from a fire fight. There was nothing remarkable about it. The second wound consisted of knife cuts in my leg. This happened when I was making a hasty retreat and ran into an NVA [North Vietnam Army] soldier. We got wrapped up in a wrestling match and tried to use our knives. We beat and bit, shouted and cursed at each other. He kept trying to work his blade into my stomach. I was stronger and pushed my blade into his vitals first. It was a bloody mess. The third wound was in my upper thigh and ended my tour of duty in Vietnam. A rocket or mortar round exploded next to me. The force of the explosion tossed me into the air. I flipped and landed on my back. I thought I was dead.

Pam: How did weather conditions affect your attitude toward fighting?

David: During the rainy season, monsoons kept the fighting down to zero. . . The climate was tough on me at first, but I got used to it as much as any Westerner could. Harsh weather conditions wear soldiers down. They seem to become the enemy, and that can be a fatal view. The only enemy is the other killer. You can't let the weather become your main concern. You have to make the elements your allies.

Pam: When you weren't fighting, how did you and other soldiers spend your time?

David: In combat areas we attended to sores and minor wounds, washing, writing letters, and sleeping. I would figure out our next moves and discuss them with my squad leaders. In areas more to the rear, we would clean up, eat, drink, write letters, go to the movies, gamble, and some guys went to local whore houses.

Pam: Have you had any problems coping with PTS since returning home from Vietnam?

David: I've had some low times over the years, but I got some help from the Veteran's Center Group. I cope well. I do have concentration problems, jump at loud noises, but I don't have rages. I'm not close to anyone except my six-year-old daughter. My only friend is your dad.

Pam: What is your most vivid memory of the war?

David: The look of surprize that registered in the eyes of the NVA soldier as my Bowie knife sank into his stomach, and how he gasped and quivered.

Pam: Before you went to Vietnam, did you think the U. S. had a right to be there?

David: Yes.

Pam: As a veteran, do you feel the same today?

David: No. We should not get involved in any fight that we don't intend to win.

Pam: What did the war teach you?

David: Just because a person has been put in charge, doesn't mean he knows what he's supposed to do. The war taught me that I have a dark side. We should not be allowed to see our dark side.

Pam: Do you feel you did your country a service in Vietnam?

David: I did my duty as I was sworn. I did my job. I did my country no service except that I kept a lot of young American soldiers under my command from being killed.

Pam: How were your treated by family and friends when you returned home?

David: My family treated me well. Their care soothed me and eased me back into the world. My friends had no time for me. They had moved on and there was a great distance between us. Upon returning from Vietnam in 1972 I was wearing my uniform at the Oakland California Airport and was beaten up by a group of anti-war demonstrators [David was on crutches, still recovering from his combat wounds]. At the University of Wyoming, where I tried to attend after my military service, I was pushed and avoided by my fellow students when they discovered I'd been a soldier in Vietnam. Steak-N-Ale Restaurants would not hire me as a manager trainee because, "at this time we are concerned about our image. The Vietnam soldier is generally seen in a negative light." I just put my soldiering days in the back of my mind. I didn't even mention my service experience on job applications. If asked, I said I was not called. As I stated earlier, I have no friends except for my relationship with your dad. My wife divorced me last year because I did not communicate with her. I love all five of my children, but I'm only close with my six-year-old. She loves me dearly.

Addendum: *David Phillips returned home from Vietnam with three Purple Hearts and a Silver Star for his bravery and leadership in battle. In 1992 he received his BA in history from the University of Central Arkansas. Since this interview, David remarried in December1993 and with his wife became self-employed in advertising promotions. He passed away, June 5, 2020.*

34.

STILL TWINS AFTER ALL THESE YEARS

The stranger nodded at Gordon and nonchalantly inquired, "How's it going so far this semester?" As a rule, men avoid chitchat with strangers while relieving their bladders in public urinals. For Gordon, this was always a potentially problematic situation when team-teaching a summer class with Gary at Oakland University in Rochester Hills, Michigan. Whenever he visited the men's room across the hall from Gary's office, there was a fair chance he would encounter someone who didn't know him and would mistake him for his brother. This time it was the college dean.

For approximately three decades, Gordon flew from Little Rock, Arkansas, to Detroit, Michigan, in early summer to supplement his regular teaching income and to work with Gary on their assorted research and writing projects. Over the years, Gordon became almost as well acquainted with Gary's sociology and anthropology colleagues in Rochester Hills as he was with his own at the UCA in Conway. But there is always a certain amount of faculty and administrative turnover at any university and, hence, the likelihood of bumping into someone new in the men's room.

Sometimes we surprise ourselves when we say something spontaneous and unrehearsed in the backstage moments of our lives. "*You don't know who I am, do you?*" Gordon artlessly responded to the new dean's innocent query. The dean reddened and turned slowly to inspect Gordon's profile. "Yesss," he carefully countered, "*I do.* You're . . . Gary Shepherd!"

"Nope, I'm Gordon," Gordon forthrightly declared, "I'm Gary's twin brother."

"Uh, hmmm, yeah, sure, I get it," said the befuddled dean, "you're actually his *twin*."

"Yes, that's right," responded Gordon.

Both men refocused their gaze on the bottom centers of their respective urinals and finished their business without further talk. Then, toweling their hands at the sink, the dean made an awkward effort to restart a conversation. "So, uh, 'Gordon,' right? Uhm, how long do you plan to be here?" the dean asked in a humoring sort of way, as they walked out to the hallway.

Gordon began an explanation of who he was and what he was doing at Oakland. But the dean, seeing Gary's office door ajar, and dubious about Gordon's claims, impulsively rushed over and threw it open. There, sitting at his desk with a quizzical look on his face, was Gary.

"Hey, dean, I see you've met my brother Gordon," he said. The stunned, disbelieving look on the dean's face and his stammered apology were priceless.

Well, we got that little misunderstanding straightened out, but then there was our night class of undergraduate students to contend with. Gary had been teaching the class two weeks before Gordon's arrival. Now it was Gordon's turn to take over. Normally, Gary would explain in advance to students about our arrangement, but this time he didn't, for reasons Gary can no longer remember. So Gordon walked into a classroom of approximately 50 students who simply assumed he was "Dr. Shepherd" and began teaching.

The vast majority of students didn't know the difference, but a few of the more attentive ones sitting on the front row were mildly disconcerted. A young woman raised her hand and said, "Dr. Shepherd, it looks like you've parted your hair on the left side tonight."

"That's true," said Gordon, who since high school always parted his hair on the left while Gary parted his on the right. (Yes, that was a time when both of us still had enough hair on the tops of our heads to part.)

A few minutes later, another student raised her hand and observed, "Dr, Shepherd, you're wearing a ring tonight and before you haven't." (Gary had lost his wedding ring some years previously and had never replaced it.)

"Okay, look," Gordon acquiesced, "I'm Dr. Shepherd alright, but *not* the Dr. Shepherd listed on your syllabus. I'm his brother, but, like him, I have a degree in sociology and am competent to teach this class. The two of us will work together in evaluating your work and assigning you a final grade for the course. If you have any concerns about this, you are more than welcome to visit with either me or my brother after class."

Nobody did. Most of the students seemed 100 percent indifferent as to who was teaching the course, and the eager, bright students on the front row seemed mostly pleased that they had correctly perceived something was amiss the moment that Gordon walked into the room and commenced the class.

Identical twins may be defined as "monozygotic" siblings, because they were formed from the exact same sperm and egg from their mother and father and therefore are siblings whose DNA is virtually the same (99.9 percent). However, *identical*—literally meaning *exactly the same*—is a minor misnomer for talking about the physical appearance and lives of identical twins, who, like everyone else, are also the products of complex environmental variables. Even when we were children and adolescents, our close friends, not to mention our parents and brother and sister, could always tell us apart. (Oddly, though, our grandmother Shepherd never could.) Nonetheless, to a remarkable degree, our lives and professional careers as adults have followed parallel paths. To this we attribute (only half-jokingly) our early need to join in cooperative efforts to stave off our older brother's resentful aggression toward us while growing up. Remember, of course, that from his point of view, our self-righteousness encroachment of his right of primogeniture was insufferable. Even though in later life we worked at reconciling our childhood differences, mutual resentment was always a hugely discordant note in our formative years. We maintain that in the crucible of this sibling conflict emerged the early solidarity of our twinship, which, in spite of the variable complexities of our adult lives, has endured to the present day. It would, of course, be unfair to completely burden or credit our older brother for all of this. Our shared disposition for collaborative alliance as twin brothers has, among other influences, been strongly reinforced by our overlapping network of friends—clearly illustrated by the stories in this volume—which we have cultivated both as kids growing up and as adults in later life. We would not be who we are without them.

One more thing. When we were young kids growing up in Salt Lake City, our Liberty Elementary School Principal, Miss Robey, conferenced with our parents about separating us into different homeroom classes. From kindergarten through the second grade, we had always been assigned to the same class with the same homeroom teacher. Miss Robey was concerned that maybe we were too close and interdependent, that it might be good for us to develop a little more individuality by putting us into separate classrooms during the school day.

When informed of this concern we were nonplused. We didn't think there was a problem. As far as we were concerned, we were perfectly capable of acting both together and independently, and that was true whether we were together in the same classroom or not. The problem, as we saw it as children (especially from Gordon's point of view) was that by assigning us to different homeroom classes for the third grade, Gordon would not get Mrs. Poulson for a teacher that year. Mrs. Poulson had been our older brother Don's teacher two-years ahead of us. He had flourished under her. Mrs. Poulson had especially encouraged the development of his art ability and, at the time, we thought we too had good art ability. For this reason, *both of us* wanted to take Mrs. Poulson for third grade. The issue to us wasn't one of developing independent personalities, it was "fairness." To Gordon, it didn't seem fair that he would miss out on Mrs. Poulson's art instruction. The other third grade teacher, Mrs. Taylor, was new and an unknown quantity. (Gordon would end up taking art from Mrs. Taylor in the sixth grade and, of course, she turned out to be terrific.) So, playing on his parents and Mrs.

Robey's sympathies, Gordon lobbied to stay with Gary in Mrs. Poulson's class "just one more year" and then it would be fine to separate them. And that's exactly what happened. Manipulative? Maybe a little. Ultimately dysfunctional? For whom and how? Both then and now we have worked both independently and in collaborative alliance; still twins after all these years.

---

122   PART II: INDIVIDUALS AND GROUPS

Figure 5-1   **Identical Twins.** Because identical twins are genetic duplicates, *any* physical or mental differences they display can be caused only by environmental factors. Thus, identical twins offer social scientists a priceless natural experiment for attempting to isolate and untangle biological, cultural, and social factors in human development. Of course, since identical twins are always of the same sex, look exactly alike, have the same parents, and usually grow up in the same home, it is more difficult than it first appears to tell whether their intellectual and psychological similarities are genetic or environmental in origin.

    The two little boys shown above are Gordon and Gary Shepherd (Gary is the one on the right). The Shepherds were born and raised in Salt Lake City and after high school they attended the University of Utah, where they both majored in sociology. Upon graduation, they entered graduate school — Gary at Michigan State and Gordon at State University of New York, Stony Brook — and each earned a Ph.D. degree in sociology. Today, Gordon Shepherd (the one on the right in this recent photograph) is a professor of sociology at Central Arkansas State University, while Gary is a professor of sociology at Oakland University. Each has done studies in the sociology of religion.

    No one thinks that the Shepherds both chose careers in sociology because of their identical genetic inheritance. But there is considerable evidence that their common heredity caused them to be very similar in terms of some more basic traits.

Page from Rodney Stark's introductory textbook, *Sociology*, on the interaction of genetic and environmental inheritance in the development of human personality. Image courtesy of Cengage Learning.

Note: At his request, we sent Rod Stark our baby picture and posed for an adult "fighting" picture for publication in the 1989 edition and all subsequent editions of his book, published by Wadsworth Publishing Company, Belmont, California.

35.

SOMEONE LIKE OUR SISTER SUE

July 15, 1955 was a bright, sunny day, and Don and the two of us sat on the thick, sloping grass on the east side of Holy Cross Hospital in downtown Salt Lake City, peering up several stories to a partially opened window. Our sister Susan had entered the world and into our lives the day before. Now, we could just make out our Mom's smiling face, looking down and waving as she held close a small, flannel-bundled figure. We waved back, barely comprehending what welcoming a little sister into our midst might portend for all of our lives in the years ahead. As a two-year old, Don had resented our sudden, disruptive appearance in his idyllic, first-born universe. Now, after eleven years of boys vying with one another in the Shepherd household, a girl had entered the family equation—an addition which, at the age of 43, our mother had long yearned for.

The dynamics of birth order, gender, and age differences between siblings can contribute to family relations in inadvertent ways. Don's relationship to Sue (which is what we always called her) was always remote; by the time Sue entered kindergarten, he had graduated from high school and then quickly married. A little closer in age and more interested in her development at home, the two of us doted on Sue, and she seemed to idolize us. Our Mom craved raising a daughter refined in social arts and tutored in domestic skills who would be close to her and follow her example. Instead, Sue became a daddy's girl and gravitated to sports.

Dad holding Sue, age about eight months.

**Our family's final configuration, circa 1958, about three years
after Sue's birth.**

Fast-forward forty years: Sue was the one who called on April 18, 1996, to tell us that Don had died at age 54 of an apparent heart attack in his Avenues apartment overlooking the city of his birth. Gary had taken a trip to Salt Lake a month earlier to check on Don when he had been admitted to LDS Hospital after collapsing from acute alcohol poisoning. Gary remembers arriving at the hospital just in time to be present at Don's bed when he was clawing at the oxygen mask and tubing that inhibited his movement and speech, hoarsely yelling that he had to have a smoke. Don recovered and was released after a few days to return home. We had been concerned about his health for some time, but none of us imagined that a month later he would be gone. This time it was Gordon's turn to make the sad trip home to help Sue finalize the disposition of our older brother's meager worldly possessions and earthly remains. (Don was an organ donor and had bequeathed his body for anatomy classes at the University of Utah School of Medicine. Ironically, during the last few years of his life, Don worked as a janitor at Holy Cross Hospital—the same hospital where all four of us had been born.)

Recently (circa November 2020), Gordon telephoned Sue who was running a few errands in her car. At the moment of Gordon's call, Sue happened to be driving past the Liberty-Wells Stake Center on the corner of 400 East and 700 South—the older central city area of our youth. "Wow," Sue said, taking cognizance of her surroundings, "I haven't been past this place in years." In their teens, Gary and Gordon had played at the Liberty-Wells Center for the Liberty Park Ward's young men's basketball and softball teams. Once this memory was spontaneously resuscitated, Gordon and Sue couldn't resist reminiscing a little more. They recalled that, following in her twin brothers' footsteps a decade later, Sue too played at the stake center for the Liberty Park Ward's young women's basketball and softball teams.

During those same years, our mom was determined that at least her *daughter* (if not her sons) was going to learn to play the piano. So Sue dutifully, but unenthusiastically, submitted to five years of piano lessons taught by our Aunt Olive's brother, Noel Fuller. At the age of 14, Sue rebelled and said no more piano for her. She much preferred hitting baseballs and tennis balls to Maestro Fuller's irksome admonitions to practice her weekly keyboard lessons.

We say that Sue followed in "our" footsteps, because, from an early age, she showed an avid interest in sports (though in comparison to the two of us, she actually appeared to have genuine athletic ability). We recall pitching whiffle balls to Sue when she was a preschooler and ducking to get out of the way when she smacked them right back at our heads with her little plastic bat. She learned to catch, throw hard, and, as a teen, could hit with power. During a South High girls' softball team practice in the early 1970s, on a small ball field then situated at the corner of 1700 South and Main, Sue walloped a pitched ball that sailed in a high arc toward Main Street and landed on the rooftop of a small business establishment facing away from the school. She developed a good outside shot when she started in basketball at Lincoln Junior High, had a strong serve and forehand in tennis, bowled a mean game during her high school years, and also learned to ski (something that the two of us never did). She also certified as a lifeguard and worked summers at the old El Rancho Lanes swimming pool on North Temple. So our little sister excelled at sports as a teen just prior to the implementation of Title IX mandates passed by Congress in 1972 for funding girls and women's athletic programs in public schools and universities. At South High, Sue was among the first to play on extracurricular girls' softball, basketball, bowling, and tennis teams, but, unfortunately, none of these was adequately funded or supported until a few years later.

The Two of us (Gordon center, Gary right) reminiscing with Sue about the good old days growing up in central Salt Lake.

As a young adult, Sue graduated from the University of Utah with a degree in psychology and a teaching certificate in special education. She went on to teach special education courses for 35 years at Highland High School. By that time, South High had closed its doors, and many of the kids who would have attended South were then enrolling at Highland. As a side note, Hal Hardcastle, one of Lincoln Junior High's outstanding PE teachers when we attended Lincoln in the 1950s, had moved on to Highland High in 1964 to coach the Ram's, wrestling, cross country, track and field, and football teams, and subsequently ended the last years of his public education career in 1987 as a student counselor at Highland. Sue confirmed for us what we already knew: Hal Hardcastle was a great guy whom Highland's students respected and revered.

As an adult, our sister Sue is a thoughtful, discreet, and unpretentious person. She likes her privacy and minds her own business. But she is also tender-hearted and liberal in her sympathies for downtrodden and misfortunate people who need a helping hand. She likewise loves animals, especially dogs, and especially golden retrievers. For over 30 years, Sue and her husband, Rod, have adopted golden fur babies [from Companion Golden Retriever Rescue which is "dedicated to the rescue and rehabilitation of homeless Golden Retrievers and placing them into permanent homes"] and patiently care for them as though they were their precocious children. A visit with Sue and Rod also necessarily entails a visit with their occasionally rambunctious but unfailingly sociable dogs.*

Gary and Sue with two of her golden fur babies.

Like our mother when we were growing up, Sue is deeply loyal to her siblings. That said, she never felt truly comfortable around Don, who was 14 years older—especially later in life when he was drinking to excess. But Sue dutifully kept tabs on him and was ready to render him her assistance whenever necessary. Sue and Rod lived a few blocks away from Don's last apartment on L Street between Fifth and Sixth Avenues. It was Sue who, concerned that she hadn't heard from Don for several days, went to his apartment, rang the bell, and, when there was no response, let herself in with the key Don had given her. She discovered his still, clothed body stretched out on his back, lying on top of his bed in the rear bedroom. It was Sue who had to call the police, an ambulance, and then us.

In our older years, the two of us often resort to sports analogies when pontificating about this and that. For example, in team sports there's nothing more important to a team's success than supportive teammates who are not only talented but also have your back and play for the team, not just themselves. On the playground when kids chose sides for different games, the question is: Who do you want to be on your side? Our advice: Pick someone like our sister Sue.

Rod, who was 10 years older than Sue, passed away after a valorous struggle with pulmonary fibrosis on January 24, 2021.

36.

ON THE ROAD AGAIN

G ary was behind the steering wheel, Gordon was riding shotgun. It seemed oddly familiar as the two of us scanned the wide-open spaces of Eastern Wyoming. Fifty years previously we had traversed this area of the country in a two-ton Utah National Guard truck on our way to summer camp near the Black Hills region of South Dakota. This time we were in the cab of a 26-foot U-Haul moving van, heading in the opposite direction, toward Salt Lake City.

Three days earlier, Gordon had flown from Arkansas to Detroit to help Gary and his wife, Lauren, pack their U-Haul with assorted furniture, books, paintings, and other belongings for transport to temporary storage units on Third West in South Salt Lake. Gary and Lauren had listed their home for sale in Rochester Hills, Michigan, and were about to close on the purchase of a house in Sandy, Utah, located near the entrances of Little Cottonwood and Big Cottonwood Canyons, overlooking the Valley of the Great Salt Lake. Lauren had insisted that if they were going to move back to Salt Lake, she wanted "a home with a view."

As we continued driving west, there was no shortage of topics for us to discuss and reminisce about. Among other things, we remembered our 1967 National Guard summer camp in South Dakota that had coincided with Israel's victorious "Six-Day War" with Egypt, Jordan, and Syria, during which we speculated about where our majors in sociology at the University of

Utah might take us as adults. We also ruefully recollected the ill-fated demise of one of our early storybook heroes—the vainglorious George Armstrong Custer—who led the Seventh Cavalry to annihilation in a greedily stupid military confrontation with Lakota Sioux and Cheyenne warriors after gold had been discovered on Indian lands in the Black Hills. And, coincidentally, we also recollected that Deadwood, South Dakota was the location for the hit musical "Calamity Jane"—starring Doris Day as Calamity and Howard Keel as Wild Bill Hickok—performed some 10 years later on South High's auditorium stage as the school musical by the South High Acapella and drama classes in our senior year.

**Howard Ashby as Wild Bill and Sally Post as Calamity Jane,
in South High's 1962 musical production.**

In slightly off-key registers, Gary began whistling while Gordon sang some lines from one of Calamity's numbers entitled, "I Just Blew in From the Windy City." Reminiscing about the high school production of Calamity Jane (Gary had had a bit-part in the chorus) reminded us of the rapidly approaching fifty-fifth reunion for South High's class of '62, which Gary was supposed to emcee. On a spur-of-the-moment impulse, Gary enjoined Gordon to dial Paul Eddington on his cell phone to see if Paul was still planning to attend the reunion. Paul was a distant cousin on their mother's side, whom the twins had met for the first time at South, and the three had become friends. As an adult, Paul ended up living in a suburb of Cleveland, Ohio, and Gary had recently renewed their friendship by making a short visit to Cleveland from Detroit. But Gordon had not seen or talked with Paul for decades. He remembered him as a mature looking, confident speaker, with a dazzling smile who had been chosen to attend Boy's State with Wayne Miller, Owen Wood, and Phil Starr. At South, Paul teamed with Bill Gehrke—another good high school buddy—as award winning debaters for the school's debate team.

Paul Eddington, circa 1962.

Yep, when Paul answered the phone, it was the same, self-confident voice that Gordon remembered from adolescence. With Gordon's phone on speaker, the three friends talked freely as the U-Haul van ate up the miles driving west through Wyoming. No, sorry," Paul explained, family conflicts would prevent him from attending the reunion. But he asked Gary to belatedly apologize to any female classmates attending whom he may have offended by his callow, adolescent glibness.

After talking with Paul, we drove on, staying awake by continuing to reminisce in a rambling stream-of-consciousness. We recalled that Paul's younger sister Susan had dated and then married, Bill Gehrke's brother Jack, who was two years younger than us. Jack blossomed athletically at South where he QB'd the football team, starred as point-guard for the basketball team, shortstop for the baseball team, and took second place at the state track meet in the 220- yard dash as a senior in 1964. At the University of Utah, Jack became the starting quarterback his junior year, continued playing shortstop for the Ute's baseball team, and, upon graduation in 1969, received professional offers to play both football and baseball. He decided on football and signed as a wide receiver with the Kansas City Chiefs, who subsequently traded him to the Denver Broncos. But to us—in junior high and his sophomore year of high school—Jack was just "Little Gehrke"—small and cocky, but already a standout, all-around athlete in competitive sports. A conscientious A-student, his older brother Bill loved sports too, but, like us, was not athletically gifted the way Jack was.

Bill and Jack Gehrke, circa 1960.

"Hey, Gar, do you remember the time we got caught skinny-dipping with Bill, Jack, and Jim Burns (another good high school friend) at Hygeia in Sugar House? queried Gordon.

"Sure," Gary replied. Here's a shorthand version of the story.

Somebody had suggested: "I know what we can do. Why don't we sneak into Hygeia?" We don't recall whose idea it was—it might have been "Little Gehrke's," who was tagging along with Bill and Jim, but it sounded agreeable to all of us. It was a warm, August night, a couple of weeks before the beginning of the 1960-61 school year. None of us had access to a car, so we'd have to hike almost two miles to get there from the Gehrke's neighborhood on Browning Avenue. But what the heck, we had nothing better to do. So off we went.

Hygeia's Iceland on 2100 South and 1200 East had opened in the late 1940s as the city's only ice-skating rink. In the 1950s Hygeia added a heated, Olympic-size swimming pool. Both the skating rink and the swimming pool were open to the public through private club memberships, which to us and our working-class parents seemed prohibitively expensive. For the likes of us, there was the free, "open plunge" at Liberty and Fairmont Parks in the summer, and also free ice skating at Liberty Park Pond, across from the Tracy Aviary, for kids who wanted to try their luck on an old pair of skates in the winter.

Hygeia fronted busy 2100 South, but the back side of the pool area was situated on a shallow ravine slope, blanketed with tall weeds and sagebrush, which served as a secluded path to the pool. When we got to the top, all we had to do was climb an eight-foot, iron picket fence and we were in! We all shed our clothes down to our tidy-whiteys and jumped into the warm water. The pool had a diving board, which we proceeded to make good use of. It had good spring, and we took turns seeing how high and far we could jump. We were having a great time, laughing, splashing, and yelling a little bit too much. Suddenly, at the other end of the pool adjacent to the dressing rooms, we heard an angry adult voice and glimpsed a man with a large flashlight hurriedly unlocking the iron gate. "What the hell do you kids think y're doin' in here!" he thundered.

Holy shit! A night watchman! We all grabbed for our clothes and carried them with us as we swiftly started scaling the iron pickets and dropping down to hide in the sage brush ravine. All but one of us made it over the fence in time. Bill was the one who got caught. The night watchman grabbed his shoulder and spun him around in the glare of his big flashlight. "I oughta whip your ass black and blue with my belt buckle! Take your clothes and git! And tell your buddies down there to never come back," he commanded, "cuz I won't be so frigg'n nice next time!"

Well, there wasn't any next time. In a few weeks, football season would be upon us (Bill was junior varsity quarterback), classes would begin, and summer swimming—whether free, paid for, or enjoyed at night by sneaking into members-only pools—was over. We didn't razz Bill as we walked home. We all knew that anyone of us could have been in his place; that he had taken the heat off the rest of us by getting caught, and that's why we had been able to escape. The mystery, of course, is why Hygeia's night watchman didn't call the Salt Lake City Police or Bill's parents. Maybe he figured it would be too much hassle, and that all he really needed to do was scare us a little bit. Or, maybe, like the downtown cops years earlier (who had let Gary and our friends Ron Swenson, Al Ebert, and Udell Stones off scot-free after Gordon had blasted their patrol car windshield with a mammoth dirt clod), he simply took a tolerant, boys-will-be-boys attitude towards adolescent escapades—as long as they were white kids, of course. We were often lucky in that regard growing up in central Salt Lake City in the 1950s.

Hygeia Iceland/Swimland, by the way, burned down in 1985, and its former location on 2100 South is occupied today by a Chick-fil-A restaurant and other commercial establishments.

By the time our U-Haul van carried us down Parley's Canyon and into the city, it was well past midnight. We stayed on Foothill Drive all the way to the campus of the University of Utah, and then headed up the northern avenues overlooking downtown Salt Lake City. We parked the truck on Ninth Avenue, just around the corner from where our sister Sue and her husband Rod Stone live on H Street. We would spend the night at Sue and Rod's and then unload the truck in the morning at the storage units in South Salt Lake. It was quiet and serene as we checked the locks on the truck before walking down to knock on Sue's door. From where we stood we had a commanding view of Salt Lake City and the twinkling radiance of a billion lights that filled the entire Valley of the Great Salt Lake. We were home.

Salt Lake City at night.

36.

FROM DUST TO DUST

April 12, 2018. Gary was delivering the eulogy for his friend and Oakland University colleague, Vince Khapoya. Listening to Gary in the company of a large assembly of other mourners (and secretly relieved that he wasn't encumbered with such a solemn assignment), Gordon reflected on the circumstances that had brought him back to Michigan again so soon and unexpectedly. Nine months previously he had returned to Michigan for what he anticipated would be the last time to help Gary pack a moving van destined for Salt Lake City and a new home for Gary and his wife Lauren in their retirement. For years prior to that, Gordon had appeared annually in Michigan to team-teach a summer night class with Gary and collaborate on research and writing projects at Oakland University, situated 30 miles due north of Detroit. During that time, he had become well acquainted with Vince Khapoya and his wife Izzy, who for 33 years had been Gary and Lauren's neighbors in Oakland University's faculty subdivision.

Kenyan by birth, Vince met and married Izzy, who is Indian (but was also born in Kenya) while both were attending college on scholarships in the United States. Both became naturalized U. S. citizens, and their children, Aman and Aisha, grew up as playmates and classmates with Gary and Lauren's children, Bethany and Snow. On uncounted occasions Gordon had shared potluck meals with the Khapoyas and other Oakland faculty subdivision neighbors during his annual summer visitation to work with Gary.

The ethnic diversity of the subdivision was one of the attractions for Gordon as a regular visitor; for Gary and Lauren as homeowners and permanent residents over the course of their working lives it was an intrinsic blessing.

For the past ten years, however, Vince had slowly been losing his struggle with Parkinson's Disease. The last time Gordon had seen him— before he entered an assisted living center in Rochester Hills, Michigan— Vince was unmistakably quieter and verbally subdued. But he had not lost his gleaming smile or personal warmth. Gary's words of eulogy for Vince penetrated Gordon's musings: ". . . his authentic, welcoming, accepting, and quietly luminous smile. A smile that reflected a man at peace with himself. A smile that signalled he accepted you as an equal and valued counterpart . . . This was a man comfortable in his own skin, perpetually inviting you to be as comfortable as he was." Vince Khapoya was the eldest son of a traditional village chieftain. In Gary's words: "He was born and raised in a humble African village in Kenya near that greatly sought-after talisman of Colonial England, Lake Victoria, mere miles distant from the village in which President Barack Obama's father was born. Examples and teachings absorbed from his grandfather, father, and mother instilled pride in himself or, better said, respect for himself and his worth as a human being."

Vince Khapoya.

Vince's memorial service was being conducted at the Birmingham Unitarian Church in Bloomfield Hills, Michigan, a scant quarter of a mile away from the LDS Detroit Temple. The adjacent LDS chapel is where Mitt Romney—President Obama's presidential opponent in 2102—attended church as a boy growing up when his father, George, had served as the LDS Bloomfield Hills stake president, president of American Motors Corporation in Detroit, and subsequently as governor of Michigan. Unlike either Mitt Romney or Barack Obama, however, Vince Khapoya, was not religious. In fact, he was intellectually hostile to most forms of organized religion. This was primarily the result of his boyhood experience growing up as a promisingly bright Kenyan boy under the authoritarian tutelage of Anglo Jesuit priests. As Gary summarized in his tribute: "When Vince qualified for admission as a youth into a Jesuit academy for promising African boys, he became directly exposed to racial prejudice, and he keenly resented it. But the experience did not embitter or demoralize him. Instead, it motivated him to contradict the low expectations heaped upon him, to excel, to demonstrate his worth as a human being when allowed opportunity and access to educational resources. He challenged the Anglo-Catholic Brothers who relentlessly tried to suppress his spirit and marginalize his status. And in the end, he far surpassed the narrow limitations they attempted to impose as he made his amazing passage from village herd boy to internationally known scholar, teacher, and humanitarian."

His antireligious sentiments notwithstanding, Vince's caring humanitarianism had led him as a committed husband and father later in life to join with his spiritually attuned wife, Izzy, to support and participate in the community-oriented programs of the inclusive and nonsectarian, Unitarian Church. Vince also had consented to Izzy's wishes before he died that a memorial service in his honor be conducted in the Unitarian Chapel on Woodward Avenue and concurred with her that Gary should be invited to deliver one of two eulogies. (The other eulogy was given by Dr. Virinder Moudgil, a long-time friend, former provost at Oakland University, and subsequently president of Lawrence Technical University.)

Elaborating further on Vince's enviable qualities of self-abnegation in his priority concern for the wellbeing of others, Gary recounted what he had observed when making periodic visits to see Vince during his residency at the Bellbrook Assisted Living Center: "While Vince was still physically mobile, passing through the hallways and rooms of the Sanctuary at Bellbrook, he was the constant recipient of heartfelt greetings from fellow residents and staff. All knew him and called out his name. All were delighted by him. He lifted everyone's spirits, even amid his own afflictions. It was touching and typical of Vince to see him caringly give helpful assistance and directions to an old friend and colleague—Venkat Reddy—who was, for a time, also a resident at Bellbrook—as the two of them walked haltingly together and haltingly conversed at meals. Vince's own condition was only marginally better than Venkat's, but, as always, he was conscientiously more focused on his friend's needs than his own."

Vince had obtained his graduate degree in political science and joined the political science faculty at Oakland University in the mid-1970s, just before Gary began his own teaching career at Oakland. As Gary recalled for the benefit of those gathered to mourn and pay tribute, "Vince's character perceptibly impacted his day-to-day working life as a faculty member at Oakland. When he became chair of the Political Science Department, Vince brought instant credibility to his role. He always remained cool and unflappable when confronted by provocations and challenges. His first instinct was to be a peacemaker and proponent of middle ways between extremes, but never at the expense of compromising his perceived duty or the principles of equal justice he held so dear." In contrast to blowhard politicians and self-anointed demagogues, "Vince was small in physical stature but a giant in moral stature. In our current Trumpian world, his honesty, integrity, compassion, unselfishness, and open-mindedness shine like diamonds in a sky of black ink."

Gary ended his eulogy by reflecting on a ten-day expedition that he and Lauren had undertaken with Vince and Izzy eight years previously to "the magnificent red rock and canyon wilderness areas of Southern Utah and Northern Arizona. We hiked together in Zion National Park, Grand Canyon National Park, Antelope Canyon, Monument Valley, Mexican Hat and the Goose Necks of the San Juan, Bridges National Monument, Capitol Reef National Park, and Bryce Canyon National Park. At Bryce Canyon—a surreal, serene, stupendous natural amphitheater of color-drenched, fantastically shaped rock formations and majestic pines—Vince was reminded of Hindu temples, both gazing down from above and walking the trails below. During a long, quiet evening stroll with Lauren around the edge of the canyon, Vince expressed a wish that upon his death his ashes might be brought to that sacred-seeming place and scattered among its beautiful spires. Surely his earthly remains will find there a compatible and fitting final resting place for a soul as beautiful as his."

Izzy and Vince at Bryce Canyon, 2008.

May 28, 2019. Gary was on the phone to describe for Gordon the simple, unadorned events connected to the realization of Vince's final resting place. Izzy had taken seriously her promise to her late husband. She had preserved his ashes to arrange a mutually available date on the calendar for meeting Gary and Lauren along with her adult children, Aman and Aisha, one of her sisters, and a nephew at Bryce Canyon. There was no established protocol or ritual to guide Izzy's actions. And the legality of releasing the ashes of a deceased loved one within the boundaries of a national park was more than dubious. Casting aside these concerns, Gary and

Lauren helped Izzy find an appropriate spot on the amphitheatre rim of the canyon's stunningly beautiful, red, orange, and pink vastness—a rock peninsula that jutted out over the temple spirals underneath. Izzy then formed her little band of congregants into a tight circle on this overhanging lookout point and read to them, in a tremulous voice, two compositions she had written for the occasion: a brief tribute to Vince's qualities as a father, husband, and human being, followed by a poetic prayer. She then invited each person to scoop a portion of Vince's ashes from a small, decorated bag and deposit them either into crevices in the rocky peninsula where they stood or release them into the desert air, where they would be dispersed on a gentle breeze over the fabulous expansion of unearthly, multi-hued formations, reaching heavenwards from the canyon floor below.

Utah's Bryce Canyon.

How strange and mysterious and simultaneously uplifting to contemplate the ultimate disposition of Vince Khapoya's life and earthly remains. Vince Khapoya was to his wife and children a conscientious husband and father. To us, he was a good and valued friend, whom we first met 2,000 miles away from the city of our birth. But unlike any of the friends we grew up with or met later in life, he was the son of a tribal chieftain from Kenya, Africa, who became a proudly patriotic American citizen, a committed internationalist, and a revered colleague and teacher of politics as an honorable vocation to the children of his adopted country. Now his atoms are mingled for the next eternity with those of the majestic, hoodoo guardians of Bryce Canyon, Utah.

38.

MUSICAL ILLITERATES
Getting By with a Little Help from Our Friends

Recently we had breakfast with Dave Lingwall at the Cracker Barrell Old Country Store on 3500 South in West Valley, Utah. We hadn't seen him for decades. Dave's thick, wavy red hair from boyhood days had faded to silvery grey, but at least he could boast of still having his hair, which we could not. As we downed our breakfasts and got reacquainted, two things became clear: Dave had a very good memory, and he had not lost his quirky, irreverent sense of humor. Naturally we reminisced about old friends and our shared pasts while growing up in central Salt Lake and then talked a little about our current lives. Dave, it turned out, had married Carla, his high school girl friend, had six children, *thirty-five* grandchildren (whose names he recited to us in perfect alphabetical order), and had worked his entire occupational career for Mountain Bell (later designated as US West). Digesting all of this information, Gary suddenly asked Dave if he still played the clarinet. Without missing a beat, Dave pulled out his phone to display a picture of himself cradling two shiny saxophones; one was a baritone and the other a tenor. Dave explained that nowadays he preferred the saxes, that they were easier for him to play in old age than the clarinet. And yeah, he still took pride in his playing.

In 1977, our great uncle, Arthur Shepherd, was posthumously awarded the Cleveland Arts Prize for Music. Arthur was a child prodigy who transcended his humble Paris, Idaho, family roots at the age of twelve to commence his musical education at the New England Conservatory in Boston. Among other adult achievements later in life, he was awarded the 1905 Paderewski Prize for best American orchestral composition, served as assistant conductor of the Cleveland Symphony Orchestra, was music critic for the Cleveland Plain Dealer, became chair of Case Western Reserve University's music department, and composed over 100 major musical works, including symphonies, string quartets, and assorted songs and their arrangements. Arthur deserved his kudos.

Regrettably, however, his Shepherd musical DNA apparently leapfrogged over the two of us. We hasten to add that our mother's side of the family cannot be blamed for this egregious misfortune. Our mother, Marjorie Coombs, was competent at the piano and had a pleasing alto singing voice. In fact, from an early age, she wanted very much for her boys to learn music. Hence, our brother Don commenced taking violin lessons in elementary school, and the two of us were slated to learn the piano. Mistake One with this plan was that our mother attempted to be our piano teacher. Mistake Two was the fact that we seemingly had little aptitude for the instrument and even less motivation to learn (the latter of these two observations quite possibly setting up a self-fulfilling prophecy for the first). As best we can recall, our lessons lasted less than two weeks of resentfully plunking out beginner tunes, like "Papa Hayden's Dead and Gone." For the sake of her own sanity, mom threw in the towel and said she would try again when we got a little older. (Due to our nearsighted intransigence, however, that never happened.)

Don continued his violin lessons for the rest of the year, but by then it was increasingly evident that he had genuine art ability. All he wanted to do with his free time was sketch and paint, so his music lessons went out the window too. As for us, we also liked art and were fairly good at drawing, but we conceded that art was Don's domain. More so than Don, we readily formed close bonds with neighborhood friends and hanging out with them dominated our boyhood interests. Instead of music or art, eventually we started gravitating towards sports, which became a consuming, adolescent passion, even though we were never very gifted athletes.

None of this means that we hated music or didn't like to sing Christmas carols at church, or songs we learned at school, or hum along or whistle to the popular tunes of the era and tap our feet to a rock'n roll beat. To the contrary. We were just not motivated to discipline ourselves long enough to study or learn music fundamentals and, to Arthur Shepherd's undoubted horror had he known, we consequently grew up musically illiterate.

But fortunately, not all of our friends shared our illiteracy. Two of our best friends, in fact, had both ability and cultivated tastes in very different kinds of music. We admired this and forgave both of them for not sharing our passion for sports. Our two musically inclined friends were Phillip Starr and, of course, David Lingwall.

To us, Phil seemed like a true prodigy. Through various church activities, our parents knew his parents, and we can remember our mother talking about Phil's blossoming piano skills before we had even started kindergarten. In every grade we passed through at Liberty Elementary, Phil was designated as the teachers' accompanist whenever we sang or learned new songs in class. He became his LDS ward piano accompanist for hymn singing in Sunday services while still an elementary schooler. Later, for three years at Lincoln Junior, he was the orchestra's pianist and the school's designated accompanist for every musical event or performance. Likewise, at South High, he played piano accompaniment for the acapella choir, all the school musicals, solo vocalists, and for our graduation ceremony. To the untutored likes of us, Phil's taste in music was indubitably classical. Classical pieces, of course, represented the most difficult and challenging music in a serious student's repertoire, so naturally we assumed those were the pieces that Phil learned and practiced. But popular Broadway show tunes and Sunday worship music were also part of his regular repertoire, and it seemed to us that he could play them flawlessly by sight-reading alone, without having to learn or rehearse them.

Phillip Starr as a sixth grader at Liberty Elementary and six years later as a senior at South High.

David Lingwall's taste in music ran in different directions. Dave took up the clarinet when he tried out for the Lincoln Junior High band and learned to play saxophone too. At South he played both the clarinet and saxophone all three years for the orchestra, pep band, and dance band. David's music wasn't just something he did to fill up his class schedule. He cultivated a genuine love for instrumental music, especially American jazz. As illiterates, the two of us were even less familiar with jazz than we were with classical music. But our friendship with Dave Lingwall changed that—a little bit, anyway. By going to Dave's house and listening to his record collection, we learned the difference between Ragtime, Dixieland, Swing, Bebop, and Cool Jazz to name a few of the variants. Some jazz musicians' names we were superficially familiar with already through their impact on American movies and pop culture (like Louis Armstrong, Duke Ellington, and Benny Goodman), but there were many others whom we had never heard of (John Coltrane,

Charlie Parker, Miles Davis, Thelonious Monk, Dave Brubeck, etc.) until Dave Lingwall exposed us to their music, for which we are forever grateful.

Dave Lingwall in the Fifth Grade at Liberty Elementary and, later, playing his saxophone for the South High dance band.

To this day we both regret muffing the chance of learning how to read music and play an instrument. We consider our musical ignorance to represent an embarrassing hole in our educations. Nonetheless, we enjoy *listening* to a wide range of different types of music—from classical to pop, to folk, to rock, to jazz—an appreciation pleasurably augmented by two of our oldest friends while growing up together in Salt Lake City. Frankly, today we even like Bob Dylan's *singing* on certain songs (and not just his lyrics). But this, perhaps, is an arcanely acquired musical taste for which Phil and Dave would prefer not to take any credit (and great uncle Arthur would disown us for sure). We'll have to ask Dave about it the next time we meet for breakfast. When you're illiterate, you try to get by with a little help from your friends.

39.

FATHER AND SON REUNION

*T*hough highly publicized topics in the 1960s, only a fraction of our generation actually involved themselves in radical student politics or abandoned
the traditions of their religious upbringing to search for salvation in alternative
new religions. Most followed 20th century career paths in life that were far more
predictable and consistent with the conventional parameters of the social worlds
in which they were raised. This does not mean, of course, that our age cohort
compatriots did not contend with some of the mean limitations of life and the
often undeserved pain which this confers. With respect and appreciation, the
following account is dedicated to Tim Christensen, South High Class of 1962.

Tim Christensen, 1962.

"Why didn't you catch that ball, daddy?" Tim Jr. earnestly inquired when the inning ended.

"Because, son," Tim Sr. patiently explained, "the ball went over the fence."

"Why didn't you jump over the fence and catch it?" Tim Jr. persisted. Little boys and their superhero dads.

A star athlete at South High, with latent artistic and musical talents (later expressed through impressive paintings and playing lead guitar as front man for a rock and roll band), Tim Sr. worked on cars for a living during his young adult years and, on weekends, hit homeruns for a local men's championship softball team.

Tim Jr. was frail and small for his age; he had been born with a serious heart defect. He struggled for breath and underwent a series of heart surgeries. The heart surgeon was Russell M. Nelson, renowned later in life as the 17th prophet and president of the Church of Jesus Christ of Latter-day Saints. The surgeries seemed to help; Tim Jr. survived and, though physically handicapped, aspired to be like his dad. The medical bills plunged Tim Sr. and his wife into virtual bankruptcy, but they didn't begrudge the cost.

Tim Sr. took his son to all of his games where he sat in the dugout as the team's six year old batboy and unofficial mascot. One hot, summer afternoon, Tim Jr. came in the house and said he was hungry: Could he have a peanut butter sandwich, please? He took his sandwich to the living room couch where he laid down and never woke up. The grief was hard, unendurable, unending.

"Who are you talking to?" his wife called out from the kitchen. Sitting in the living room in lingering, stolid grief, Tim Sr. didn't answer, but his voice could still be clearly heard, as though in conversation with an unannounced visitor.

Decades later, catching up with one another's lives over breakfast at a local café in Sandy, Utah, Tim confided to us: "I don't know, maybe you think I was crazy or on drugs, or something weird, but when I was on the living room couch, my son came to me, only he wasn't a child, he was grown. He said, 'Dad, I just want you to know that I'm alright, that I'm not in pain anymore.'" Tim Sr. volunteered his story to us with a slow, steady voice, but his eyes were misty.

"That was a long time ago," Gordon commented; "have you seen or talked with your boy since then?"

"Yes," Tim Sr. acknowledged, "on occasion we have talks."

"What does he say now?" Gary inquired.

"The last time he came to me," Tim replied, "he said, 'Dad, are you ready to come with me now?' And I said, 'No son, not yet, not yet.'"

Let us not embrace false hope

On this bleak and broken day

But the father and son reunion

Is only a glimmer away

These raw moments our minds repeat

In perpetual pain and sorrow

But the father and son reunion

Will surely come tomorrow

It's hard to believe life ends

In such a mysterious way

But the father and son reunion

Is only a glimmer away

40.

SHEIK CAPUTO AND
THE BIG DUGOUT IN THE SKY

"Caputo," Gordon thought to himself, "his last name was Caputo, but what was his first name?" Gordon was trying to remember the first name of the man who, in the early 1960s had been the director of the Elks Club (and coach of the Elks Club softball team we played against during the summer of 1960). The Elks Club was a squat, Quonset hut shaped building on Main Street and 1300 South in Salt Lake City situated on the other side of Derks Field's left and center field fences. Technically, the Elks Club was "The Boys and Girls Elks Club," but very few girls ever went there to avail themselves of the cramped basketball court and other modest sports facilities and equipment that the club offered for inner-city kids living in the area. Among area boys it was known simply as the Elks Club. As young teens, we began frequenting the Elks Club in the winter months during our sophomore year at South High in 1959-60. The "Club" was a mile hike from our home at 1166 Denver Street, a half block from Liberty Park on Fifth East. Unlike many of the local LDS Ward chapels, the older Liberty/Liberty Park Ward Chapel did not have a basketball court included as part of its amusement hall wing of the building. So, if we wanted to shoot baskets and work on lefthanded layups after school, our first (and often only) option for practice was the Elks Club.

The two of us had been reminiscing about the summer we played fast-pitch softball for the Salt lake County Recreational league and faced the Elks Club team in the championship game. Gordon clearly remembered that the Elks Club's coach was, in fact, Coach Caputo, but what was his *first* name? It's funny in older age how frustrating minor memory lapses concerning retrospectively trivial things can be. What *was* his first name? We had known and played baseball with Kenny Caputo in junior high and (not to mention Joe Caputo, a same-aged cousin of Kenny's, who was a superb athlete and feared fighter). Was the Caputo in charge of the Elks Club a relative? This nagging question was about to open up some unanticipated discoveries.

Kenny Caputo as a sophomore at South High, 1959-60. As recounted in other stories in this volume, Kenny played baseball with us on Cops League and Automotive League teams and was a starter for the South High nine at second base.

A few days later, out of nowhere, it suddenly came to Gordon: Coach Caputo's first name was *John*. John Caputo. Was that right? How could one be sure? Well, that's what Google is for. Gordon googled the name "John Caputo, Salt Lake City." A number of obituary entries flashed on his laptop screen. In particular there was one for Frank John Caputo and another for John

Joseph Caputo that seemed promising. Gordon tried Frank John first. The opening lines of the obituary read:

> August 4, 1915 ~ August 9, 2015. Our beloved father, grand-father and dear friend, Frank John Caputo, known to many as "The Sheik," passed away shortly after his 100th birthday, on Sunday, August 9, 2015 in Holladay, UT. The son of Rosario and Christina Mary Brunino Caputo, Frank was born on August 4, 1915 in Sunnyside, UT. He was the third of 11 children in the family.

Okay, interesting, but this didn't seem like the right description of the Caputo Gordon was looking for, so he clicked on the obituary for John Joseph Caputo: Eureka! This had to be the right guy.

> John J. Caputo died March 30, 2010 after a courageous battle with cancer. He was born in Salt Lake City on April 3, 1924 to Cristina Brunino and Rosario Caputo. John graduated from West High School and Utah State University where his athletic prowess is legendary. He is still remembered for stealing the football at the 1948 Aggie/Wyoming game which was touted to be the play that won the game.

Hmmm, Gordon thought to himself, reflecting on the two obituary notices, John must have been a younger brother to *Frank*, the other Caputo he had just read about. Frank Caputo was born in 1915, compared to John's birth in 1924, and both Frank and John were identified as sons of Rosario and Christina Caputo. Nine years younger than Frank, John J. had been a star athlete at both West High and Utah State University. Sure, of course. Gordon remembered that, as director of the Elks Club, Coach John hailed from Salt Lake City's westside and seemed to know all the kids who played sports at West High. But who knew he had been such a great athlete in his youth? He certainly knew sports, and you could tell he was a tough competitor, but he wasn't a big guy, and, in his late thirties, he was already getting a little paunchy.

John Joseph Caputo, 1924-2010.

Reading further in John Caputo's obituary, Gordon learned that:

> John taught in public schools for 35 years in Utah and California,
> serving as classroom teacher, coach and vice principal... For 18
> years, he meticulously groomed the Ken Price Field [in Murray,
> roughly ten miles south of Temple Square in Salt Lake] into one
> of the most beautiful youth ballparks in the Country. He valued
> education and encouraged many youth to pursue educational
> and athletic opportunities.

Coach Caputo had been a classroom teacher and even a vice *principal* somewhere? Holy Toledo, who would have guessed that? Both of us remembered
Coach Caputo as a profane, no-nonsense, tough-as-nails sports adept who
seemed perfectly at home on a basketball court or athletic field, but, to us at
the time, not so much in the halls of a school building or classroom. Such
are the narrow impressions formed in youth of other people who are briefly
encountered in narrow circumstances and whose full lives and histories are
scarcely considered or ever appreciated.

Following Gordon's search efforts to remember Coach Caputo's first name, Gary coincidentally sent him a link to an interview with well-known sports writer, John Schulian (illustrating the sort of serendipity that our wives claim transcends the rules of probability). Along with the link, Gary noted that "we should have given Schulian a second look when we knew him back in the day," which was acknowledgement of yet another too hastily formed impression. The relevance of John Schulian for the two of us was that we remembered him joining us as kids for some games of over-the-line at Municipal Ball Park between 700 and 800 East on 1300 South. He was friends with Kenny Caputo, and acquainted with Bill Gehrke and Johnny Parker, but ended up attending East High rather than South. In our youthful opinions, Schulian was only an average ball player and gratingly argumentative about the rules during our pickup games. Following several disagreements over the course of one game, Schulian called a line drive Gordon hit past him in left field to be a foul ball. In disgust, Gordon yelled, "The only thing foul around here is your breath!"—a fatuous insult, but it cracked up Jonny Parker, and we all laughed like crazy as Schulian simmered in crimson anger and embarrassment. We regret that we didn't make an effort to get better acquainted with Schulian. We belatedly realize that we share a fair number of his interests and sports opinions as adults and think we would appreciate him much more than when we were kids. And in fairness to Schulian's ballplaying ability, we should also report that later he matured into an outstanding catcher and solid hitter in high school and went on to win an MVP award playing amateur league ball for Utah Power and Light in 1967. So much for our youthful small-mindedness and prejudicial prognosticating.

Schulian was offered a baseball scholarship by the University of Utah but decided to concentrate on his major in journalism and went on to become a nationally respected sports columnist and author of well-regarded books on sports (not to mention a later and continuing career as a well-known writer of movie and TV screenplays and novels). The interview Gary sent Gordon was dated October 11, 2011, and was titled, "Bronx Banter Interview:

John Schulian," by Alex Belth (Bronx Banter Interview: John Schulian Bronx Banter (bronxbanterblog.com). Gordon read the interview with great interest. In it, Schulian was insightful, articulate, highly knowledgeable about a wide range of sports topics, and generous in his own appraisals of the sports heroes and their moments on the field, in the ring, and on the court that he had written about over his sports writing career, including such luminaries as Muhammad Ali, Willie Mays, Reggie Jackson, Nolan Ryan, Walter Payton, and Julius Erving (Dr. J), among many others.

Midway through the interview, Belth suddenly asked Schulian, "Why do you have such a feel, an affinity for doing pieces of players from the past?"

Schulian's loving response was:

> I've always been fascinated by the past . . . I mean from childhood on. No matter where I was living, I gravitated to talkers and storytellers, older guys usually, the kind who could weave a spell with words whether they realized it or not. I had a neighbor in Salt Lake City who was like that, a railroad machinist named Sheik Caputo who had played semipro baseball until he was in his 40s. He'd start talking about the team he ran at the Naval Depot during World War II, or how his mother used her broom to hit the feds who busted her father for bootlegging wine during prohibition. I ate it all up. When I started writing for newspapers and magazines, I was still that same kid, forever eager to sit down with old timers who had stories to tell, filing away everything I heard and imagining what the world I was hearing about must have been like.

Wait a second! Go back: *Sheik Caputo in Salt Lake City*?

Gordon immediately returned to Google and entered "Frank John Caputo" again. This time he read the entire, lengthy obituary. According to the obituary,

In 1923, the Caputos moved to Salt Lake City, UT where they lived in the upstairs quarters of the family-owned grocery store. Caputo's Grocery was the heart and soul of the family's existence for the next 57 years, a place remembered fondly for both the wine the father made and the sweaters the mother knitted for her bambini. If there was a clotheshorse in the family, it was Frank, who wore his brand new knickers to Jackson Junior High and instantly became known as "The Sheik," a nickname that stayed with him the rest of his life. But he was far more than just another teenaged dandy. He starred in football, basketball and track at West High, and if you asked him what his fondest memory of those days was, it was not receiving a diploma. It was smearing his football uniform with garlic, a tactic that sent more than one opponent reeling.

So Frank Caputo, older brother to Coach John and the son of Italian immigrants, was "*The Sheik*," a nickname bestowed on him no doubt by his mostly Mormon classmates because of the handmade sweaters and cool knickers he sported as a boy. Well in advance of his kid brother John, he *also* had been a star athlete at West High—and, one infers from the garlic anecdote, the owner of a big, gregarious personality who delighted as an adult in telling stories about his wine making father and his broom swinging mother during prohibition days in Salt Lake City. Reading further, Gordon learned that

The only sport missing from Frank's athletic resume in high school was baseball, which happened to be his best sport. It didn't become part of interscholastic sports in Salt Lake until the 1940's, and by then Frank had already made a name for himself as a first baseman in the Catholic Youth Organization's baseball program, the legendary Utah Industrial League and the Salt Lake Amateur League. In later years he managed a powerhouse team for the Utah Naval Supply Depot in Davis County and coached the American Legion teams from East and Granite high schools, happily chewing tobacco and encouraging his players to "squat low, take squirrel's aim and swing parallel."

Alright then, as an adult, Sheik was good enough to play amateur and semi-pro baseball and (his tobacco chewing notwithstanding) also coached high school age American Legion teams in the summer. "Squat low, take squirrel's aim and swing parallel"—still excellent advice to young hitters learning the game. But it was what followed next that caused Gordon to do another doubletake:

> As much a fan as he was a participant, Frank and his son Kenny traveled to New York for the 1956 World Series and saw all seven games between their beloved Yankees and the Brooklyn Dodgers. When the Yanks' Don Larsen pitched his perfect game, they were standing there watching, right behind the home-plate box seats.

Frank and his son *Kenny*? Frank "Sheik" Caputo was our boyhood friend Kenny Caputo's dad! When the two of us were playing summer baseball at Municipal Park, Kenny lived four streets south of the ball field on the corner of Eighth East and Kensington Avenue and we got acquainted with his dad, not as "The Sheik," of course, but as Mr. Caputo. Mr. Caputo was stocky, had a full head of dark wavey hair, and wore thick-framed glasses. He came to all of Kenny's games and would distinctively bellow-out each time Kenny came to bat: "Bow your neck, Kenny! Keep your neck bowed!" (Bowing your neck is how a batter takes "squirrel's aim.")

What impressed us most was Mr. Caputo's friendly, outgoing manner. He wasn't aloof and didn't talk down to us as kids. He engaged us about baseball and was more than willing to play catch with us when we were warming up before a game. Gordon vividly recalls warming up with Mr. Caputo when he and Kenny were teammates for Ken Garff Oldsmobile in the Automotive League. Mr. Caputo said to Gordon, "Hey, you've got a little hop on your throw. Throw harder and let's see what you've got." Gordon started throwing hard and Mr. Caputo said, "You've got a live fastball, son. Have you ever pitched before?"

Gordon conceded that, yeah, he had pitched a little when he was twelve, "but that was a a long time ago."

Mr. Caputo said, "That long ago, huh?" and smiled generously. "Well, I'm going to tell your coach to take a look at you. He may want to try you out on the pitcher's mound some time." (Which is what happened, but the account of Gordon's wild pitching debut in a subsequent game is a story for another time.)

Back to Kenny and his dad: They went to New York to watch the 1956 World Series together and saw all seven games, including Don Larsen's perfect game! Son-of-a-gun. The two of us never knew that. We were also huge Yankee fans and watched the whole series with bated breath on television. Not many of our friends or their dads, as we remember, liked the Yankees. But, in retrospect, Frank "Sheik" Caputo, a first-generation son of Italian immigrant parents, would naturally have been a Yankee fan and pass his fan loyalty on to Kenny. In 1936, when Sheik Caputo was 21 years-old, the Yankee's starting lineup included Frank Crosetti at shortstop, Tony Lazzeri at second base, and the rookie sensation Joe DiMaggio in centerfield. In later years the Yankees would acquire Vic Raschi (pitcher), Phil Rizzuto (shortstop), and Yogi Berra (catcher), all Italian Americans. It was Yogi Berra who caught Don Larsen's perfect game in the fifth game of the 1956 World Series.

As recounted in "The Sheik's" obituary,

Frank told the story of that great adventure many a night as the back porch of his home on the corner of Eighth East and Kensington Avenue, which was transformed into what was affectionately known as "The Dugout." There was always cold beer on hand to wash down the pepperoni, cheese and olives that he laid out in a seemingly endless parade of characters from his life in baseball.

"The Dugout" is where John Schulian remembers listening as a kid to Sheik Caputo hold forth on sports and the good old days of growing up on Salt Lake City's west side. In a subsequent correspondence we developed with Schulian, John elaborated on his relationship with Mr. Caputo:

> When my parents and I moved [away from their initial home] to the area near 17th East and Yalecrest, I hadn't made friends there yet. So every day I would jump on my bike and ride down to Muni or the Caputo's, to see what was going on. Every night without fail, Monday through Friday, the Sheik and his wife, Nell, would set a place for me at the table and feed me dinner. And when darkness had fallen, the Sheik would load my bike in the trunk of his green Mercury and drive me home. I've never met anyone with a bigger heart.
>
> Peace, John
>
> P.S. I still say the damn ball was foul.

Too bad the two of us didn't spend more time getting acquainted with Kenny's dad, let alone with John Schulian. We think that we too would have eaten up the Sheik's stories.

Other tidbits gleaned from The Sheik's obituary confirmed that he worked as a machinist for the Union Pacific Railroad for 37 years; that in retirement he jogged five miles every day around Liberty Park and played golf at the Rose Park Golf Course, while "merrily bickering with his kid brother John" (Coach Caputo to us). The last three years of Frank's life were spent at Sunrise at Holliday, an adult care facility, where "he always enjoyed his 2:00 a.m. sirloin burger, Bud Light and the conversations that were had."

Frank John "Sheik" Caputo, 1915-2015.

Frank John "Sheik" Caputo lived to be an amazing hundred years old. "He will always be remembered," his 2015 obituary stated, "for his big heart, helping others and treating everyone as his own family." That's how we remember him too—as an adult who liked everybody and who took an interest in boys and their games, encouraging them to develop their youthful potential. Rest in peace Mr. Caputo. We can't help but wonder, when you turned one hundred, if St. Peter greeted you at the Pearly Gates, proclaiming, "Welcome Sheik! Welcome to The Big Dugout in the Sky!"

41.

AUTHORS MEET CRITICS
IN THE CITY OF OUR BIRTH

Inarguably, it was more fun being a critic than an author in these types of professional settings. Both of us were eying the clock as we listened to a panel of critics review our recently published book, *Jan Shipps: An Intellectual and Social Portrait* (Greg Kofford Books, 2109). The setting was a session of the annual conference of the Mormon History Association (MHA), which was holding its 2019 annual meeting at the Sheraton Hotel in Salt Lake City on Fifth South and Second West. The critic-commentators were all distinguished Mormon scholars (Tom Alexander, Phillip Barlow, Kathryn Daynes, Elbert Peck, and Andrea Radke-Moss) who were well acquainted with Jan Shipps and her important contributions as a non-Mormon historian to the advancement of Mormon Studies as a respectable field of academic scholarship. Jan, in fact, had served as MHA's first woman president in 1980 and had been actively involved in the Association's affairs over the span of her entire professional career.

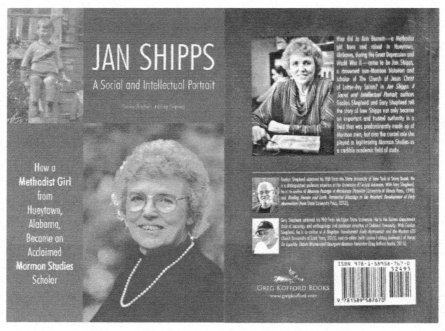

Front and back covers of our Jan Shipps Book.
Images courtesy of Greg Kofford Books.

Prior to our session, we had met University of Utah Sterling M. McMurrin Professor of Religious Studies historian Colleen McDannell for lunch, hoping to get better acquainted and reassure her that she hadn't made a mistake in agreeing to contribute a chapter to a new book we were proposing to edit on global Mormonism in the 21st century. Colleen has a lively sense of humor and seemed pleased that we could hold our own in the zinger department. Right in the middle of downing our house salads, who should materialize at our table? None other than Warner Woodworth! Warner is a well know BYU professor emeritus in organizational leadership, management, and entrepreneurial development in underdeveloped countries. But long before he acquired those credentials, we had known Warner as boys growing up in the 1950s. Warner was the same age as our brother Don, and he lived a couple of blocks from us on Denver Street near Liberty Park. We attended the same

LDS chapel, the same public schools, and when we were sophomores, he was elected student body president at South High. As children, we had battled Warner, his musically talented brother Mark, and other neighborhood boys playing war games in "the field" behind Ron Swenson's house.

We were pleased to introduce Warner to Colleen. Gary invited him to sit down and share some of our lunch, and Warner readily accepted. Warner was in an expansive mood. He freely admitted he hadn't paid his registration fee for the conference, but that he would stealthily drop by our Authors meet Critics session after lunch anyway. Colleen mostly listened with a mixture of tolerance and bemusement as we reminisced with Warner about our families and childhoods growing up as Mormon boys in Salt Lake while also trying to keep her involved in the conversation.

Colleen, by the way, was raised Catholic in neighboring Colorado, received her BA and MA degrees in history from the University of Colorado (like Jan Shipps, whose Ph.D. was also from the University of Colorado) and the University of Denver respectively, and obtained her Ph.D. from Temple University in Pennsylvania. As a scholar, Colleen has written acclaimed books concerning religious beliefs about heaven, modern Catholic reforms, and Christianity's contributions to popular culture. A non-Mormon scholar like Jan Shipps, Colleen also has become a recognized authority on Mormon history topics, especially women's unsung roles in the history of the LDS Church. Furthermore, like the two of us, Colleen, was preparing to face a panel of critics later that afternoon in review of her recently published, *Sister Saints: Mormon Women Since the End of Polygamy* (Oxford University Press, 2019).

A good feminist, Colleen seemed reassured to learn of Warner's own progressive upbringing and uniquely liberal bonafides as a Marriott School of Business professor at BYU. One set of boyhood memories we rehearsed with Warner in this regard concerned a neighbor family in the Liberty Ward by the name of Marchant. The Marchant's had a total of *fifteen* children. Yep, that's not a typo: eight daughters and seven sons. One of the boys, Byron, was Don and Warner's age, one of the girls, Karen (who could sing like an angel), was our age, and another boy, Dwight, who used to play a little tennis with Gordon at Liberty Park, was just a year younger. There were a dozen more siblings, both older and younger. We attended classes with Marchant kids from elementary school all the way through high school.

The thing is, the Marchant's *mother*—Beatrice Alvaretta Peterson (sister Marchant to us growing up in the Liberty/Liberty Park Wards)—was anything but a stay-at-home mom. Over the years she was a public school teacher, ward relief society president, Young Women's Mutual Improvement Association president, ward librarian, president of the VFW Auxiliary for women, recipient of the Susa Young Gates Award, AND, was hugely active in politics for the Democratic Party. She served for years as a legislative and voting district chairperson for the Democratic Party and also as its Salt Lake County secretary. We distinctly remember sister Marchant energetically going door to door every election year with campaign and voter registration literature. At the age of 65, she herself was elected as a Democrat to two terms in the state legislature, where she championed bills for taxation reform, and social services and healthcare reform. Warner's childhood friend, Byron Marchant, incidentally, was excommunicated from the LDS Church in 1977 for his public protests against the church's refusal to ordain males of African descent to its lay priesthood (a ban ironically lifted a year later).

Our pleasant lunch with Warner and Colleen was over. It was time to go face the music. We wished Colleen well in her pending panel session, and she likewise wished us well in ours. We agreed to stay in touch.

As we listened to the mostly kind comments of our critics, it become increasingly clear that the time allocated on the program for our responses was going to be highly abbreviated. In organizing the panel, we probably should have kept participation to three commentators instead of five. But every one of our panelists was a knowledgeable and respected scholar with unique qualifications for talking about the career of Jan Shipps in Mormon Studies, and we didn't regret our selection of critics in the least. Instead, we were mostly relieved that the two of us would only have a few minutes left between us to say something in response. Gary spoke first. He of course thanked the panelists, explained to the audience in attendance that Jan's health didn't permit her to travel, but that she sent her appreciation and good wishes to all, and then summarized why and how we, as sociologists, had collaborated on the book. Gordon also thanked the panelists for perhaps being more generous in their critiques of his and Gary's work than they deserved and said that they would be happy to discuss the book further with anyone who had questions. There, in fact, followed a few audience questions, but time quickly expired and the session was over.

All in all, it had been a good day. We had published our book on Jan in the nick of time for a conference setting that would help publicize it in the Mormon intellectual community, and we appreciated the courteous and positive treatment it had received from prominent Mormon historians. We also had enjoyed getting acquainted with Colleen McDannell and renewing an old friendship with Warner Woodworth—in a setting not too many blocks distant from where our lives had first connected decades earlier. And, as it turned out, Warner wasn't the only old friend attending our conference session. There, in the first several rows of seats, were Kay Hellstrom Gaisford, Janet Burton Seegmiller, and Marian Peck Rees, all women with whom we had attended South High in the early 1960s. Kay was the editor of the South High yearbook our junior year, had worked closely with our brother Don on yearbook staff the previous year, and went on to attend Stanford University with our childhood friend, Phillip Starr. Janet, a published author in her own right, was the editor of the South High Scribe our junior year when the two of us were sports reporters and, as Gary reminded her, she was the first peer "critic" of our writing efforts. We were less well acquainted with Marian in school, but she was good friends with some of the girls Gary dated, and we had become better acquainted as adults when she and her husband, Dale, became regular attenders at Mormon History conferences and Sunstone Symposia.

It was a mini-reunion of sorts. Now that Gary and his wife Lauren had moved back to Salt Lake in retirement, there would be many more opportunities to renew friendships that had endured for sixty years or more. As a regular visitor from out-of-state, Gordon could also look forward with Gary to the satisfying promise of renewing their solidarity as twin brothers through continued contact with professional colleagues and old friends in the city of their birth.

Driving back to Gary's new residence in Sandy when our conference session was over, we decided to call Jan Shipps, who at this point had moved into an assisted living unit in Bloomington, Indiana with her husband Tony. Jan was still recovering her mobility from a painful fall at home the previous year. We put Gordon's phone on speaker while Gary negotiated light traffic on Foothill Drive and Interstate 215 and listened to Jan greet us in her customary firm voice, nuanced by lingering traces of the Alabama accent she grew up with before she had ever heard of the Mormons and their mountain empire headquartered in the Valley of the Great Salt Lake.

You should, of course, read our book for the details, but southerners Jan and Tony moved north to Chicago, Detroit, Logan, Utah (where Jan discovered the Mormons), Colorado, and ultimately Bloomington, Indiana as Tony pursued an academic career in English literature and library administration. Jan belatedly acquired a bachelor's degree in history at Utah State University, a Ph.D. from the University of Colorado (where she wrote her dissertation on 19th century Mormons in politics), and ultimately gained a joint academic appointment in history and religious studies at Indiana-Purdue University in Indiana. The constellation of shaping influences along the way that explain how a Methodist girl from Hueytown, Alabama, became an acclaimed Mormon studies scholar is precisely what our book about Jan aims to depict and understand.

Jan was glad to get our call but had forgotten that Gordon was also in Salt Lake for our authors meet critics session at the Mormon History Association's annual meeting, a meeting she very much had wanted to attend. But she excitedly reported to us that a copy of the book had just arrived in the mail. and that she and Tony were taking turns reading it out loud to each other. Tony interjected from the background and said, "Yes, and I'm learning many things about myself I never knew before!" which made us smile. Tony would turn 93 in several more months; Jan would be 90.

Jan and Tony Shipps, circa 1989.

Our objective in researching, interviewing, and writing about Jan Shipps was never to produce a definitive biography but primarily to obtain Jan's own recollections about her childhood, young adulthood in marriage to Tony, her early educational experiences, and her transformative career encounter with Mormons and the scholars who shaped her academic interests and outlook as a professional historian while she was still around to recount them. Other professional historians could follow up with much more detailed and comprehensive narratives of Jan's life and contributions to Mormon Studies. In the meantime, however, we had succeeded in obtaining her own account. Furthermore, we had been anxious to get our book published while she was still with us to see the results of our many hours of interviews. Mission accomplished! We took collaborative pride in that and, at the same time, felt fortunate in the process to have formed appreciative friendship bonds with Jan and Tony Shipps.*

It was rewarding to celebrate all of this with the two of them via speakerphone while gazing across the Salt Lake Valley from the vantage point of the city's eastern foothills as we motored toward the Sandy suburbs between Big and Little Cottonwood Canyons. Life was good.

Anthony (Tony) Wimberly Shipps died April 9, 2021 at the age of 94 from natural causes.

42.

THE LITTLE GIRL WHO
LOVED THE LIBRARY

One hundred and twelve books. Quite a haul! The number is so appealingly precise that it couldn't be the mere product of faulty memory or nostalgic imagination. That was the number of library books that Lavina remembers checking out on her first trip to the library in Moses Lake, Washington. There was no such thing as a library in the tiny hamlet of Lost River, Idaho—her family's previous residence (after moving from Shelley, Idaho)—nor in the rural community of Warden, Washington, where once again her father had moved his growing, Mormon family. But thirty miles distant from Warden, the public library in the flourishing town of Moses Lake featured a very generous checkout policy: *No limit* on the number of books a patron wished to check out.

No-limit? Wow! The two of us would have loved to have enjoyed that degree of munificence when visiting the old Salt Lake City Library on State Street and South Temple when we were young. We're sorry we didn't know Lavina—who's the same age as us—when we were kids growing up in Salt Lake. We think we would have hit it off great. But as kind fate would have it, our paths were to cross later in life with the little girl who loved the library. First, though, let's get back to that record-setting Moses Lake book haul.

Her dad found Lavina in the library wing of the city and county building—after he had finished licensing his rickety old truck—where she had wandered while bored, waiting for him to fill out the necessary paperwork. We never met Lavina's father, but infer that he must have been a kindly indulgent man for carrying armsful of books out to his truck rather than reprimanding his daughter's unrestrained delight in discovering the library. And we also infer that the Moses Lake librarians were equally indulgent (and probably secretly delighted by the little girl's craving for books) in issuing Lavina her very own library card and then approving of every one of her one-hundred twelve selections without a hint of dismay or discouragement. From such seemingly small and oft forgotten moments, turning points emerge and lives are shaped.

And what snapshot image from this story do we get of Lavina as a child, the little girl who loved the library? Bright, maybe even precocious; dutiful but also self-confident, trusting, and comfortable around adults; curious, not afraid to explore, not afraid to avail herself of opportunities to learn and grow; and open to the transporting beauty and world-expanding inspiration of books. Thank God for books. If kids learn to love to read when they're young, chances are they'll do well in life. As for Lavina, when she grew up she became a writer and editor of books. That's when we got to know her.

We had been struggling for several years to come up with a workable format for our Mexican missionary memoirs, (eventually entitled, *Mormon Passage*). In 1991, our sociology colleague, Armand Mauss, recommended that we get in touch with Lavina Fielding Anderson in Salt Lake City, who was the best editor of Mormon related materials he knew. Having secured a visit-date via email to talk with Lavina, Gordon—who was in Salt Lake on a family trip—found himself knocking on the door at 1519 Roberta Street on the corner of Kensington Avenue, a scant block away from South High's old auditorium (now the Grand Theater in the Salt Lake Community College) on State Street. A modestly proportioned, two-story, Old World architectural gem, the house at this address had given the little side-street a distinctive look for decades.

Lavina and Paul Anderson's Roberta Street house in Salt Lake City.

Gordon fondly remembered passing by this same house every afternoon with Gary and their boyhood friend, Lorin Larsen, as a shortcut to the playground of Whittier Elementary, where they attended the sixth grade for half a year while their school, Liberty Elementary, was being remodeled. When Lavina came to the door, the first things that instantly impressed Gordon were her warm, welcoming smile, authentic cheerfulness, and quick wit that made him feel like he had known her for years.

Lavina Fielding Anderson.

By the time Gordon left Lavina and Paul Anderson's home on Roberta Street, he was vastly reassured about his and Gary's project and especially by the fact that Lavina had agreed to review and critique their manuscript.

Over the years, both of us would return on occasion to Lavina and Paul's home for drop-by visits. On sabbatical leave from Oakland University in 1998, Gary spent several afternoons interviewing Lavina about her involvement in the Mormon Alliance (a lay support group organization for disenchanted or struggling church members) and her determined, continued activity in the local Whittier Ward of the LDS Church, in spite of having been excommunicated in 1993 for her critical writings on ecclesiastical and spiritual abuse of church intellectuals. Another twenty years down the road, Lavina—concurrent with her own research and writing on the same subject—gave us encouragement and critical support in preparing our manuscript on Mormon patriarchal blessings for publication by Penn State University Press (*Binding Earth and Heaven: Patriarchal Blessings in the Prophetic Development of Early Mormonism*, 2010). At the same time, it was Lavina who strongly encouraged us to update our earliest book, *A Kingdom Transformed* for the University of Utah Press (which we subsequently did in 2016). And most recently, we teamed with Lavina as coeditors of *Voices for Equality* (Greg Kofford Books, 2015), a book of original essays on resurgent Mormon feminism and the Ordain Women movement.

This latter publication would never have gotten off the ground without Lavina's intervention. She's the one who pushed us to pursue the project and connected us with Greg Kofford Books as a receptive outlet for publishing a controversial volume on the issue of Mormon women and ordination to the LDS lay priesthood. Kofford managing editor, Loyd Ericson, informed us that, yes, they would be interested in publishing the book, but only on condition that Lavina joined us as an editor of the projected volume. Absolutely! We've never been prouder to collaborate with a valued colleague than we were with Lavina. Her connections within the LDS feminist community and ours among social science colleagues interested in contemporary religious issues produced an ideal mix of contributing authors and analytical perspectives.

As an editor, what Lavina excels at is not just her eagle eye for careless punctuation and grammatical miscues, or even her mastery of English prose and good writing mechanics; it is her generous capacity for providing other writers with challenging, positive encouragement and not just blunt criticism of their work. Even experienced writers need a good editor. Work with Lavina and we guarantee you will become better at your craft than you were before. Most of the books we have co-authored over the past thirty-five years bear the editorial imprint and stimulating encouragement of Lavina Fielding Anderson. We are most grateful to the little girl who loved the library.

It was a Saturday morning in late March 2019, and, once again, we were sitting in the comfortable living room at 1519 Roberta Street. We had been ushered into the house by Lavina's daughter-in-law, Marina, after arriving on the front steps unannounced and unexpected. We were there to return an ear bud that Lavina's son, Christian had left at Gary and Lauren's home in Sandy the night before. That night Lavina and Christian had attended our dinner party with other guests, including: former *Sunstone* editor Elbert Peck; Utah Valley University anthropologist David C. Knowlton; Utah landscape artist Kathy Carling Wilson; Washington University in Saint Louis professor of history and religious studies, Laurie Maffly-Kipp; Utah Historical Quarterly editor and author, Jedidiah Rogers, and his expert copy-editing wife, Holly Hansen Rogers. Gordon was also on hand after overseeing a one-day conference of the Mormon Social Science Association on the campus of Utah Valley University in Orem.

It had been a difficult twelve months for the Andersons. On March 23 of the previous year, Lavina's beloved architect/artist husband Paul had died suddenly of heart failure. On the day following our dinner party of the previous evening, we found ourselves in the Andersons' living room, surrounded by a small sampling of the lively oil paintings Paul had begun turning out following his retirement as curator of exhibits at BYU's Museum of Art, whose hospitable and elegant building he had helped design. Lavina, beaming as always, made light conversation with us about our current projects and family commitments. Then she voluntarily brought up the topic of her excommunication and possible member reinstatement, which Lauren had asked her about the previous evening at dinner. Lavina reiterated to us what she had told Lauren, namely that, following Paul's memorial service at the Whittier Ward chapel, she had been approached by her ward bishop, who recommended she apply for rebaptism in the Church. He would initiate and strongly support her petition up the channels of church bureaucracy, he told her. Now, she further revealed to us, she had in fact submitted a petition, the Liberty Stake president (who, unbelievably, was the son of our old Liberty Park Ward bishop and next door neighbor, Gilbert McLean!) had signed it with a positive endorsement from him and the high council, and it was now presumably wending its way to the desk of the Church's First Presidency. The First Presidency bore ultimate responsibility for rendering a final verdict on Lavina's request.

What did she think her prospects were, and how did she feel about this now, after the passage of so many years? Gary asked. It wasn't a done deal, Lavina replied, and in any case it would probably still be months before any decision was announced. In the meantime, her fundamental beliefs and feelings had not changed. She never felt she had left the church; she still believed in its fundamental teachings and that God had never abandoned her. She had written honestly and carefully about the abuses of men in authority that needed exposure and rectification. They were men, not gods. She had never denied the religious principles of her family faith, but she could not recant or apologize for what she had truthfully reported. She would welcome reinstatement as a member in good standing, but, if not, she could continue to live her life with a clear conscience before God. Ecclesiastical officials could withhold official recognition of her church standing, but they could not withhold God's love for her or Lavina's love for her fellow Latter-day Saints and the faith tradition she had embraced her entire life. She would continue being a Latter-day Saint regardless of the First Presidency's decision.

On September 5, 2019, the headline of an article by *Salt Lake Tribune* religion writer, Peggy Fletcher Stack, read: "Writer excommunicated during 'September Six' purge loses her bid to rejoin the LDS Church." The headline was followed by a picture of Lavina at her Roberta Street home, standing in her living room and surrounded by oil paintings by her husband Paul Anderson.

Lavina in her Salt Lake City Roberta Street home, September 2019. Image courtesy of Trent Nelson, *Salt Lake Tribune*.

"Lavina Fielding Anderson, one of the famed 'September Six' writers and scholars disciplined by The Church of Jesus Christ of Latter-day Saints in 1993," Stack wrote, "got a big 'no' last week to her request for rebaptism from the men who matter most: the faith's governing First Presidency. 'I was not surprised or angry about the outcome,' Anderson said Wednesday, and she has no plans to try to open that door again. 'I have kept my covenants, remained close to the church and have felt that what I have done is accepted by the Lord,' the Salt Lake City editor and writer said. 'If there is unfinished business, it's the First Presidency's, not mine.'"

The woman who loves libraries was not backing down.

EPILOGUE

We sometimes ask people if they pray, and they say different things.

It's the different things they say that tell us something about who they are.

We asked a 90 year-old Methodist woman historian of Mormon studies fame if she prayed.

She said yes.

She prays out loud every night before bed, because her 90 year-old librarian, skeptic husband wants to hear her words of comfort and say amen.

Why doesn't *he* pray?

He believes in his wife's prayers, that she can say for him what he can't say for himself.

It makes him sleep better at night.

She prays for protection.

She prays that their home will be protected from fire, because his childhood memories of smoke and flame in his bedroom have never been extinguished.

She prays for immigrants, because she fears for their safety in a calloused country that no longer welcomes their aspirations.

She prays for her born-again son, who prays for her redemption; and she prays for her grandchildren's children and their generations to come.

She prays for her country.

She prays for the protection of many, but not for herself.

More forbearing than fearful, her faith is simple.

She believes in a just God—who knows her heart—and in herself.

She sleeps at night without her husband's prayers in her ears.

We asked an ambitiously accomplished juvenile justice advocate if she prayed.

She too said yes.

But her prayers are not meek prayers of petition.

She dialogues with Mother God about frustrating obstacles in her path.

She likes rules; she wants a plan; she wants things to make sense.

She wants The Mother to know what her concerns are.

Will it help her sleep better at night knowing that Mother God has been clearly informed of her frustrated concerns?

Sleepless nights are still the norm for this ambitiously accomplished woman.

In stoic envy, she indulges her taste for wry irony by kvetching about her agnostic husband and his brother's super-power of morning catnapping.

Do the agnostic twin brothers pray?

Yes, they occasionally pray, in a manner of speaking.

Not with heart-melting conviction or penance; not with desperate need or high-minded benediction for the welfare of the world.

They abjure prayers for themselves.

But they might pray for others, if asked with sincerity of purpose.

They impose conditions on these prayers, however.

They must be proffered in Spanish, and they only permit themselves to address *La Madre*.

The latter is an idiosyncrasy of their wives' influence and the former an artifact of their days as

callow emissaries of the Lord in 1960s Mexico.

They can pray and speak of godly matters in the sonorous tongue of Mexican angels but not in

the blunt and practical tongue of their British ancestors.

Why is this? Only God (or psychiatry) knows.

What *they* know is that they always look forward to a morning catnap.

Once we even asked the girl who loves libraries if she prayed.

Of course! she answered, I love feeling the presence of God in my prayers.

Presence of God? Really?

Yes, really, she affirmed.

We don't always love or respect ourselves, she said, but when in prayer I'm listened to with love and respect, I know God is there.

Tell it, sister, we won't fault you for your faith.

We think God loves libraries too.

If God can speak to people in prayer, why not in books and libraries?

If a little girl wants to read one hundred and twelve books from the library, who's to say she won't discover a God who talks and listens to her with love and respect?

Sometimes we ask people if they pray, and they say different things.

It's the different things they say that tell us something about who they are.

Let us pray.

Querida Madre,

[Dear Mother]

Te pedimos que nos bendigas con el deseo de mejorar nuestras vidas,

[We ask you to bless us with the desire to improve our lives,]

Con el deseo de obtener más entendimiento y sabiduría),

[with the desire to obtain more understanding and wisdom,]

Y también con el deseo de fortalecer nuestra compasión por los extranjeros,

[And also with the desire to strengthen our compassion for strangers,]

Por los que faltan las necesidades de la vida,

[For those who lack the necessities of life,]

Por los que luchan contra persecución injusta.

[For those who struggle against unjust persecution.]

Y Madre, te pedimos ayudarnos a ser mejor ejemplos por nuestras hijas e hijos,

[And Mother, we ask you to help us be better examples for our daughters and sons,]

Para que ellos lleguen a ser adultos maderos,

[That they might become mature adults,]

Preparados a guiar nuestro país y comunidades en una dirección más derecha en los años que venir.

[Prepared to guide our country and communities in a better direction in the years to come.]

Especialmente aquí, Madre, en La Ciudad de Los Santos

[Especially here, Mother, in the City of the Saints.]

Hope for the future.